Getting Paid While Taking Time

Getting Paid While Taking Time

The Women's Movement and the
Development of Paid Family Leave Policies
in the United States

Megan A. Sholar

TEMPLE UNIVERSITY PRESS
Philadelphia • *Rome* • *Tokyo*

TEMPLE UNIVERSITY PRESS
Philadelphia, Pennsylvania 19122
www.temple.edu/tempress

Library of Congress Cataloging-in-Publication Data

Names: Sholar, Megan Anne, 1978– author.
Title: Getting paid while taking time : the women's movement and the development of paid family leave policies in the United States / Megan Anne Sholar.
Description: Philadelphia : Temple University Press, 2016. | Includes bibliographi-
  cal references and index.
Identifiers: LCCN 2016003374| ISBN 9781439912942 (hardback : alk. paper) |
  ISBN 9781439912959 (paper : alk. paper) | ISBN 9781439912966 (e-book)
Subjects: LCSH: Feminism—United States. | Women's rights—United States. |
  Parental leave—United States. | United States—Social policy. | BISAC:
  POLITICAL SCIENCE / Labor & Industrial Relations. | SOCIAL SCIENCE /
  Women's Studies. | SOCIAL SCIENCE / Sociology / Marriage & Family.
Classification: LCC HQ1426 .S446 2016 | DDC 305.420973—dc23 LC record
  available at http://lccn.loc.gov/2016003374

♾ The paper used in this publication meets the requirements of the American
National Standard for Information Sciences—Permanence of Paper for Printed
Library Materials, ANSI Z39.48-1992

Printed in the United States of America

9 8 7 6 5 4 3 2 1

In memory of my grandmothers, Carolyn Rose and Norma Lee,
who showed me what it means to be strong

Contents

Acknowledgments

I begin by thanking my colleagues at Loyola University Chicago who have assisted me through various stages of this project. Olga Avdeyeva and Vincent Mahler read numerous drafts in the early phases, asking tough questions and offering valuable insights that helped me strengthen my arguments. Claudio Katz has continuously supported me in both my research and my teaching. His encouragement helped me overcome my uncertainties as I wrote and rewrote the pages. I especially thank Susan Gluck Mezey for her help at every stage of the process. The detailed comments she provided on the chapters were invaluable, and she was always available to discuss them with me. She is extremely generous with her time and encouragement, and I am truly grateful for both her guidance and her friendship.

Working with Temple University Press has been a wonderful experience. Senior editor Aaron Javsicas provided me with enthusiastic support from the very beginning; I thank him for his confidence in the project. I am also grateful for the support of marketing director Ann-Marie Anderson, publicity manager Gary Kramer, and art manager Kate Nichols. I could not have asked for a better production editor than Rebecca Logan at Newgen North America, who was always available to address any questions and concerns. I also thank copyeditor Amy Schneider; the finished product is much stronger as a result of her meticulous review. Anonymous readers provided comments and suggestions that forced me to clarify my ideas and sharpen my analysis. I am especially grateful to Steven Wisensale for his detailed feedback on the manuscript. His insight on family leave and the policy-making process was invaluable.

Family leave policies are changing at a rapid pace throughout the United States. As a passionate advocate of paid leave, I am thrilled! As a scholar trying to complete my analysis of current leave policies, my reaction upon discovering that I needed to make yet another last-minute revision was often less enthusiastic. I therefore extend my deepest gratitude to my interview subjects. I could not have written this book without the help of the activists, politicians, and scholars who provided me with a firsthand look into family leave policy making across the country. Their willingness to give up hours of their time to answer my questions—as well as the follow-up questions that would invariably pop up at a later date—is immensely appreciated. I also acknowledge the role that the librarians at both Loyola University Chicago and Northwestern University's Library of Special Collections have played in the completion of this text. In particular, Susan Lewis went above and beyond to help me gather resources.

Finally, I thank my family and friends for their encouragement over the years. Thanks go to my Alton girls, my Chicago girls, and the Lebowskis for their understanding during those times that work kept me from spending time with them, as well as for their readiness to celebrate with me after meeting a deadline. Most important, I thank my parents, Mike and Michelle. There is not enough space in this book for me to acknowledge all that they have done for me. I can only hope that they know how much I appreciate the love and support that they have given me.

1

Women's Movements and the Passage
of Family Leave Policies

amily leave policies vary enormously throughout the world. At
one extreme, Sweden offers 480 days of paid leave to new parents.
Ninety of those days are reserved for the father; the other days can
be shared between the parents any time within the first eight years of
their child's life. Although most nations have policies that are far less
generous, almost all of them guarantee some amount of paid leave to
new mothers. Benefits are typically the most substantial in European
states. For example, Finland provides eighteen weeks of paid maternity leave, nine weeks of paid paternity leave, and twenty-six weeks of
paid parental leave. In an attempt to increase gender equality, Iceland
gives each parent the nontransferable right to three months of paid
leave, as well as three months that may be shared between the parents. The United Kingdom has also recently amended its family leave
policies to promote a more egalitarian division of labor in the family.
After an initial two weeks of paid maternity leave and two weeks of
paid paternity leave, parents in the United Kingdom can share thirty-
seven weeks of paid leave.

Although European countries generally provide the most generous benefits to parents, paid maternity leave is now customary around
the world. With the exception of Suriname, every country in Latin

America and the Caribbean offers at least twelve weeks of paid maternity leave. Across Africa, most countries provide between twelve and fourteen weeks of maternity benefits; Tunisia is an outlier, with only four weeks of paid maternity leave. There is greater variance throughout Asia, but the continent still averages approximately twelve weeks of paid leave for new mothers. In the Middle East, maternity benefits hover around eight weeks. Leave benefits for fathers have also become more common in recent years; eighty-seven countries currently provide paid leave to new fathers in the form of either paternity or parental leave. For example, Canada provides seventeen weeks of paid maternity leave and up to thirty-seven weeks of paid parental leave.

Of the 185 countries that the International Labour Organization examined for its 2014 study, only Papua New Guinea and the United States do not guarantee paid family leave for either men or women (Addati, Cassirer, and Gilchrist 2014). The World Policy Analysis Center adds the Marshall Islands, Micronesia, Nauru, Palau, Suriname, and Tonga to the list of primarily low- or middle-income states without paid maternity leave. The United States remains the only industrialized nation in the world that does not provide paid family leave at the national level for either men or women (World Policy Analysis Center, n.d.).

The purpose of this book is to explain the development of family leave policies at both the national level and the state level in the United States, with special attention paid to the ways in which women's movement actors and other activists influence the policy-making process. The United States has continually lagged behind the rest of the developed—as well as developing—world with regard to family leave benefits. The Pregnancy Discrimination Act (PDA) of 1978 mandates that pregnant women receive the same sick days and disability benefits as other employees. The law also prohibits an employer from firing or refusing to hire or promote a woman because of her pregnancy. However, the PDA does not provide time off to care for a new child. It was not until 1993 that the United States passed the Family and Medical Leave Act (FMLA), granting certain categories of women and men up to twelve weeks of *unpaid* job-protected leave to care for a new child. Yet because of the stringent parameters of the law, only about 6 percent of corporations and 60 percent of the workforce is covered (Ray, Gornick, and Schmitt 2009; Heymann and Earle 2010, 57).

In the more than two decades since the passage of the FMLA, there have been numerous unsuccessful attempts to expand family leave benefits at the national level. However, in the United States innovations in family policies often arise at the state level. In the American federal system, states can legislate social policy not addressed by the federal government. Subnational governments have more freedom to design policy that is consistent with the dominant political culture of their state. Local elites and activists may campaign for different goals than federal policy makers. As a result of the greater leeway subnational governments have in the policy-making process, there is significant variation in family leave policies among states. Before the FMLA was implemented in 1993, nearly forty states had crafted some type of unpaid family leave policy, although there was little uniformity across state lines. Since 1993, more than two dozen states have proposed paid family leave. Three states—California, New Jersey, and Rhode Island—have successfully implemented paid leave programs. Beginning in 2018, New York will become the fourth state to guarantee paid family leave. Although Washington State passed a paid parental leave bill in 2007, budgetary constraints have delayed implementation indefinitely, and family leave advocates have largely abandoned that law and are working toward the passage of a more expansive policy.

In this chapter, I define the different types of family leave policies, describe the importance of family leave for society, and detail the current policies in the United States. I then review the literature on public policy making and social movements. Because family leave policy is a gendered issue, I situate it within the larger context of the literature devoted to the study of women's movements in shaping gender-based policies. I also introduce other key variables that influence the policy-making process in the United States, such as unions, critical actors in the legislature, and party control of the government. After detailing my methods and data sources, I conclude with a brief outline of the remainder of the book.

Family Leave Policies

Defining Family Leave Policy

Family leave policy encompasses a variety of leave types. Maternity leave is granted to mothers for a limited period around the time of childbirth or adoption; paternity leave is given to fathers for a limited period around the time of childbirth or adoption (Gornick and Meyers 2003, 112). After maternity and paternity leave expire, parental leave provides longer periods of gender-neutral, job-protected leave for parents to care for small children (Haas 2003). Most countries typically have separate programs that cover leave to care for a sick family member. For example, the Employment Insurance program in Canada provides "compassionate care benefits" for this purpose (Service Canada 2016). However, in the United States, family leave often encompasses both parental and disability leave, including leave to care for a family member with a serious illness or because of an employee's own illness or injury.

Family leave policies are measured on two dimensions: availability and generosity. Availability refers to the inclusiveness of the policy. Individuals must meet certain requirements to be eligible for leave, such as the sex of the claimant, amount of time spent in the labor force, and income earned. Generosity refers to the duration and the wage replacement levels of the leave, as well as job protection (Gornick and Meyers 2003, chap. 5).

The Evolution of Family Leave Policies

There are many reasons nations may decide to grant family leave. Most early leave policies arose as a result of governments' concern for the health of mothers and children (Gauthier 1996, 50). In some cases, leave policies are part of a larger pronatalist campaign to increase birthrates;[1] other countries offer leave to allow parents—usually women—more time with their children. Some governments use such policies as a way to increase participation in the workforce, while allowing employees to balance work and family life. Urie Bronfenbrenner (1979) found that allowing parents time with their new child may benefit both the child and the whole family system. Only within the past few decades has gender entered the debate over family benefits in the form of concern about women's double burden in the home and workplace.[2]

In 1877, Switzerland passed the first maternity leave policy, allowing women eight weeks of unpaid, job-protected leave surrounding the birth of a child. Six years later, Germany became the first country to provide paid maternity leave. The plan was part of Bismarck's social security system, which recognized that the government and employers were responsible for assuming the risks facing employees, such as illness and accidents (Gauthier 1996, 50–51). By World War I, fourteen countries had enacted paid maternity leave laws (Kamerman and Moss 2009, 1).[3] In the 1920s, the International Labour Organization (ILO) recommended that member countries enact maternity leave laws; leave policies in most European countries today took root from these recommendations (Radigan 1988, 5). By World War II, almost all developed countries provided women workers with some form of paid maternity leave (Gauthier 1996, 50). As described earlier, almost every country in the world today provides paid maternity leave, though the generosity of these leaves varies significantly. Moreover, paternity leave is becoming more common as an increasing number of governments recognize the benefits of allowing all workers to take the time that they need to care for their families. As the population ages, leave for elder care has also taken on increased significance.

The Importance of Family Leave Policies

Demographic shifts in the United States have made it increasingly difficult for many Americans to reconcile their work lives with their family lives. Most notable among these changes is women's increased labor force participation. In 1938, most workers had a family member at home—usually a woman—who was a full-time caregiver (Boushey and Mitukiewicz 2014, 1). Such an arrangement is much less common today. Women currently make up 46.8 percent of the American labor force (U.S. Department of Labor, n.d., "Labor Force by Sex"); their participation rate is 57 percent. The labor force participation rate of mothers with children under eighteen is 70 percent; it stands at 57.3 percent for women with children under age one (U.S. Department of Labor, n.d., "Women in the Labor Force"). Since the majority of women now work outside the home, it is much less likely that families will have a stay-at-home parent to provide care. Indeed, in 2012 only 28.3 percent of married couples consisted of a father in the labor force and a mother who stayed home (Glynn 2014, 5). Also contributing to greater demands for time off from paid work for caregiving responsibilities is the rise in the number of single-parent households. In 2012, 26.1 percent of families with children were headed by single mothers; single fathers headed 8.2 percent of them (3).

As the structure of the family continues to change in the United States, it has become clear that family leave is not just a women's issue. It is no longer assumed that men will be the exclusive bread-winners in families. From 1977 to 2008, the percentage of employees who agree that it is better for all parties if the man earns the money and the woman takes care of the home and the family dropped from 64 percent to 39 percent (Galinsky, Aumann, and Bond 2011, 9). During that same period, there has also been a change in men's roles and behaviors at home. The amount of time that fathers spend with their children under age thirteen on workdays has increased from two to three hours; women's time with children has remained steady at 3.8 hours (14). Although men and women have not reached parity in caregiving, the gender gap continues to narrow. It is therefore not surprising that the proportion of men who reported work-life conflict increased from 34 percent in 1977 to 49 percent in 2008. Fathers in dual-earner families had a more pronounced increase, from 35 percent to 60 percent (18; see also Hill et al. 2003). A recent poll finds that 56 percent of working parents say that it is difficult for them to balance their work responsibilities with their family responsibilities. Slightly more working mothers (60 percent) are likely to report this difficulty than working fathers (52 percent) (Pew Research Center 2015, 5).

With most mothers entering the labor force and more fathers contributing to the care of children, increasing attention has been given to the availability of leave for men in the form of either paternity or parental leave (Brandth and Kvande 2009; C. Miller 2014; Morgan 2009; Otani 2015). Although FMLA leave is extended to both men and women in the United States, there has been little change in men's usage of unpaid leave since the law's passage (Han and Waldfogel 2003). Men are less likely than women to know that they qualify for FMLA leave, and they often use vacation days to take parental leave (Kaufman, Lyonette, and Crompton 2010; Baird and Reynolds 2004). When fathers do take leave, it positively affects their level of involvement in child care and housework, and it ultimately improves outcomes for both children and the fathers themselves (Cabrera,

Shannon, and Tamis-LeMonda 2007; Haas and Hwang 2008; Huerta et al. 2013; Nepomnyaschy and Waldfogel 2007; O'Brien, Brandth, and Kvande 2007; Tanaka and Waldfogel 2007).

America's rapidly growing elder population also highlights the need for greater family leave policies. In 2013, the number of Americans age sixty-five or older reached 44.7 million, which is about 14.1 percent of the total population. The number of older Americans increased by 8.8 million (24.7 percent) between 2003 and 2013; this rate was only 6.8 percent for the population under age sixty-five. It is estimated that the number of people age sixty-five or older will reach 56.4 million in 2020; by 2060, the number is expected to be 98.2 million (U.S. Department of Health and Human Services, Administration on Aging 2014). In 2008, 42 percent of the workforce (54.6 million employees) indicated that they had provided elder care within the previous five years; 49 percent of the workforce expected to provide elder care in the next five years (Aumann et al. 2010). As the elder population continues to increase at a dramatic rate, greater demands will be placed on the younger generations to care for them. Indeed, it is estimated that by 2020, one in three households will be responsible for caring for an elderly relative (Wisensale 2009, 261).

Today most workers have some level of responsibility for the care of either children or older family relatives (Boushey and Mitukiewicz 2014). Policies that recognize these changes and allow employees the job-protected leave that they need would ease the pressure on both workers and their families. Indeed, the effects of family leave policies—or the lack thereof—are far reaching. The availability and generosity of leaves affect parents' time for caregiving, their ability to participate in civil society, and their families' economic well-being (Gornick and Meyers 2003, chap. 5). Numerous studies have also found a connection between parental leave and the health and welfare of mothers, fathers, and children (Human Rights Watch 2011). Moreover, employers are positively affected by family leave policies. Workers who receive paid leave are more likely to return to their same employer, which greatly reduces turnover costs (Milkman and Appelbaum 2013; Bell and Newman 2003, 4). Companies in the United States that are required to provide unpaid leave under the FMLA have reported that the policy has either a positive or neutral effect on profitability and growth (Cantor et al. 2001).

Family leave policies are especially important for women because—even with the growing involvement of men—they are still typically the primary caregivers in the family. Indeed, 60 percent of caregivers for adults are female (American Association of Retired Persons Public Policy Institute and National Alliance for Caregiving 2015, 16). Likewise, women are more likely to provide care for children. As caregivers, women often need time off from work to fulfill their unpaid duties. Throughout the Western world, women take an overwhelming majority of leave available, even when it is extended to fathers (Morgan 2006, 9; Bruning and Plantenga 1999). Without leave benefits, women often must exit the workforce or end up in low-paid, part-time, irregular, and unstable jobs after they have children. Family leave coverage helps raise women's earning capacity because it allows them to remain with the same employer throughout the period of childbirth (Waldfogel 1998). This increases both women's and their employers' incentives to invest in firm-specific training for women, which can help them advance in their careers. Maintaining workplace ties is also important because social benefits such as health care and pensions are often contingent on labor force participation (Orloff 1993).

Clearly the availability of leave is crucial for gender equality. But even policies that are nominally gender neutral often affect men and women in different ways.[4] Because public policy has typically been based on traditional ideas of women's roles, it has reinforced women's subordinate status (Conway, Ahern, and Steuernagel 2005, 6). Therefore, it is important to examine both the availability and the generosity of leave policies in order to understand their full gendered repercussions. The length of leaves can negatively affect women's participation rates in the workforce, lowering their earning capacity, increasing occupational segregation, and contributing to continuing gender inequality in the home. For example, women who take leave for a year or longer are much less likely to return to their jobs. Likewise, if women are granted only a minimal amount of time away from work, they are more likely to quit after giving birth (Gornick and Meyers 2003; Waldfogel 1998). Finally, as is discussed in detail in Chapter 3, wage replacement during leave is crucial for women. Many women cannot afford to take unpaid leave and must return to work early (Lerner 2015; Jacobs and Gerson 2004; Heymann 2005).

Shortened leaves can be harmful to the physical and emotional health of both mother and child (Tanaka 2005). Moreover, unpaid leave decreases women's lifetime earnings, which can affect gender equity in the workplace and the home (Rose and Hartmann 2004, iv; Waldfogel 1997, 1998; Appelbaum and Milkman 2011).

Many advocates of the expansion of family leave policies hope to strengthen women's position in society by providing them with better ways to reconcile their work lives with their family lives. Often they point to laws that promote a dual earner-carer model to achieve balance.[5] The countries that have the most supportive policies for dual earner-carer families have prioritized gender neutrality in leave benefits and created incentives for men to take advantage of the benefits (Gornick and Meyers 2003, 101).[6] National-level leave policies in the United States are gender neutral in name yet do little to encourage men to use them. At the same time, women are often excluded from coverage because of the stringent parameters of the law, and only three states currently provide wage replacement during leave.[7]

Temporary Disability Insurance

In the United States, there is no federal-state insurance system for short-term disability that compares with the federal-state system of unemployment insurance. However, in 1946 Congress amended the Federal Unemployment Tax Act "to permit states where employees make contributions under the unemployment insurance program to use some or all of these contributions to pay disability benefits." Rhode Island had already passed the first state law in 1942; California, New Jersey, and New York followed throughout the 1940s. In 1969, Hawaii became the last state to adopt such a program (U.S. Social Security Administration, Office of Retirement and Disability Policy 2014). Funding and coverage varies among the five states; Table 1.1 summarizes these differences. Temporary Disability Insurance (TDI) programs provide paid leave to employees during a temporary illness or injury unrelated to work; however, the benefits did not apply to pregnant women until the passage of the PDA in 1978 (Fass 2009, 6). At that time, TDI covered about 50 percent of all women and over 80 percent of working women in the five states that

TABLE 1.1   EXISTING STATE TEMPORARY DISABILITY INSURANCE PROGRAMS, 2016

	California	Hawaii*	New Jersey	New York	Rhode Island
Year enacted	1946	1969	1948	1949	1942
Eligibility	Earned at least $300 from which State Disability Insurance (SDI)[†] deductions were withheld during any quarter in the base period	(1) Worked at least fourteen weeks in the previous year; (2) received pay for at least twenty hours of work during each of those weeks; (3) earned at least $400 in that year	(1) Worked at least twenty calendar weeks of New Jersey covered employment; (2) earned either at least $165 during each of the twenty weeks or at least $8,300 during the base year	Must work for a New York covered employer for at least four consecutive weeks	Earned at least $11,520 from which TDI/TCI deductions were withheld during the twelve-month base period or alternate base period[‡]
Benefit level	55 percent of an employee's weekly earnings, up to $1,129 per week	58 percent of an employee's weekly earnings, up to $570 per week	66 percent of an employee's weekly earnings, up to $615 per week	50 percent of an employee's weekly wages, up to $170 per week	4.62 percent of an employee's wages paid in the highest quarter of the base period; minimum is $84 per week; maximum is $795 per week[§]

Length of benefits	Fifty-two weeks	Twenty-six weeks	Twenty-six weeks	Twenty-six weeks	Thirty weeks
Funding source(s)	Employee only	Employee and employer	Employee and employer	Employee and employer	Employee only

Sources: California Employment Development Department, n.d., "State Disability Insurance"; Hawaii Department of Labor and Industrial Relations, Disability Compensation Division, n.d.; New Jersey Department of Labor and Workforce Development, n.d.; New York State Workers' Compensation Board, n.d.; Rhode Island Department of Labor and Training, n.d., "Temporary Disability Insurance."

* Although Hawaii has a TDI program, it has largely been privatized.

† SDI is California's TDI program.

‡ If this amount has not been met, an employee may still be eligible for benefits if he or she earned at least $1,920 in one of the base period quarters, the total base period taxable wages are at least one and one-half times the employee's highest quarter of earnings, and the base period taxable wages are at least $3,840.

§ An employee may also be entitled to a dependency allowance if he or she has dependent children under age eighteen or over age eighteen and incapacitated. This allowance is limited to five dependents and is equal to the greater of $10 or 7 percent of the benefit rate.

had adopted it, so access to paid maternity leave expanded dramatically under the policy (Stearns 2015).

Although TDI allows biological mothers to take paid leave from work around the period of childbirth, it is considered disability leave rather than some type of family leave. These programs do not provide benefits for fathers or adoptive mothers. Because the leave is aimed only at women, it may be considered the type of special treatment that women's movement actors in the United States fervently opposed during the fight for the FMLA. Indeed, a study by Sylvia Guendelman and colleagues (2006) demonstrates the reluctance that many women felt when using TDI for maternity leave. The authors examined the rates at which women in Southern California used the paid leave available to them through TDI from 2002 to 2003, a year before paid family leave was implemented. Although the state provided them with four weeks of paid antenatal leave and six to eight weeks paid postnatal leave, women were hesitant to take advantage of the full time allotted to them, especially antenatally. Of the women surveyed, 52 percent worked until they gave birth, 32 percent took antenatal leave with the expectation that they would return to their job sometime after giving birth, 9 percent quit their jobs, 5 percent cut back on their hours, and 2 percent were fired during pregnancy (66). More telling is the fact that 52 percent of the women who took leave cited medical problems as the reason; only 25 percent named maternity leave benefits as their motivation. Most women did not want to be classified as an employee needing special treatment beyond the disability leave that was afforded all employees.

In addition to allowing women to take paid maternity leave, TDI programs have facilitated the implementation of paid family leave in California, New Jersey, and Rhode Island. Since those states had already developed the necessary infrastructure to fund TDI, it was relatively easy to expand the program to be used for paid family leave. Beginning in 2018, New York will administer paid family leave through its TDI program as well. Because of the ease of use, it is somewhat surprising that no other states have adopted similar TDI models. As Steven K. Wisensale (2001, 122) indicates, it is also rather curious that none of the five states has abandoned the program.[8]

Family Leave Policies in the United States

At the National Level

In the United States, under the Family and Medical Leave Act of 1993, eligible employees can take up to twelve weeks of unpaid job-protected leave for the following reasons: the birth and care of a newborn child of the employee; the placement with the employee of a son or daughter for adoption or foster care; to care for an immediate family member (spouse, child, or parent) with a serious health condition; and the employee's own illness. However, there are many restrictions in the act: the company must have at least fifty employees within a seventy-five mile radius, the employee must have been employed by the company for at least one year and have worked at least 1,250 hours in that year, and employees in the top 10 percent of the company's pay scale may be excluded.[9] This means that many employees of small businesses, those who cannot afford to lose twelve weeks of pay, and those at the top of their organizations will not be able to capitalize on this leave (Conway, Ahern, and Steuernagel 2005, 189).

At the State Level

There is no federal paid leave in the United States, but California, New Jersey, and Rhode Island have implemented paid family leave policies. In 2016, New York adopted paid family leave that will take effect in 2018. In May 2007, Washington State passed a law providing five weeks of paid leave to parents to care for a newborn or newly adopted child (Washington State Legislature, n.d., "SB 5659"). This law was originally scheduled to take effect in October 2009, but the implementation date has been postponed indefinitely because of budgetary conflicts. As detailed in Chapter 5, activists have largely abandoned this law to work toward more comprehensive family leave legislation.

In July 2004, California became the first state to provide paid family leave to all workers who are covered by the State Disability Insurance (SDI) program. The Paid Family Leave (PFL) insurance program offers up to six weeks of benefits during a twelve-month period in order to care for a seriously ill family member or to bond with a new minor child.[10] Employees receive approximately 55 percent of their lost wages during this time, up to a maximum of $1,129 per week. Administered by the California Employment Development Department, the PFL program is funded by employees through the SDI program, rather than employers. To be eligible, an employee must have earned at least $300 from which SDI deductions were withheld during any quarter in the base period, which is approximately five to eighteen months prior to the claim (California Employment Development Department, n.d.). Although California's PFL program does not protect the employee's job during leave, many employees are covered under the FMLA and the California Family Rights Act (CFRA).[11]

On May 2, 2008, New Jersey governor Jon Corzine signed a bill to allow up to six weeks of paid leave during a twelve-month period to care for newborns and newly adopted or foster children, or for seriously ill family members.[12] Funded though the state's TDI program, the plan provides workers with up to two-thirds of their usual wage, with a weekly maximum of $615. The benefits extend to employees who have worked for a New Jersey employer for at least twenty weeks and who have earned at least $168 in a base week, or $8,400 during the base year, which is the fifty-two weeks prior to the start of leave (New Jersey Department of Labor and Workforce Development, n.d.). This law does not guarantee the employee's reinstatement upon return from leave; only employees covered by either the FMLA or the New Jersey Family Leave Act (NJFLA) receive this protection.[13]

On July 23, 2013, Rhode Island enacted the Temporary Caregiver Insurance (TCI) program. Taking effect on January 5, 2014, TCI provides Rhode Island workers with up to four weeks of benefits during a twelve-month period to bond with a new child or care for a family member with a serious health condition.[14] As in California and New Jersey, the program is funded completely by employee payroll deductions. While on leave, employees receive 4.62 percent of the wages paid to them in the highest quarter of their base period; the maximum benefit is $795. Rhode Island's program also provides job protection and health benefits protection for all employees eligible for TCI. Employees in Rhode Island are eligible for benefits if they have earned at least $11,520 in either the base period or an alternative base period (Rhode Island Department of Labor and Training, n.d., "Temporary Disability Insurance").

On March 31, 2016, government leaders in New York announced that they had reached a budget agreement that included the country's most extensive paid family leave program to date. On April 4, 2016, Governor Andrew Cuomo signed into law a bill providing employees eight weeks of job-protected, paid leave during a twelve-month period. The law will take effect in 2018, with the length of leave increasing to twelve weeks by 2021. Workers will be able to take leave to bond with a new child, care for a seriously ill family member, or address certain military family needs. Benefits will start at 50 percent of an employee's weekly earnings, up to a cap of $648. By 2021, the wage replacement rate will be 67 percent, up to a cap of $868. As in California, New Jersey, and Rhode Island, New York will provide paid family leave through its existing TDI system. Although New York's TDI program is financed by both employers and employees, only employees will pay into the paid family leave fund (A Better Balance 2016; Katz et al. 2016).

Explaining Public Policy Variation

A vast literature seeks to explain why governments decide to adopt certain public policies while eschewing others. Typically, scholars point to the effects of social and economic conditions and political institutions, processes, and behaviors on public policies. For example, the existence of multiple veto points in a political system often slows the pace of policy change (Tsebelis 1995; Huber and Stephens 2001). Numerous studies have examined the effects of public opinion on the policy-making process (Key 1961; Page and Shapiro 1983; Burstein 2003). Other scholars have focused on the role of political parties, interest groups, elites, and social movements (Aldrich 2011; Blaise, Blake, and Dion 1996; Schattschneider 1960; McConnell 1966; Wright 1996; Burstein and Linton 2002).

Family leave policy is clearly a gendered issue, as women are much more likely than men to take leave to care for a new baby or a sick family member (Boushey, Farrell, and Schmitt 2013; Lewis 1993; Morgan 2006). Therefore, I place the issue within the larger literature that studies the role of women's movements in shaping gender-based policies. In recent decades, an increasing number of women's issues have found a place on the public agenda in postindustrial democracies. Also, a growing body of research examines the role of political actors in shaping such gender policies.

Differences in actors' characteristics and strategies and the political environment in which they work are central to explaining changes in gender policies (Banaszak 1996; Haussman and Sauer 2007; McBride and Mazur 2010; Morgan and Zippel 2003; Weldon 2002b, 2006, 2011). With regard to family leave in the United States, women's movements have a significant influence on the policy-making process.

Women's Movements

A women's movement is a type of social movement aimed at promoting the well-being or status of women (Tilly 1978). Therefore, to understand women's movements fully, a brief discussion of the broader social movement literature is necessary. A social movement is "a sustained series of interactions between power holders and persons successfully claiming to speak on behalf of a constituency lacking formal representation, in the course of which those persons make publicly visible demands for changes in the distribution or exercise of power, and back those demands with public demonstrations of support" (Tilly 1984, 306). Such a movement entails a wide-ranging social group, rather than the isolated activity of a few people, where there is "solidarity in pursuit of common goals" (Molyneux 1998, 70). Social movements affect democratic political systems in a number of important ways, including stopping or prompting government action, changing social values, influencing policy debate, improving substantive representation for marginalized groups, reducing social conflict, and transforming government institutions (Rochon and Mazmanian 1993; Tarrow 1994; Tilly 1995; Diani 1992; Wolbrecht and Hero 2005; Weldon 2011).

Social movements work to get particular ideas recognized as problems by both the general public and policy makers through tactics such as protests, voter mobilization, the creation or co-optation of interest groups, and the endorsement of and work for specific candidates and referenda proposals. Once a social movement has drawn attention to an issue, the issue has the opportunity to be seen and adopted by government officials, legislators, and other policy makers. Thus, getting an issue on the agenda is crucial to policy change (Kingdon 1984; Cobb and Elder 1972).

Social movements attempt to frame issues in terms that will enhance their goals (Benford and Snow 2000; Snow and Benford 1992). "Framing" refers to the "conscious strategic efforts by groups of people to fashion shared understandings of the world and of themselves that legitimate and motivate collective action" (McAdam, McCarthy, and Zald 1996, 6; see also Schattschneider 1960). Movement actors attempt to link their ideals to popular beliefs in order to rally support for their cause. If the movement's frame of the issue gets incorporated into the dominant frame of debate, the movement can then claim to have a place in the policy-making process (Schneider and Ingram 1993).

Women's movements share most characteristics of social movements; they are set apart from other social movements in that they are "consciously and explicitly gendered" (McBride and Mazur 2010, 145).[15] A women's movement consists of both "the discourse of women's movements—the ideas, aspirations, and identities developed from gender consciousness that inspire collective behavior— and the actors articulating these points in public" (McBride and Mazur 2010, 144; see also Ferree and Hess 2000). Because it is difficult to adequately observe the formation of women's movement ideas and discourse, empirical studies focus on women's movement actors (WMAs). WMAs are the individuals and formal and informal organizations that "are inspired by movement thinkers to promote what they see as women's interests" (McBride and Mazur 2010, 30). By definition, WMAs are nonstate actors.[16]

Scholars have repeatedly identified women's movement strength as a predictor of policy success (Amenta et al. 2010; Katzenstein 1989; Mazur 2002; Weldon 2002b, 2011).[17] Strength can be gauged by the level of political support the movement garners and the resources it commands (Weldon 2006). It can also be assessed through an examination of the narrative accounts of the movement, specifically looking for descriptions such as "strong" or "powerful." Likewise, the number of women's organizations or the number of members they have can signify the strength of the women's movement. Movements that are strong or influential "can command public support and attention, while weaker ones have trouble convincing the media and others that their positions and opinions are important for public discussion" (Weldon 2002b, 80).[18]

When women's movements are strong, they increase their chances of advancing women's rights. WMAs play a crucial role in getting their priority issues on the governmental agenda because they are often the first to articulate the matter. Indeed, agenda setting is one of the main ways in which WMAs influence public policy (Mansbridge 1995; Morgan 2006; Weldon 2002b). A strong movement will be better poised to influence the government's agenda, for it can successfully mobilize grassroots action and electoral support, and its spokespeople become legitimate contributors to public discourse (Kingdon 1984; Rochon and Mazmanian 1993). Legislators are also more likely to respond favorably to women's demands when women's movements are highly mobilized (Costain 1998).

Clearly, the strength of women's movements plays a role in determining gender policy outcomes. However, in the case of family leave policy, strength does little to explain the lack of paid leave at the national level, for the American women's movement has historically been strong. Indeed, the United States has produced one of the strongest women's movements in the Western world (Gelb 1989; Morgan 2006, 19–20; Weldon 2011). Although there is some variation at the state level, it does not correspond to the variation in family leave policies. In other words, the states with the strongest women's movements have not automatically adopted the most generous family leave policies. At the same time, the states that have already passed paid family leave do have strong, autonomous women's movements. To gain a fuller understanding of the ways in which women's movements affect policy development, I also examine the cohesiveness and issue prioritization of movements. When the women's movement is united in its support of a piece of legislation and positions it as a priority on its agenda, WMAs can better influence the policy-making process.

Cohesion

Even when a women's movement is strong, it may be internally divided on certain issues; such fragmentation decreases the amount of influence the movement can have on the policy-making process. Therefore, it is necessary to examine the cohesion of the women's movement in the context of family leave policy making. Cohesion "is present when movement groups active on the issue agree on the frame of the debate and the policy proposal" (Lovenduski 2005, 16).

Framing is a key function of women's movements. Because the way in which the major policy actors depict policy issues can greatly affect the content of both policy debate and the policy itself, WMAs continually try to insert their own ideas and frames into the dominant discourse (Lovenduski 2005, 6–8; Mazur 2001). Once successful in framing the issue in terms that would improve the status of women, the women's movement will attempt to maintain these frames so debates surrounding the issue will always be conducted in such terms. Problems arise when WMAs cannot agree on how to frame an issue. But when a movement is cohesive, it will be more likely to successfully influence the policy-making process (Lovenduski 2005; Outshoorn 2004; Stetson 2001b).

In the United States, there has historically been dissent within the women's movement regarding discourse on family leave. Many WMAs are wary of pressing for "maternity leave" for fear of drawing too much attention to gender differences in the workplace. Major women's groups, such as the National Organization for Women (NOW), have gone as far as to protest against protective labor legislation, including paid maternity leave (Barakso 2004). These "equal-treatment" feminists argue that by singling women out for special privilege, leave that is provided only for women will further the belief that they should be treated differently. Such WMAs clash with "special-treatment" feminists who claim that women are different from men and that pregnancy presents job obstacles for women that men do not face. For that reason, these WMAs advocate maternity leave that compensates women for their special needs (Kay 1985; Vogel 1990, 1995; W. Williams 1984–1985). Equal-treatment feminists have generally won out, which is why the first bill introduced in Congress in 1985 identified "parental" leave instead of "maternal" leave (Wisensale 2001, 139).[19] This disagreement between equal-treatment feminists who want formal equality and special-treatment feminists who advocate substantive equality weakened the bargaining power of the women's movement during the fight for the FMLA. Likewise, discord regarding the details of the legislation, such as whether leave should be paid, diminished WMAs' influence on lawmakers. For the most part, these divisions have not been present within more recent campaigns, as legislative proposals that include formal equality and wage replacement have become the norm. However, in some cases there is still disagreement over issues such as length of leave, wage replacement levels, sources of funding, and definition of "family member."

Issue Prioritization

Issue priority refers to the attention WMAs devote to an issue and the position of that issue on the list of overall movement concerns (Outshoorn 2004, 17; Lovenduski 2005, 16). To effect policy change, WMAs must mark an issue as a movement priority; movement strength and cohesion mean little if actors are not committed to the issue. Agenda setting is one of the key contributions that women's movements can make to the policy process. However, WMAs will not exert much energy trying to get an issue on the government's agenda if they are not passionate about it. WMAs are more likely to success-fully pressure policy makers to adopt family leave policies if the issue is among the top priorities on the movement's agenda (Lovenduski 2005; Outshoorn 2004).

In the United States, the national women's movement has his-torically focused much of its energy on issues like reproductive rights and violence against women. For most of the early part of the second wave of feminism, family leave policies were not even on the women's movement agenda in the United States. Although the issue has gradu-ally received more attention, it has never become a top priority at the national level. A number of women's movements at the state level have recently begun to reposition paid family leave higher on their agendas; however, other issues such as domestic violence and sexual assault, equal pay, gay rights, and reproductive freedoms may take precedence.

The Interaction Effect

WMAs can influence the policy-making process in a number of ways, such as agenda setting, framing, and lobbying. However, there is not usually a direct relationship between women's movements and policy outcomes (Katzenstein 1987, 13). Rather, women's movements often effect policy change through their alliances with other orga-nizations, interest groups, state actors, and political parties. For ex-ample, Susan J. Carroll (2006) finds that female legislators feel more freedom to fight for women in the policy process when they have alternative spaces—like those that women's organizations provide—that reinforce their feminist identity and support their legislative actions. Women's policy agencies within the state, such as women's commissions or women's bureaus, also benefit from political support from women's movements (Weldon 2002a, 1160).

Policy makers are unlikely to pass generous family leave policies in the absence of a strong women's movement that is united in its support of the legislation and has made it a priority. But when WMAs meet these conditions, they can exert significant pressure on legislators. However, women's movements do not act alone, and no one factor can fully explain the outcomes of the policy-making process. Therefore, I examine other actors that may influence the passage of family leave policies, such as unions and organizations representing the interests of families, children, seniors, and individuals with disabilities. I look for critical actors in the legislature, women's policy agencies within the bureaucracies, and party control of both the executive and legislative branches. I also analyze the strength of the countermovement that works to prevent the passage of paid family leave.

Labor Unions

Labor unions, which promote and protect the welfare of workers, are sites of resistance in the fight against corporate rule (Francia 2006). Historically, unions have used strikes and collective bargaining to gain improved rights and benefits in the workplace. Over time, unions have evolved into interest groups that work primarily within existing institutional channels to bring about change (Asher et al. 2001). They influence congressional policy through tools such as lobbying, campaign contributions, issue advertising, and grassroots activities. They help women press their demands for legislation concerning equal opportunity, pay equity, and protection against sexual and racial harassment. In general, unions have played a critical role in working to expand the social welfare state (Frank and Lipner 1988). Union membership in the United States has declined significantly in recent decades, falling from 24.0 percent of workers in 1973 to 11.1 percent in 2015 (Hirsch and Macpherson 2003, 2016). Although this has weakened unions' ability to drive paid family leave efforts at the national level, union membership has not dropped at the same rate across the states. Membership levels range from 2.1 percent in South Carolina to 24.7 percent in New York; the degree of influence that unions are able to exert in state-level paid leave campaigns will vary in similar fashion (Hirsch and Macpherson 2003, 2015). Even with the drop in union membership, Ruth Milkman and Eileen Appelbaum (2013) still assert that support from organized labor is crucial to the passage of paid family leave in the states. However, they stress that it "cannot be taken for granted, since some labor leaders, most of whom are still male, may not see this issue as a high priority" (23). Therefore, it often falls to WMAs to press unions to take up the issue.

Critical Actors

Numerous studies demonstrate a positive correlation between an absence of women in positions of power and gender-biased policies that discriminate against women (Lovenduski 1986; Gelb 1989; Sainsbury 1994). Female politicians are more likely to represent women and introduce bills that support women's rights (Mansbridge 1999; Thomas 1994; Caiazza 2004; Swers 2002; Dodson 2006). Recent studies have found that the presence of women in the legislature has a positive effect on the adoption and generosity of leave policies (Kittilson 2008; Lambert 2008; Williamson and Carnes 2013). At the same time, women or men can be "critical actors"—individuals in office who significantly move the policy process forward—in the fight for paid family leave (Childs and Krook 2006; Dahlerup 1988).

Women's Policy Agencies

A women's policy agency (WPA) is a structure that is both formally established by government statute or decree and officially charged with addressing women's status and rights or promoting sex-based equality (Stetson and Mazur 1995, 2–5; Mazur 2001, 3–4). WPAs go by a variety of names. The United Nations refers to them as "national policy machinery for the advancement of women" (Stetson and Mazur 1995, 3); in the United States they are typically called women's bureaus or commissions. More generally, these agencies are known as state feminist offices, and the women who staff them and promote a feminist agenda are called "femocrats" (Eisenstein 1990, 1996; Sawer 1990, 1996; Naumann 2005). Now seen as legitimate state structures, women's policy agencies are present in most countries at the federal level (Weldon 2002b). WPAs can "facilitate [women's] movement success by gendering issue definitions used by policy actors in ways that coincide with movement frames in policy debates, leading to both access and policy change" (McBride and Mazur 2010, 5).

Party or Coalition in Power

At the national level, leftist parties are generally more committed to gender equality (Carroll 2001; Costain 1992; Htun and Power 2006). Olga Avdeyeva (2010) observed a connection between the ideological makeup of national parliaments and the level of access women's groups have in the policy-making process. Specifically, she found that "strong women's movements are able to influence government decisions when they find ideological supporters within the government" (212). Since leftist parties are more likely to be "ideological supporters" of women's movements, WMAs will have a better chance of accessing and influencing the policy-making process when leftist parties are in power.

A similar pattern is found at the state level in the United States. Jeff Cummins (2011) observes that political party control significantly affects the percentage of citizens who gain access to health insurance coverage. In a study of abortion policy at the state level, Marshall H. Medoff, Christopher Dennis, and Kerri Stephens (2011) conclude that party control in the legislative and executive branches affects the likelihood that a state will enact a parental involvement law. With regard to parental leave, Sarah Williamson and Matthew Carnes (2013) find that states with a pattern of Democratic-controlled legislatures typically adopt more generous protections.

Strength of Opposition/Countermovement

Movements attempt to challenge the dominant culture, which often triggers the formation of opposition or countermovements (Staggenborg 1998; Zald and Useem 1987; Meyer and Staggenborg 1996).

Because women's movements frequently seek to alter the status quo of gender and family relations, they tend to provoke strong counter-movements. A countermovement, then, refers to the actors who are actively working against the WMAs' goals in the policy arena. For example, many antifeminist organizations, such as the Eagle Forum and Stop ERA, have formed specifically to fight against the passage of the Equal Rights Amendment (ERA) and to preserve traditional gender roles in the family (Soule and Olzak 2004; Ashley and Olson 1998). Antiabortion groups such as Operation Rescue have engaged in both peaceful demonstrations and sometimes violent confrontations to shut down abortion clinics (Meyer and Staggenborg 1996, 1629). Business interests are typically the primary opponents of family leave policies (Bernstein 2001; Elving 1995).[20]

Methods and Data

To date, there have been numerous cross-national works that compare and contrast the generosity of family leave policies (Ray, Gornick, and Schmitt 2009; Gornick and Meyers 2003, chap. 5; Bruning and Plantenga 1999). There are also many quantitative studies that seek to explain variation in family leave policies (Williamson and Carnes 2013; Kittilson 2008; Lambert 2008; Morgan and Zippel 2003). A number of scholars have qualitatively examined the passage of the FMLA (Elving 1995; Wisensale 2001; Radigan 1988; Bernstein 2001; White 2006). However, there is little qualitative analysis on the process of family leave policy making in the United States since that time. Therefore, I employ qualitative methods—specifically process tracing—to explain developments in family leave policies throughout the United States at both the national and the state levels. David Collier defines process tracing as "the systematic examination of diagnostic evidence selected and analyzed in light of research questions and hypotheses posed by the investigator" (2011, 823). Using this form of within-case analysis, I investigate the chain of events that has led to the adoption of different family leave policies (see George and McKeown 1985; George and Bennett 2005, chap. 10). Telling "policy stories" enables me to detect patterns in successful and unsuccessful policies (Jacobs and Davies 1994, 2). Tracing the evolution of family leave policies allows me to examine the various explanatory factors and interactions in a way that cannot be captured in a quantitative analysis.

I begin my investigation on the national level in the 1960s, at the onset of the second wave of feminism in the United States. Public policy with regard to pregnant women was beginning to change at this time. In the United States, the 1972 Equal Employment Opportunity Commission (EEOC) guidelines applied the 1964 Civil Rights Act principle of equal treatment to pregnancy. These guidelines defined disabilities resulting from pregnancy, such as miscarriage, abortion, or childbirth, as "temporary disabilities," which meant that women experiencing pregnancy disabilities should receive all of the usual benefits associated with a temporary disability. As I expand on in Chapter 2, the guidelines did little to change pregnancy discrimination practices in the workforce. However, they signaled a starting point in the national debate on family leave policies. Since that time, there have been numerous campaigns at both the national and the state levels for the expansion of family leave benefits.

To understand the family leave policy-making process in the United States, I gather information from a variety of sources, including archival data and documents put forth by women's organizations. For example, I review over four decades of *National NOW Times*, the official journal of the National Organization for Women, to determine the organization's issue prioritization during that time. Because NOW is arguably the largest and most powerful women's organization in the United States, an examination of its activism will shed light on the ways in which it helped shape the policy-making process. I also consider the significant influence of other women's groups, such as the League of Women Voters and the National Partnership for Women and Families.[21] I collect original data in the form of interviews with activists who have been involved in the fight for the passage of family leave, supplementing my findings with secondary accounts of the process.

This book contributes to the theoretical understanding of policy-making processes. It adds to the growing body of work on family policy, and the results of the analysis can help explain other governments' experiences with the development of such policies. The model can also be applied to women's movements' experiences with other work-life policies, such as government-sponsored child care. More broadly, this work adds to the literature on women's movements—and social movements in general—and their effects on the policy-making process. Most work on social movements still identifies male-led movements as the norm; therefore, more research is needed on women's movements (Ferree and Mueller 2004, 577). Jennifer Marchbank claims that "if we understand the methods used by patriarchal systems to keep WIIs [Women's Interest Issues] off the agenda, marginalise and delegitimise them, then we shall be able to devise strategies for effectively challenging the patriarchal status quo" (2000, 1). This book helps illuminate the ways in which activists have overcome opposition to the passage of family leave policies; such knowledge may inform the ways in which WMAs work for the passage of other policies aimed at improving gender equality in the future.

Finally, this book highlights the increasing demand for family leave policies in the United States—as well as the need for research addressing such policies. The United States is notorious for its position as the only developed country in the world without any type of mandated paid family leave. The expansion of paid leave within the country over the last decade demonstrates that need and demand for family leave are shifting. Moreover, the fact that some of these policy changes are currently in progress means that little analysis has been done on them yet; this reinforces the necessity for more qualitative work. Such analysis will provide a better understanding of family leave policy variation throughout both the United States and the rest of the world.

Overview of the Book

In the following pages, I analyze the factors that have influenced the family leave policy-making process in the United States. Chapter 2 focuses on the national level, describing the circumstances surrounding the passage of the FMLA in 1993. I highlight the role that women's movement actors played in the campaign leading up to the passage of the law, evaluating the movement's strength, cohesion, and issue prioritization. I address the ways in which other actors, such as labor unions, groups representing the interests of children and seniors, and individual legislators, played a significant part in the eventual passage of the law. Likewise, I assess the ways in which business interests shaped the policy-making process.

In Chapter 3, I describe the effects of the FMLA on Americans' work-life balance, including the repercussions from the fact that leave is unpaid. I examine the numerous attempts to expand the FMLA since its passage and describe the alterations that have been adopted. The first change to the FMLA expanded coverage to an individual whose military family member either is called to active duty in support of a military operation or has incurred serious injury or illness in the line of duty. Although this amendment did not pass until 2008—fifteen years after the law's initial passage—the increasing visibility of state campaigns has recently reinvigorated activism at the national level. There have been new proposals for paid leave for federal employees, the creation of a state paid leave fund within the U.S. Department of Labor, and most recently the introduction of the Family and Medical Insurance Leave (FAMILY) Act, which would provide virtually all workers up to twelve weeks of paid family leave.

In Chapters 4 and 5, I shift my focus to the state level. Chapter 4 highlights the states that have passed paid family leave legislation: California, New Jersey, Rhode Island, and New York. Using interview data, primary documents, and secondary accounts of the policy-making process, I analyze the role that WMAs and activist organizations played in the passage of leave in each case. I also examine the political environment, including partisan control and the presence of critical actors in the government, as well as the intensity of the countermovement. In Chapter 5, I explore four states that have proposed paid family leave legislation but have not yet passed such laws: Washington, Oregon, Massachusetts, and Hawaii. Although Washington adopted a paid parental leave law in 2007, it never implemented the program because of the lack of a funding mechanism. In 2015, a new bill with significantly expanded provisions was introduced but has yet to pass; I focus on this bill in Chapter 5. Using techniques similar to those employed in Chapter 4, I trace the progress of the bills to discover the role that various actors have played in the policy-making process and the primary reasons that paid family leave has not passed in these cases.

Chapter 6 summarizes the main findings of the book. I revisit the discussion on the importance of social movements in influencing public policy and evaluate the role that WMAs and other activists have played in the particular issue of paid family leave. I explore the growing number of private companies and municipal governments that—in the absence of comprehensive legislation at the federal level—are providing family leave to their employees. Drawing lessons from the case studies, I conclude by addressing the future of paid family leave policies in the United States.

2

The Passage of the National Family and Medical Leave Act (FMLA)

As described in Chapter 1, the United States is the only developed country in the world that does not guarantee paid family leave. Passed in 1993, the Family and Medical Leave Act (FMLA) provides twelve weeks of unpaid, job-protected leave for employees to care for a new child or sick family member, or because of the employee's own serious illness.[1] However, because of the stringent eligibility requirements, only about 60 percent of U.S. workers meet the requirements for leave under the FMLA (Ray, Gornick, and Schmitt 2009; Heymann and Earle 2010, 57). Of those covered, many cannot afford to take unpaid time from work (Lerner 2015; Jacobs and Gerson 2004; Heymann 2005). Despite these shortcomings, the FMLA was a major accomplishment for the coalition that worked for its passage for almost a decade. Not only would the law go on to help millions of individuals by ensuring their job security while on leave, but it was also a symbolic victory because it demonstrated the growing recognition that policy makers have a significant role to play in improving work-life balance of those individuals.

In this chapter, I discuss the circumstances surrounding the passage of the FMLA, paying special attention to the women's movement actors (WMAs) who played a major role in this historic achievement. After establishing the United States as a liberal welfare regime, I describe the historical environment preceding the drafting of the first national-level family leave bill in 1984. I then detail the development of the FMLA through its four name changes, describing the women's movement's strength, cohesion, and issue prioritization throughout the campaign. I address the significant contribution that other actors made to the campaign as well, including unions, Catholic groups, and organizations representing the interests of children, seniors, and those with disabilities. Likewise, I note the importance of individual legislators, both in moving the legislation forward and in blocking its passage. Finally, I address the significant influence wielded by business interests.

The United States as a Liberal Welfare Regime

The United States has long exemplified a political culture that is suspicious of "big government." In general, the government has taken a limited role in providing social welfare benefits. As a liberal[2] individualist country, the United States places greater emphasis on the private sector to provide such protections, and Americans tend to be wary of allocating resources through the national government (Esping-Andersen 1990).[3] In other words, citizens are "encouraged to seek their welfare in the market" (Myles 1998, 344). There is a focus on "negative liberty," which entails freedom from state regulation of personal and economic affairs (O'Connor, Orloff, and Shaver 1999, 28). When benefits are provided, they are generally modest and may be means-tested.

The American liberal welfare state differs considerably from most European states, which are generally classified as either conservative/corporatist or social democratic. In the conservative/corporatist states common throughout continental Europe, benefits are more generous than those in liberal regimes. However, benefits are typically linked to earnings in the labor market and therefore maintain existing social patterns. Social democratic welfare states are found in the Nordic countries. They generally work to promote equality through the provision of high levels of universal benefits and services by the state (Esping-Andersen 1990). It is not surprising that the United States and Europe have developed such different family leave policies; they are reflective of a larger welfare state divergence (see Alesina and Glaeser 2004; Alesina, Glaeser, and Sacerdote 2001; Flora and Heidenheimer 1981; Gilens 1999).

Even in comparison to other liberal welfare states, the United States is considered a welfare state "laggard" (Lipset 1990, 4; Alesina and Glaeser 2004; Gilens 1999). Citizens embrace an individualist culture and free market rhetoric, and they are less likely to support large welfare programs and an active role for government than most other Western democracies (Shapiro and Young 1989). Since the late 1970s, there has been a rise in popularity of those ideologies and political forces that celebrate market liberalism (O'Connor, Orloff, and Shaver 1999, 1). This neoliberal discourse "helped to shift and justify citizens' perceptions from a vision of states as activist centers of policy initiatives to one of states as limited, morally and economically, in their responsibilities" (Banaszak, Beckwith, and Rucht 2003, 8).[4]

In the United States, there is substantial faith in the free market, and "women and men are *in principle* treated as equals, without any attention being given to the current differences between the sexes with regard to their care duties" (Van Doorne-Huiskes 1999, 100–101; emphasis added). In reality, liberalism contributes to and perpetuates the inequality between the sexes (MacKinnon 1989, 1991; O'Connor, Orloff, and Shaver 1999; Pateman 1989; Okin 1989). Although liberalism portrays the "public" (paid work, law, and politics) and "private" (home and family) spheres as independent of one another, they are inextricably linked.[5] The distinction between the spheres has often been used to legitimize practices that are oppressive to women (Randall 1991). This construction of a public-private dichotomy results in a sexual division of labor that presupposes that women should take the responsibility for unpaid work (Baker 1999, 14).

Many claim that the U.S. welfare state has neglected the needs of women and their children; some go so far as to describe it as hostile to them (O'Connor, Orloff, and Shaver 1999, 3). Indeed, the neoliberal arrangement is often most helpful to those who need the least from the state (Meyer 2003, 294). For example, the FMLA is targeted at workers who are more likely to have family and financial resources, as well as employer-provided leave benefits (Elison 1997). In this liberal setting, little attention is given to the need to combine care and paid work. Such matters are seen as the responsibility of individual families, rather than of the government (Staggenborg 1998, 131; Okin

1989). However, American women find themselves in a difficult position. Although the tendency of a liberal welfare state is to provide low benefit levels in order to ensure attachment to the paid labor market, many women must cut their ties with the market when they become pregnant. Certainly the absence of family leave policies in the United States weakened women's position in relation to men because women were considered the primary caregivers. This meant that when no family leave policy—such as maternity, paternity, or parental leave— existed, women would be the ones to sacrifice their careers in order to care for the children (Glass and Estes 1997, 296–297; Anthony 2008, 473). Therefore, the provision of leaves, even relatively short and unpaid ones, is significant for women in that they allow them a better chance to successfully balance work and family life.

Historical Context

Female Participation in the Labor Force

At the beginning of the twentieth century, women's participation rate in the workforce was slightly below 20 percent.[6] In the lead-up to World War II, women were still treated as temporary workers, assumed to be in the workplace only until they got married and began to raise children. Indeed, many employers refused to employ women who were married. In businesses where women were allowed to work, they were typically fired or forced to resign upon becoming pregnant (Conway, Ahern, and Steuernagel 2005, 186). From 1930 to 1960, women's participation rate rose from 22 to 37.7 percent. During World War II, many women entered the workforce to replace their departed husbands' salaries and to support the war effort. After the war ended, only about half of those women left the workforce, and attitudes toward the employment of married women slowly began to change (Gornick and Meyers 2003, 28).

Women's participation rates in the workforce continued to climb in the last quarter of the twentieth century. With the onset of the recession of the 1970s, many women had to join the workforce in order to maintain their families' standard of living (Mishel, Bernstein, and Schmitt 2001; Evans and Nelson 1989, 30). At the same time, the education rates of women in both high school and college substantially increased (Blau, Ferber, and Winkler 2002). Their earning potential in the workforce—and therefore the opportunity costs of staying home—rose with their educational status. The introduction of the birth control pill in 1960 gave women the opportunity to decide when to have children, which afforded them more time to pursue education or employment.

Many women—especially married women—were attracted to the workforce as more jobs opened up in clerical services, rather than in manufacturing sectors (Evans and Nelson 1989, 24). From 1960 to 1989, the participation rate for married women increased from 31.9 to 57.8 percent; the rate for married women with children under six years old rose from 18.6 to 58.4 percent. As the number of divorced people more than quadrupled from 1970 to 1996 (Saluter and Lugaila 1998), more women entered the workforce. Similarly, as women began to wait until they were older to marry, many single women needed to work in order to support themselves. From 1970 to 1981, the participation rate for single mothers increased from 53 to 61 percent (Freedman 1988, 25).

By 1990, women's participation rate was up to 69.1 percent. Although women were not entering the workforce at the same rate as men (89.3 percent), they had made massive gains throughout the century. However, the world of work remained gendered. There was still an assumption that a full-time homemaker—the woman—would be available to care for the family; therefore, most jobs were not organized to allow people time at home. Employees were expected to put in long hours and take little time off (Gornick and Meyers 2003). Many women did not fit well into this mold, as they needed time off for giving birth and raising children. As the number of working women grew, they became increasingly aware of the gendered nature of the inequalities they were facing.

Protective Legislation

Modern labor regulations were first developed in the United States during the Progressive Era, starting in the late nineteenth century. Early legislation highlighted women's maternal roles and the need to protect both mothers and their unborn children. In *Muller v. Oregon* in 1908, the Supreme Court institutionalized this view of women, upholding a labor law that restricted only women.[7] The Court decided that Curt Muller, the owner of a laundry business, violated an Oregon labor law by making a female employee work more than ten hours a day, which was viewed as detrimental to her health. The case came only three years after *Lochner v. New York*, in which the Court overturned a New York law that restricted the weekly working hours of bakers.[8] The difference between the rulings in *Muller* and *Lochner* demonstrates that the courts were only upholding protective legislation for women, rather than for all workers.

At the time, many women, working with organizations like the Women's Trade Union League, the League of Women Voters (LWV), and the National Consumers League, participated in great numbers to pass protective legislation for female workers such as minimum wage and maximum hours laws (Frank and Lipner 1988, 10–11). However, such legislation caused employers to view women as less desirable employees (Anthony 2008, 463) and likely kept them from making inroads into the higher-paying jobs dominated by men (Piccirillo 1988, 296–297; Taylor 1991). Other women's groups, such as the National Women's Party under the leadership of Alice Paul, supported a version of feminism based on the concepts of equal treatment and economic independence (Evans and Nelson 1989, 21). This division between proponents of special treatment and those advocating equal treatment would later hurt women's organizational power and prove to be problematic for the passage of family leave in the United States.

In the early 1960s, with a Democrat in the White House, the labor movement had a significant amount of power; a number of measures were passed that benefited women in the workforce. A 1963 report by the President's Commission on the Status of Women, which reintroduced women's rights onto the national political agenda, called for better child care services for women in the workforce and an end to workforce discrimination. It was quickly followed by the passage of the Equal Pay Act, the first national legislation forbidding discrimination against women workers (Evans and Nelson 1989, 27). Shortly after that, Title VII of the 1964 Civil Rights Act, which prohibits discrimination in employment on the basis of sex, was passed.[9] However, at that time the denial of benefits to pregnant employees was not considered discrimination based on sex, as it only affected pregnant women, rather than all women. For the most part, individual employers could decide how to treat pregnancy in the workplace (Piccirillo 1988, 298).

In 1972, the Equal Employment Opportunity Commission (EEOC) guidelines were revised to define disabilities resulting from pregnancy—such as miscarriage, abortion, or childbirth—as "temporary disabilities" and to award individuals with such disabilities all of the usual benefits associated with a temporary disability (Conway, Ahern, and Steuernagel 2005, 186). Women's policy agencies played an important role in this decision. In 1970 the Citizens' Advisory Council on the Status of Women proposed defining pregnancy as a temporary job-related disability, which was a gender-neutral concept. Following this proposal, Women's Bureau director Elizabeth Koontz pressured the EEOC to change its guidelines so that pregnant women could not be excluded from disability benefits. In this way, femocrats "provided a policy definition that allowed reconciliation of maternity leave with liberal feminist beliefs" (Stetson 1995, 264–265). However, after this victory, WPAs did little else to advance family policies in the United States; women's movement actors and unions became more prominent players in the battle over leave.

A number of Supreme Court decisions in the 1970s challenged the new EEOC guidelines. As many feminists had feared, the earlier demand for protective legislation "introduced into law and judicial decision-making a focus on women workers as different from men and justified discrimination based on that difference" (Evans and Nelson 1989, 21). In the 1974 case *Geduldig v. Aiello*, the Supreme Court decided that the denial of insurance benefits for work loss resulting from a normal pregnancy did not violate the Fourteenth Amendment.[10] Failing to cover pregnancy-related services was not found to be sex discrimination because the plan excluded individuals only on the basis of pregnancy, not sex. Two years later, in *General Electric Company v. Gilbert*, the Court made a similar distinction between pregnancy and sex under Title VII.[11] It was again decided that excluding pregnancy from a company's disability plan did not constitute sex discrimination because women were also included in the group of nonpregnant workers who did not face discrimination. In the 1977 case *Nashville Gas v. Satty*, the Court decided that the denial of sick pay to an employee on maternity leave does not violate

Title VII.[12] These three cases demonstrate that the Supreme Court did not believe that discrimination against pregnant women constituted sex discrimination. However, since only women can become pregnant, they are the ones directly hurt by the lack of legislation protecting pregnant women from discrimination.

The response to the *Gilbert* opinion was immediate: "The ink had barely dried on the Supreme Court's 1976 opinion . . . when a coalition began drafting legislation to nullify the Court's ruling" (Pedriana 2009, 1). Made up of mostly union groups, the coalition also included members of the National Organization for Women (NOW), the Women's Legal Defense Fund (WLDF), the Women's Equity Action League, the National Women's Political Caucus, and the Women's Rights Project of the American Civil Liberties Union (Gelb and Palley 1987, 167–168).[13] The group dubbed itself the Campaign to End Discrimination against Pregnant Workers and made it a top priority to overturn the *Gilbert* decision and similar legislation that discriminated against women. Describing the Supreme Court ruling, president of NOW Karen DeCrow called it a "slap in the face to motherhood. If people are paid sick leave when they're out for nose jobs, hair transplants and vasectomies, why not for childbirth?" ("Feminist Leaders Plan" 1976, 40).

The campaign's swift and strong response to *Gilbert* had the desired effect; in early 1977 Congress introduced legislation aimed at reversing the decision. At the legislative hearings, a long list of supporters testified, including feminist lawyers, physicians, labor activists, and members of Congress, as well as representatives of the Equal Employment Opportunity Commission, the American Civil Liberties Union, and the National Association for the Advancement of Colored People (Pedriana 2009, 12). Those supporters made clear their belief that pregnancy discrimination was discrimination against all women in the workplace. Susan Ross, cochair of the campaign, captures this idea in her testimony:

> These groups [of the campaign] were united by one concern— the realization of *Gilbert*'s enormous potential for harm in eradicating the rights women workers had fought so hard to achieve in the thirteen years since Congress enacted Title VII of the Civil Rights Act of 1964. . . . The Court's logic could be

extended to any disfavorable treatment of pregnant workers. And since most women workers do bear children at some point in their working lives, this one decision could thus be used to justify a whole complex of discriminatory employment practices designed to insure that women worker's [sic] role in the market place be confined to low-paying, dead-end jobs. . . . Employers routinely fire pregnant workers, refuse to hire them, strip them of seniority rights, and deny them sick leave and medical benefits given other workers. Such policies have a lifetime impact on women's careers. Together, they add up to one basic fact: employers use women's role as childbearer as the central justification of and support for discrimination against women workers. Thus, discrimination against women workers cannot be eradicated unless the root discrimination, based on pregnancy and childbirth, is also eliminated. (U.S. House Committee on Education and Labor 1977, 31–32)

Sensing the mood of the public, few were willing to speak out against the campaign. Therefore, in 1978 Congress overwhelming voted to amend Title VII with the passage of the Pregnancy Discrimination Act (PDA), which prohibited discrimination on the basis of pregnancy and required employers with fifteen or more employees who offered health or disability policies to provide coverage to pregnant women, including covering all conditions related to pregnancy and childbirth.[14] According to Pedriana, "It was a resurgent women's movement unequivocally committed to full legal equality for women workers that was arguably most responsible for constructing, mobilizing, and diffusing an aggressive equal treatment discourse that partly transformed both the cultural norms and legal rules governing the rights and opportunities of working women who might become pregnant" (2009, 13). Indeed, the women's movement was united on this issue in a way that was not seen during the fight for family leave in the 1980s and 1990s. This can likely be attributed to the fact that the blatant discrimination against pregnant women was considered more of a black-and-white issue. Even business interests did not put up much opposition to the PDA because they did not want to go on record as opposing protections for pregnant women (Gelb and Palley

1987). This position would change dramatically in the fight for family leave.

Although the PDA helped many women in the workforce while they were pregnant, there was still no statute in place to assist women after the birth of a child. It was generally assumed that the private sector was responsible for family leave policies, which would be included in fringe benefits packages negotiated between employers and unions (Conway, Ahern, and Steuernagel 2005, 187). Therefore, some activists began to organize in support of family leave. However, during the 1970s the Equal Rights Amendment (ERA) and reproductive rights, rather than labor or family issues, united the women's movement and dominated its agenda (Stetson 2001a).[15] Moreover, WMAs were divided on the question of whether pregnant women were entitled to special accommodations in the workplace (Mezey 2011).

Equal Treatment versus Special Treatment

Many feminists were concerned that maternity leave would have a detrimental impact on the advances women had already made in the workplace. Thus a debate began between feminists advocating "special treatment" for women and those fighting for "equal treatment" (Symes 1987; Vogel 1990, 1995; Huckle 1981; Pateman 1992). Special treatment advocates claimed that women are different from men, and pregnancy presents job obstacles for women that men do not face. For that reason, "positive action to change the institutions in which women work is essential in achieving women's equality because those institutions are, for the most part, designed with a male prototype in mind" (Krieger and Cooney 1983, 515; see also Finley 1986). For this group, maternity benefits were necessary to recognize women's particular needs.[16]

Equal treatment advocates believed that "the special-treatment approach accepts the male norm in defining disability coverage and merely tacks on special provisions for women's differences rather than adopts a perspective encompassing and defined from inception by the needs of both men and women" (Piccirillo 1988, 312). These feminists argued that by singling women out for special privilege, leave that was provided only for women would further the belief that they should be treated differently (W. Williams 1984–1985). If employers believed that female employees required more benefits than male employees, they would be apprehensive about hiring women. Moreover, maternity leave would strengthen society's belief that women's primary responsibility is taking care of the home and family (Taub 1985). As long as that idea remained prevalent, passing legislation that allowed women space outside the home would be difficult. Equal-treatment feminists had made similar arguments prior to the passage of the PDA. Writing in 1977 for *Do It NOW*, the monthly newsletter for NOW, Nina Haegstadt asserted that "pregnancy must be covered only to the same extent which other disabilities are covered" (National Organization for Women 1977, 6). Likewise, NOW filed an amicus brief in the 1974 Supreme Court case *Cleveland Board of Education v. LaFleur*, which held that a mandatory pregnancy leave time period is arbitrary and discriminatory because no other prolonged medical ailments were subject to such restrictions.[17]

This division in the United States between equal-treatment feminists and special-treatment feminists has its roots in the ongoing tension between formal equality and substantive equality. Formal equality requires that the law treat all individuals alike; gender neutrality in the law is thought to make men and women equal (Rosenfeld 1986; Rebouché 2009; Fredman 2003; Melnick 2000). However, this model assumes that men and women are similarly situated and have equal access to power and resources, which is rarely the case. On the other side of the debate, proponents of substantive equality believe that "women as a group are disadvantaged, and that equality measures must address the economic, social, legal, and political dimensions of that group disadvantage" (Day and Brodsky 1998, 45). Therefore, the effects of a law, rather than just its form, need to be examined (Kay 1985). In this model, the government must work to remove the barriers associated with a group's special characteristics in order to achieve equality of opportunity for all individuals. In the United States, WMAs involved in the fight for family leave were divided between equal treatment feminists who wanted formal equality and special-treatment feminists who advocated substantive equality.

The Courts and the Debate over Protective Legislation

California state legislator Howard Berman was responsible for the state's 1978 law that provided a four-month disability leave for new mothers. As part of his 1982 campaign for the U.S. House of Representatives, he promised to introduce a similar bill at the national level if elected. But in 1983, California's pregnancy leave law was challenged in court. Lillian Garland, an employee of the California Federal Savings and Loan Association, had lost her position in the company after taking leave following the birth of her child. She charged that her dismissal violated the California Fair Employment and Housing Act, which had been amended prior to the passage of the PDA to require that employers with fifteen or more workers provide pregnant women with four months of unpaid leave and a guaranteed position upon returning. However, Garland's employer, together with the California Chamber of Commerce and the Merchants and Manufacturers Association, claimed that the law was discriminatory because men did not receive similar benefits for other kinds of disabilities. In their view, this special treatment of women discriminated against men and violated the PDA. In 1984, the federal district court agreed that the California law violated Title VII of the 1964 Civil Rights Act because it did not allow men to take maternity leave (Wisensale 2001, 134–135).

This ruling intensified the debate on equal versus special treatment among women. Groups like NOW, WLDF, LWV, the National Women's Political Caucus, and the Women's Rights Project of the American Civil Liberties Union saw the maternity leave statute as a well-meaning measure that was nonetheless protective and in conflict with the principles of equal treatment of male and female workers. San Francisco mayor Dianne Feinstein elucidated this viewpoint: "What we women have been saying all along is we want to be treated equally. . . . Now we have to put our money where our mouth is. What we were asking was to create a special group of workers that in essence is pregnant women and new mothers. I just don't happen to agree with that" (quoted in United Press International 1984, C5). Because they opposed any type of special treatment for women, these activists were in effect supporting the challenge to the maternity law. They claimed that the law's benefits for women should extend to all temporarily disabled workers. In this way, pregnant women would gain job protection without being set apart from the rest of the workforce (Radigan 1988, 8–9). Other women's organizations, such as 9to5 National Association of Working Women and the Coalition for Reproductive Equality in the Workplace (CREW) disagreed with the district court's ruling. These groups argued that the California law actually made women equal to men by recognizing their differences and allowing both sexes to exercise their reproductive rights without risking their jobs. Indeed, Christine Littleton, cofounder of CREW, claimed, "Sometimes equal treatment is what is necessary for long-term equality. Sometimes it is not" (quoted in Leo, Castronovo, and Hackman 1986, 63). Even noted feminist Betty Friedan, author of *The Feminine Mystique*, came down on the side of special treatment, arguing that women are different from men and the concept of equality needs to take into consideration the fact that women are the only ones who can bear children (Stetson 2004, 284). Moreover, supporters of the law argued that businesses were unlikely to discriminate against women as a result of maternity leave protection because they had come to rely heavily on female productivity in the workforce (Radigan 1988, 8). Clearly the Court's ruling forced the equal- versus special-treatment debate into the spotlight, which meant that WMAs would have to deal with it before they could design any kind of family leave policy.

In 1985, the Court of Appeals for the Ninth Circuit reversed the district court's ruling that California's pregnancy disability leave violated the PDA. Two years later, in *California Federal Savings and Loan v. Guerra*, the Supreme Court affirmed the appellate court's decision.[18] The Court upheld California's law requiring employers to provide protectionist policies for working women who are temporarily disabled by pregnancy, reasoning that the PDA represented a floor of protection for pregnant employees beneath which they could not fall, rather than a ceiling limiting how much they could achieve. The California law was not preempted by the PDA because the intent of the state law was not inconsistent with that of the PDA. Moreover, the Court decided that there was no conflict between the California law and the PDA because an employer could comply with both laws by extending disability leave and guaranteed job reinstatement to all workers (Mezey 2011, 168–169).

Guerra revealed the intensity of the debate about the role of the legal system in protecting pregnant women. On one side, NOW, the American Civil Liberties Union, the League of Women Voters, and the National Women's Political Caucus demonstrated their preference for equal treatment by filing amicus curiae briefs in which they argued that the California law conflicted with the PDA. These activists believed that giving pregnant women special treatment would hurt all women's chances for equality. Instead, disability leave should be awarded to all disabled workers. California Women Lawyers stood on the other side of the debate. They claimed that the preferential treatment found in the California law was crucial to women's equality in the workforce (Stewart 1987, 44).

A similar case was proceeding in Montana at that time. In 1979, Tamara Buley was hired as a sales clerk by the Miller-Wohl Company in Great Falls, Montana. Shortly after she began her job, she discovered she was pregnant and missed a few days of work because of morning sickness. Because Miller-Wohl had a policy of denying sick leave to employees with less than one year of seniority, Buley was fired for these absences. She filed a complaint with the Montana Human Rights Commission, claiming to have been fired because of her pregnancy, which violated the 1975 Montana Maternity Leave Act (MMLA) (Krieger and Cooney 1983, 513–514). As in *Guerra*, Miller-Wohl responded by asking the federal court to overturn the MMLA because it violated the equal protection and due process clauses of the Fourteenth Amendment and was preempted by the PDA (Mezey 2011, 171–172). After six years of litigation in the state and federal courts, the Montana Supreme Court spoke the last word and upheld the MMLA (Fitzgerald 1988, 149).

The American women's movement was never able to completely reconcile the debate between equal treatment and special treatment. However, regarding family leave policies, ultimately the equal-treatment advocates won out and the movement predominantly employed frames of gender equality. Seeking to degender (Ferree et al. 2002) the issue by shifting the emphasis away from gender difference toward gender-neutral terms, activists pressed for leave policies that would protect more than just pregnant women. However, this strategy backfired in two ways. First, it intensified the clash between "equality" and "difference" feminists. There were also disputes among activists over whether the leave should be paid. Although some actors argued that paid leave would be more difficult to pass and therefore should be abandoned, others believed that unpaid leave would not benefit the millions of workers who could not afford to take time off without pay (Bernstein 2001, 45). This infighting ultimately weakened women's position. Second, opposition from businesses and the government intensified when faced with family and medical leave, rather than just maternity or parental leave (White 2006, 321). A maternity leave bill would have been easier to pass in the United States because it did not promote role change; rather, it reinforced the idea that women are the primary caregivers.[19]

Women's Movement Actors

In the United States, the second wave of feminism began in the 1960s, as women gained the education, employment, and resources necessary for such an endeavor (Dahlerup 1986; Lovenduski 1986; Katzenstein and Mueller 1987; Gelb 1989; Costain 1992; Teske and Tétreault 2000). Women started to mobilize in growing numbers in order to confront the structures and cultures that oppressed them. One of the main issues on the movement's agenda in the beginning of the second wave was women's participation in the paid workforce. Activists also began to examine the ways in which the nuclear family affected women's status, concluding that "persistent gender inequality in the labor market is both cause and consequence of women's disproportionate assumption of unpaid work in the home" (Gornick and Meyers 2003, 3). However, WMAs at that time did not prioritize policies aimed at mitigating the gendered division of labor in the home, such as family leave. Instead, they concentrated on women's emancipation through wage work, believing that increased numbers of women in the paid workforce would lead to more equality in the home. But it quickly became clear that even when women began working outside the home in escalating numbers, they were still responsible for most of the domestic work and caregiving. Groups like NOW came together to voice women's concerns regarding these inequalities.

NOW was founded in 1966 and continues to be one of the strongest feminist organizations in the United States.[20] It was created in part as a response to the lack of action on the part of the EEOC to enforce the gender provisions of the 1964 Civil Rights Act. Because NOW is part of the women's movement and it attempts to influence the government with its organizational activities, it is both a social movement organization and an interest group (Henderson and Jeydel 2007, 44). Initially

NOW—like most organizations in second-wave feminism—looked to the state to rectify its grievances (Baker 1999, 12). The organization primarily concentrated its efforts on institutionalized political channels and on networking both inside and outside established governmental and nongovernmental organizations. At the same time, leaders of NOW also expected the organization to use a variety of tactics to effect change, such as forming alliances with other organization, lobbying industry, and holding demonstrations (Barakso 2004, 42).

In 1967, NOW drafted the Bill of Rights for Women, which included, among other things, a demand for maternity leave rights and the enforcement of equal employment opportunity laws (Barakso 2004, 41). But after the document's publication, the organization spent little time actually promoting the passage of family leave policies, for its agenda was dominated by other issues. Indeed, a careful examination of *National NOW Times*, the official journal of the National Organization for Women, from 1970 until the passage of the FMLA in 1993 turns up little mention of family leave.[21] In the eight years leading up to the passage of the PDA in 1978, only one article covered family leave. This 1973 article discussed the recent court cases in which mandatory pregnancy leave time periods were found to violate Title VII, and then offered advice to women who were affected by such a policy (National Organization for Women, 1973). During the eight-year period, coverage of the ERA was in every issue, and reproductive rights were mentioned in at least 75 percent of the issues.[22] Workplace discrimination unrelated to pregnancy and childbirth, violence against women, and marriage and divorce matters were also priorities for the organization at this time.

In the early stages of the second wave, WMAs had few inroads to established politics.[23] Because the public was largely unfamiliar with the concerns and demands of this new women's movement, it also attracted little public support (Banaszak, Beckwith, and Rucht 2003, 20). By the mid-1970s, the movement had entered a stage of growth, as demonstrated by an increase in new recruits to the movement organizations,[24] events, and activities, and a rise in feminist consciousness (Rosenfeld and Ward 1996).[25] Through the use of political parties, formal interest groups, legislatures, media, academia, and bureaucracies, the women's movement became increasingly consolidated and institutionalized (Haussman and Sauer 2007, 3).[26] What started as a loose collection of beliefs became more organized and structured, with specific policy goals and plans for implementation. It was also moderately close to the left, having allied itself with the Democratic Party. Therefore, WMAs at this time were well poised to challenge pregnancy discrimination in the workplace, which had become a problem for a growing number of women.

Immediately after the *Gilbert* decision in 1976, in which the Supreme Court upheld a General Electric disability insurance program that excluded pregnancy, WMAs sprung to action (Sawyers and Meyer 1999, 192). Activists waited for the decision outside the courthouse, and then photocopied it and distributed it among women's organizations. They also scheduled meetings in major cities to discuss ways to fight the Court's decision and were able to attract significant media attention (Costain 1992, 129–130). The result of the WMAs' lobbying campaign was the 1978 Pregnancy Discrimination Act. This demonstrates that a strong and unified women's movement can achieve policy success when it prioritizes an issue. However, the movement declined dramatically after this accomplishment; many point to the PDA as one of the last major legislative victories of the second wave (Spalter-Roth and Schreiber 1995). Indeed, the PDA "provides a counterpoint to failed and stalled feminist efforts in the 1980s" (Sawyers and Meyer 1999, 193).

After the economic downturn that began in the mid-1970s, a conservative resurgence emerged in 1980 that "combine[d] hostility to 'big government' and the welfare state with a social traditionalism rooted in a conservative religious revival" (Morgan 2006, 136). Following Ronald Reagan's election in 1980 and the defeat of the ERA in 1982, the women's movement found itself in a state of disarray and facing an antifeminist backlash (Bashevkin 1998).[27] NOW was $1 million in debt and its membership had fallen from a peak of 200,000 members to 130,000. Feminist projects lost their government funding, and the needs of low-income Americans took priority for many organizations as social programs were slashed across the board. Many Americans blamed the women's movement for putting women in a position where they "struggled to do justice to both job and family" (F. Davis 1991, 471). The media implied that feminists had lured housewives from their homes at the expense of both them and their families (474). Nancy Chodorow and colleagues concluded that the American public decided that the United States had "tried feminism and it didn't work" (1984, 102).

At a time when the movement most needed to maintain women's support, some women felt that feminism had already achieved its desired goals: "Sex discrimination in education and employment had lessened just enough that many young, white middle class women believed the battle was over" (F. Davis 1991, 472). Therefore, WMAs set out to build a new agenda that would attract women who were in the paid workforce, were single or divorced, or were under thirty years old by focusing on so-called special needs issues such as child care, abortion, and equal pay and working conditions (Costain 1992, 120). But family leave was still absent from the organization's agenda. From 1978 to 1983, there were no articles in *National NOW Times* that focused on family leave.[28] The ERA, reproductive rights, and workplace discrimination unrelated to pregnancy continued to dominate the journal. Discrimination against women in the military, in education, and based on sexual orientation also began to garner more attention from NOW at that time.

As the women's movement lost momentum, WMAs' chances for getting a family leave bill through the legislative process were slim, especially since the issue was low on its agenda. In this environment, the first version of family and medical leave, the Family Employment Security Act of 1984, was drafted. In theory, most feminists supported the idea of some type of leave for women after the birth or adoption of a child, believing that it would help neutralize the effect of childbearing on career advancement while underscoring the need for a system of family support in the United States (Conway, Ahern, and Steuernagel 2005, 188). However, as discussed earlier, many of the most powerful women's organizations had a number of issues that were higher priorities than family leave. Moreover, as the eight years of debate following the first draft of the bill demonstrate, women were divided on both the type of family leave to ask for and whether it should be paid.

The Evolution of Family Leave Policies

Family Employment Security Act of 1984

After the California federal court's 1984 decision that the state's four-month job-protected pregnancy disability leave law violated Title VII, activists on both sides of the equal-treatment versus special-treatment debate went to work designing new federal legislation.[29] Siding with the special-treatment advocates, Representative Berman, in conjunction with other Democratic California legislators, began drafting a federal family leave bill similar to the California law he had authored. Although the bill included job-protected leave for mothers and fathers after the birth or adoption of a child, it also allowed women to take leave before the child arrived to cover any pregnancy-related disabilities (Radigan 1988, 9). Groups such as CREW and 9to5 backed this special coverage (Wisensale 2003, 139).

Equal-treatment activists did not support the inclusion of disability leave only for women, so they formed their own committee to draft a bill. Led by Donna Lenhoff and Judith Lichtman of the Women's Legal Defense Fund,[30] this drafting committee included a number of WMAs, such as feminist law professors Wendy Williams and Susan Deller Ross of Georgetown University Law School and Sherry Cassedy of the Congressional Caucus for Women's Issues. They also incorporated other groups, including the American Association of University Women, the National Organization for Women, the Association of Junior Leagues, the National Council of Jewish Women, the Women's Equity Action League, the League of Women Voters, and the Children's Defense Fund (Radigan 1988, 9–10; Wisensale 2001, 136; Elving 1995, 29). The result of their work, the Family Employment Security Act (FESA) of 1984, was the first version of the FMLA.

Although the FESA was never formally introduced into Congress, it set the stage for future bills. As its name implies, the bill prioritized job security. Employees who were temporarily unable to work because of disability could take job-protected leave of up to twenty-six weeks. During this time, seniority and benefits would continue to accrue. Perhaps more significant is the inclusion of the word "family." In addition to disability leave for the employee, the FESA covered care for a newborn or newly adopted child, a child's illness, and a spouse's disability, regardless of the employee's gender. The creation of the FESA gave legislators an option to consider that was very different from Representative Berman's proposal that gave special coverage to women. But Berman continued to advocate for a narrow bill that covered only birth and adoption, claiming that it would easily gain the support of social conservatives who called themselves pro-family and pro-life (Elving 1995, 29–31). Some WMAs sided with Berman because they too favored special treatment for pregnant women. Others were attracted to the idea of a bill that would pass without much difficulty. After the loss of the ERA in 1982 and a general lack of support from the Reagan White House, some advocates wanted a bill that had a good chance of passing quickly (Bernstein 2001, 94).

Although the women's movement was strong at this time, as a whole it did not prioritize family leave. In 1984, when the *National NOW Times* printed a chart that listed the position of the Republican and Democratic presidential candidates on a number of issues that were most important, family leave was not included among the twelve issues. But this is not to say that there was no support for the issue from other organizations and critical actors within the movement at that time. As noted earlier, the Women's Legal Defense Fund stepped up to spearhead the early days of the campaign. Judith Lichtman and Donna Lenhoff were key actors in the creation of the FESA, and they enlisted a number of WMAs to work with them on the issue. Still, there was some disagreement within the movement regarding the issue of equal treatment versus special treatment. Equal-treatment feminists would only accept a bill that provided the same leave options for both women and men; the FESA accomplished this by guaranteeing disability leave for all workers. Some special-treatment advocates were uneasy about the fact that the bill equated maternity leave with disability leave because it did not take the unique characteristics of childbirth into account (Kaitin 1994, 106). They felt that by focusing on disability rather than pregnancy, the bill was designed for male subjects, as men only experience disabilities, not pregnancies (Cavarero 1992). WMAs also disagreed on the issue of wage replacement. Most of the activists felt that the leave should be paid so that workers at every level could participate; however, they ultimately decided that a bill mandating wage replacement could not gain sufficient legislative support (Radigan 1988, 11). Later, organizations like NOW were especially vocal about the fact that they saw this decision as a big mistake.

WMAs initially put the concept of family leave on the federal agenda and informed the public about it (Bernstein 2001, 64). After the first bill was introduced, the coalition grew to include a variety of other actors, including the American Association of Retired Persons, the Alzheimer's Association, the U.S. Catholic Conference,

Hadassah, and the American Academy of Pediatrics (Asher and Lenhoff 2001, 116). Labor organizations, such as United Auto Workers, the Service Employees International Union, United Steelworkers of America, the Communications Workers of America, and the International Ladies' Garment Workers' Union, were also crucial to the legislation's success; this can be seen in the fact that the bill was recast as a piece of labor legislation (Kaitin 1994, 103). The coalition eventually grew to include over one hundred groups focused on women, children, seniors, and issues of labor, religion, disability, and civil rights (Asher and Lenhoff 2001, 116). Much of the credit for the size of the coalition goes to the Women's Legal Defense Fund. As Judith Lichtman described, "From its earliest inception, we [WLDF] wanted to have a broad-based coalition" supporting family leave. According to Lichtman, the coalition received "enormous support" from women's communities. Moreover, there was strong support from labor groups, religious interests, senior organizations, and others "because we [WLDF] brought it in." [31]

Parental and Disability Leave Act of 1985

Women in elective office are more likely to advocate women's issues and ideas (Mansbridge 1999; Thomas 1994; Caiazza 2004; Swers 2002; Dodson 2006). In the United States, female representatives were typically the critical actors who moved the family leave policy-making process forward in the legislature, especially when the issue was first introduced. Representative Patricia Schroeder (D-CO) played the primary role in the fight for family leave in the mid-1980s. By 1985, Representative Berman had given up on his special-treatment approach and turned the issue of family leave over to the Congressional Caucus on Women's Issues, which was cochaired by Schroeder. The most senior Democratic congresswoman, Schroeder was a champion of women's and children's issues. She also held a seat on the Education and Labor Committee, which was the likely setting for the development of a new family leave bill (Wisensale 2001, 137). She quickly offered her leadership for the family leave bill, in large part because she had been looking for a popular issue to renew interest in women's rights. Family leave especially appealed to her at this time because "it not only broadened the appeal of a women's initiative but it also stole the thunder of the new right" (Radigan 1988, 13). She introduced the Parental and Disability Leave Act (PDLA) on the floor of the House of Representatives on April 4, 1985.

Advocates for family leave had changed the name of the Family Employment Security Act to the Parental and Disability Leave Act prior to its introduction in 1985. The change revealed that equal-treatment feminists had largely won the debate. Using "parental" instead of "maternal" demonstrated that equal coverage would be granted to women and men, thereby avoiding claims that the law would unfairly favor women (Lewin 1986). Moreover, drafters of the bill were worried that the word "family" that was used in the proto-type bill would indicate that the legislation was the property of the far right (Radigan 1988, 15). Including the word "disability" indicated that conditions other than pregnancy and childbirth would be covered (Wisensale 2001, 139).

This new bill required all employers to provide eighteen weeks of unpaid, job-protected leave for mothers or fathers of newborn or newly adopted children, as well as twenty-six weeks of unpaid leave for workers with temporary disabilities unrelated to work and for employees with sick children (Elving 1995, 42). During the leave, employers had to continue employees' health insurance and other personal benefits, as well as guarantee the employee's job upon returning to work. Originally, the bill did not limit leave to companies of a certain size, but an early compromise raised the employee exemption to five (Kaitin 1994, 91). It also required the creation of a commission to investigate the possibility of wage replacement in the future (Wisensale 2001, 139). Many family leave advocates had wanted paid leave but felt that it would make the bill much harder to pass.

The Parental and Disability Leave Act was introduced in a climate dominated by conservatives who were not eager to expand government programs or promote liberal ideas like universal child care and family leave.[32] In 1985, conservative Ronald Reagan was starting his second term as president. Faced with a major budget deficit, the Republican-majority Congress was also ready to make cuts. Thus it is not surprising that the bill was assigned the number 2020, for the higher the bill number, the less likely it will pass during a legislative session. WMAs were not pressuring members of Congress to take up this cause; therefore, politicians did not believe they would gain political capital by endorsing the bill. In her haste to write the bill and get it on the agenda, Schroeder did not recruit any cosponsors. This is also indicative of the low levels of organized support for a family leave bill at that time.

From the beginning, the bill gained little congressional support and faced numerous delays. The first subcommittee hearing on it did not take place until October 1985, six months after its introduction. Forty members eventually cosponsored the bill, but that list did not include some key women legislators or the chairs of the two committees assigned to the bill, Education and Labor and the Post Office and Civil Service Committee. Moreover, there was no companion bill in the Senate. Although the bill was able to get through two House subcommittees, it died in the summer of 1986 (Wisensale 2001, 138–140).

Most WMAs supported the idea of family leave, believing that it was a necessary measure to promote gender equality in the workforce. The disagreements within the movement concerned the way in which the leave should be codified. In the August–September 1985 issue of *National NOW Times*, the organization dedicated an article to family leave for the first time. The piece began with a description of the court cases that challenged state maternity laws in California and Montana. Asserting that NOW does not approve of protective legislation for women because it singles women out for special—and ultimately discriminatory—treatment, the article then declared NOW's support for the Parental and Disability Leave Act, which took the equal-treatment approach (National Organization for Women 1985).

NOW also continually tried to persuade the family leave coalition to demand paid leave, believing that unpaid leave merely reinforced the male breadwinner model (Minow 1990). At one of the first hearings on family and medical leave, NOW president Eleanor Smeal briefly departed from her prepared text and noted that NOW would have liked to see the proposed bill establish paid leave (Bernstein 2001, 96). Most other WMAs did not want to include paid leave in the bill for fear that it would be quickly rejected. But NOW had become more radical over time and less willing to accept compromises that it felt did not actually challenge patriarchal authority (Taylor and Whittier 1997; Whittier 1995).

Parental and Medical Leave Act of 1986

For the new legislative session, the title of the family leave bill was changed again in response to pressure from advocates of people with disabilities who felt the term "disability" was offensive. Thus, the Parental and Medical Leave Act was introduced in the House on March 4, 1986. A month later, Senator Christopher Dodd (D-CT) put forth a bill in the Senate that was almost identical. Changing "disability" to "medical" meant that the bill would appeal to a wider constituency (Wisensale 2001, 141–142).

At this time, most WMAs still supported the family leave bill. In both the May–June and the July–September issues of *National NOW Times* in 1986, the organization published articles about the status of the family leave bill. Moreover, NOW stated that it "strongly supports the FMLA as an important step in bringing parental labor policy to this nation."[33] The president of NOW, Ellie Smeal, urged activists around the country to lobby their House members for passage of the bill (National Organization for Women 1986, 8).

When the Supreme Court agreed in the beginning of 1986 to decide the ultimate fate of California's pregnancy leave statute, press coverage of family leave issues increased (Radigan 1988, 20). As the bills moved through committees, they began to attract bipartisan support. However, Representative Marge Roukema (R-NJ)—a supporter of family leave—led the call for massive changes in the bill that would draw more Republican support.[34] She wanted to reduce the twenty-six-week medical leave to thirteen weeks and cut parental leave from eighteen weeks to eight weeks. She also advocated tougher eligibility requirements, including a set period of employment that workers had to complete before qualifying for leave, as well as the provision that the bill would apply only to companies with fifty or more employees. Although bill supporters did want to appeal to a wider Republican base, they did not implement all of Roukema's recommendations. Company size was raised from five to fifteen employees; eligibility requirements were set at five hundred hours or three months; and the total time for either medical or parental leave was changed to thirty-six weeks over a two-year period. Significantly, they also expanded the coverage beyond parents. New provisions in the bill specified that an employee could take time off to care for a child, spouse, or elderly parent (Wisensale 2001, 142–143). This last revision was key in gaining the backing of the American Association of Retired Persons (AARP), one of the largest and most powerful lobbying groups in Washington. The organization had withheld its support early in the debate because of the fear that women might lose their pensions and other retirement income if they were forced to leave their jobs for family care. Once care for elder family members was added to the bill, AARP joined the coalition and "moved inexorably to the front rank." Its first act was to promote the addition of spousal care to the bill. Some members of the coalition balked at this suggestion, worried that such expanded coverage would increase the ire of the business community. At the very least, it removed any remaining hope among the coalition for the possibility of paid leave, for the cost of covering elder care would be too great. Moreover, groups like the Association of Junior Leagues backed away from the effort as a result of this suggestion because they felt that the original focus on young children was disappearing (Elving 1995, 157–158). Although the support of the AARP—including a significant financial contribution to the campaign's efforts— was ultimately crucial to the passage of the FMLA, its entrance into the coalition also exposed some of the rifts that had formed among the members.

The renaming of the House bill to the Family and Medical Leave Act exacerbated divisions in the coalition of leave supporters. Organizations like the Children's Defense Fund and the Junior League favored the term "parental" because it denoted care for children. Because these groups were also trying to pass a child care law at this time, they wanted Congress to think in terms of children rather than the family. On the other side, the AARP and the U.S. Catholic Conference cheered the name change because it highlighted the importance of the extended family and multigenerational relationships (Wisensale 2001, 143). These groups also claimed that switching to "family" would appeal to a wider audience because more workers would be covered. But supporters of keeping "parental" in the bill's title pointed out that a focus on parents would mean that fewer workers would be covered, which would be less expensive for businesses. This was especially important as the business community began to organize against family leave.

The Rise of the Countermovement

The countermovement against family leave was led by businesses (Bernstein 2001, 2). In general, business interests oppose any type of government intervention on behalf of employees in business activities (Evans and Nelson 1989, 83). After the introduction of the Parental and Medical Leave Act in 1986, the U.S. Chamber of Commerce sent a letter to its members encouraging them to fight against the coalition that supported family leave. In response, numerous mom-and-pop shops delivered their complaints to Capitol Hill. They argued that the bill would be too costly for businesses, many businesses were already voluntarily providing job-protected leaves, employers would become reluctant to hire women, and other employee benefits would be cut as a result of mandated family leave (Radigan 1988, 20). The National Association of Manufacturers, the National Federation of Independent Business, and the Society for Human Resources Management also took up the fight against family leave (Asher and Lenhoff 2001, 117; Elison 1997, 42–43). From 1986 to 1992, the National Federation of Independent Businesses conducted a continuing poll among its 600,000 members to determine their views on the issue. Over and over again the organization reported that 85 percent of its members were against a family leave policy mandated by the government (Wisensale 2001, 143).

In 1987, Mary Tavenner created the Concerned Alliance of Responsible Employers (CARE), which became the lead organization in the fight against family and medical leave. Members labeled family and medical leave an "unfunded mandate," claiming that such a policy would set a precedent that would lead to government-mandated paid family leave, health care, and vacation time, costing businesses a large percentage of their profits (Anthony 2008, 471). The U.S. Chamber of Commerce argued that mandatory leave would especially hurt small businesses because they would not be able to afford to find and train the temporary help necessary to replace workers on leave (Conway, Ahern, and Steuernagel 2005, 188). Many opponents in the business world argued that leave policies would hurt U.S. businesses' ability to compete abroad and create an investment disincentive (Radigan 1988, 3).[35] Therefore, the business community claimed that family leave policies should be voluntary, not mandatory.

In liberal welfare states, businesses are said to represent the central good of capitalism. Moreover, business advocates tend to be wealthy and well connected; therefore, they are better positioned to influence the political system (Kaitin 1994, 109–110). Businesses can be particularly strong in a system like the United States because its fragmented institutions allow many veto points where opponents can block policy reforms they believe to be harmful to their interests (Pierson 1995). Businesses resented being forced to provide women with employment opportunities "because the 'ideal worker' was still based upon the male standard of someone who has a spouse available to take care of the domestic and caregiving needs of the family" (Anthony 2008, 471). Many cultural and religious conservatives shared this vision of the "ideal worker."

Studies of feminist movements "seldom consider the possibility that the same changes in women's status that prompted the emergence of feminism may also have fueled activism among conservative or nonfeminist women" (Baldez 2001, 13). However, counter to the women's movement for gender equality, there was also a conservative, antifeminist movement in the United States. As the United States shifted to the right, this countermovement was allowed more political space to express its beliefs.

Conservatives argued that regulation policies put forth by the government are "an unnecessary intrusion in people's lives" (Conway, Ahern, and Steuernagel 2005, 190). Organizations like Stop ERA, Eagle Forum, and Concerned Women for America (CWA) worked to stop feminist bills, such as the Equal Rights Amendment, from passing (O'Connor, Orloff, and Shaver 1999, 207). With regard to family leave policies, many members of the New Right[36] opposed family and medical leave, for they believed it encouraged women to enter the workforce instead of focusing all their energies on the home and family (Asher and Lenhoff 2001, 117).[37] In the United States, there is a long-standing belief that caregiving is a private—primarily female—responsibility; therefore, the government should play little role in shaping it (Gornick and Meyers 2003, 5; see also Teghtsoonian 1993). Influential conservative political activist Phyllis Schlafly (1986) described parental leave as a "windfall for yuppies" because it would give preferential treatment to two-wage-earner families who could afford to take leave without pay. However, cultural and religious conservatives did not mark family leave as a priority for two reasons. First, these organizations were focusing on other issues at the time, such as the defeat of child care bills. In addition, conservatives were torn on the issue of family leave. Although much of the New Right was against a family leave bill because it allowed women to work outside the home, it also encouraged families to spend more time together, which was viewed positively by a significant number of conservatives (Bernstein 2001, 103). This ambivalence led many members of the New Right to stay out of the debate.

Family and Medical Leave Act of 1987

In January 1987, family leave supporters were optimistic because Democrats had gained the majority in both houses of Congress. However, it would be six years before the Family and Medical Leave Act (FMLA) would become law. Critical actors continued to play a role in keeping family leave policies on the agenda. Representative Schroeder, who sponsored the Parental and Disability Leave Act of 1985 and coauthored the FMLA, maintained her support for the passage of a family leave bill. In 1988 she wrote a chapter for an edited volume titled "Parental Leave: The Need for a Federal Policy." In the piece, Schroeder outlined the ways in which the PDA is limited and called for the passage of the FMLA to fill these policy gaps. After taking control of Congress in 1987, Democrats were able to pass the bill. However, because they lacked the necessary votes to override a veto, the bill could not make it past the desk of Republican president George H. W. Bush.

Legislators continued to debate the details of the bill. Representative Roukema maintained that the cutoff for company size should be increased and that leave time should be reduced. She also wanted to allow employers to deny leave to the top 10 percent of earners in a company. Lawmakers compromised again and set the company size at fifty, family leave at ten weeks every two years, and medical leave at fifteen weeks over a one-year period. In the Senate, Dodd made similar changes to the bill, allowing ten weeks for family leave and ten weeks for medical leave, as well as applying the bill to businesses with fifty or more employees (Wisensale 2001, 144–145). Significantly, Dodd also challenged the Chamber of Commerce's claim that implementing the FMLA would cost between $2 billion and $16 billion annually, calling on the General Accounting Office (GAO) to do a fiscal impact study. The GAO found that the cost would actually be between $188 and $236 million (U.S. General Accounting Office 1988). But the business community continued to object to family leave on principle. Christine Russell, a spokesperson for the Chamber of Commerce, claimed that benefits like family leave should not be federally mandated, and businesses "resent the government's intrusion" (quoted in Kantrowitz and Wingert 1989, 65).

These compromises attracted more supporters of the bill, such as moderate Republicans. At the same time, family leave advocates gained support from some conservative Republicans and the U.S. Catholic Conference by convincing them that the bill would lead to fewer abortions because it would allow women to have children and still work (Bernstein 2001, 9; Radigan 1988, 23). Republicans who wanted to back the FMLA used this argument as political cover (Wisensale 2001, 146). However, the compromises also further divided the original coalition of leave proponents. Activists who had strongly supported the bill in its early form began to worry that the FMLA would endorse a relatively low ceiling for benefits, rather than inspire businesses to do more to protect workers (Kaitin 1994, 106). Within the women's movement, family leave was not near the top of its agenda (McBride and Mazur 2010; Staggenborg 1991). There continued to be a tension between proponents of equal treatment and those favoring special treatment, and the inclusion of wage replacement in the bill had become a deal breaker for some WMAs.

Shifts in the Women's Movement
By the mid-1980s, the women's movement as a whole had become less visible and lost the political influence it had during the 1970s (Boles 1991; Costain 1992; McBride 2007). In large part this decline was a result of the significant challenges the movement faced in the early 1980s, such as the rise of the New Right, Reagan's election as president, the defeat of the ERA, and the economic recession that exacerbated the feminization of poverty (Morgan 2001, 2006; Faludi 1991; Costain 1992; Hyde 1995; Mansbridge 1986; B. Ryan 1992). In response, the women's movement felt compelled to temper itself in order to protect gains it had already made. It also became

fragmented: "The movement's radical wing retrenched, institutionalized feminists became more moderate . . . and potential mainstream
supporters left the political struggle" (Sawyers and Meyer 1999, 197).

In 1988, NOW still stood behind the FMLA. Indeed, the organization managed to have twenty-five thousand Mother's Day cards
sent to members of Congress from around the country that urged
action on the family leave bill (Elving 1995, 105). But a year later,
NOW's support for the FMLA was waning. The *National NOW Times*
provided the following statement about the bill: "NOW supports this
legislation with reservations. It is not paid leave, which we believe is
critical, and the numbers required in the House version eliminate
most employees from coverage. We will monitor the legislation for
unacceptable amendments, such as abortion riders or further reduc-
tions in the number of employees covered" (National Organization
for Women 1989, 10). In the fall 1990 issue, NOW president Molly
Yard said that the organization would encourage Schroeder to introduce a much stronger family leave bill in the next session of Congress
(National Organization for Women 1990). By 1991, the language had
become much harsher: "NOW has nominally supported the bill, but
is very unhappy with the weakening clauses and amendments that
reduced it to have little more than a token impact. What NOW has
continued to call for is paid leave and a policy that applies equally to
all workers in this country" (National Organization for Women 1991,
12). These statements demonstrate that NOW, arguably the leading
women's organization in the United States, was in favor of the idea of
family leave. However, its support for the FMLA continually diminished because of the numerous compromises that had been made to
appeal to a more widespread audience (Elving 1995, 225).[38]

Looking at the *National NOW Times* from 1984 until the passage of the FMLA in 1993, I found that the pages were dominated by
abortion. Although NOW still strongly supported the ERA, coverage
of the amendment had diminished because of its failure to gain ratification before the 1982 deadline. The organization started to spend
more time highlighting race and sexuality issues, global feminist
movements, and problems encountered by women in the military.
During this nine-year period, family leave was discussed much more
than it had been in the previous fourteen years; I found twenty references in those issues. However, most of these citations were short

excerpts within the "Legislative Updates" section that described the status of bills dealing with women's issues that were currently being debated in Congress. There were only five articles specifically dedicated to family leave, and none of them were on the front page of the journal. Moreover, many of the articles spoke negatively about the FMLA because of the numerous concessions the family leave coalition had made to gain support—or at least less hostility—from opponents such as the business community.

Although NOW's support for the FMLA waned over time, the Women's Legal Defense Fund did not waver in its sponsorship of the bill. WMAs from the WLDF wrote the first draft of the legislation that would become the FMLA, and they maintained a leadership role in the family leave coalition that steadily grew to include a wide array of interest groups throughout the late 1980s and early 1990s. Donna Lenhoff recounts that the family leave legislation was a "huge priority" for the WLDF.[39] She says that during the 1980s, when she was working as a lawyer for the organization, she spent about half of her time on the issue; her job was to bring other groups into the coalition. She started primarily with women's organizations and then moved to unions, noting that a bill on labor would not pass at the time without unions. As the campaign progressed, groups for the interests of children and senior citizens came into the fold. After the Americans with Disabilities Act passed in 1990, disability groups concentrated more of their energy on family leave as well. So at a time when NOW was gradually losing enthusiasm for the family leave bill, the Women's Legal Defense Fund maintained its ardent support throughout the entirety of the legislative process. Indeed, Lenhoff says that when the Democrats retook the Senate in 1987, thereby improving the political environment for the coalition, the WLDF redoubled its efforts.[40]

In addition to the disagreements that arose in the women's movement as the family leave bill began to reflect an increasing number of compromises, some WMAs were torn between working on the passage of the FMLA and trying to get a child care bill enacted. In November 1987, the Act for Better Child Care Services (ABC) was introduced in Congress. For the most part, WMAs who were working on the FMLA were also working on—or at least ideologically committed to—the ABC. However, many in the ABC coalition, such as the Children's Defense Fund, believed that child care legislation was more important than family leave, and therefore focused primarily on pressuring legislators to pass their bill (Kaitin 1994, 100).

The fact that the FMLA was ultimately framed as a labor issue demonstrated the weakness and growing fragmentation of the women's movement. Deborah J. Anthony criticizes WMAs' inability to frame the debate in terms of gender equality: "In an interesting dynamic, proponents of the law emphasized its benefit to men and children as a major selling point, indicating that its importance to women was not valuable enough to warrant its passage, but instead required demonstration of how useful the law would be for everyone else" (2008, 470). During the 1970s, when the movement was at its strongest, WMAs found success framing a variety and work and family bills as gender equality issues (Burstein, Bricher, and Einwohner 1995). But by the time family leave was introduced to Congress, neither political party was willing to frame it as a "pro-woman" issue. Instead, the Democratic Party claimed it was a "pro-labor" measure, while the Republicans who helped pass it used the legislation to bolster their image as a "pro-family" party (Mazur 2002, 113). WMAs had not pressured legislators to advocate family leave on their behalf, and they were worried that a bill centered on "women's rights" would not pass (Stetson 2004, 284–288; Kaitin 1994, 109).

Unions, Businesses, and Partisan Politics

During the 1980s, child care legislation and family and medical leave became top priorities on labor's legislative agenda. Unions believed that the FMLA would provide a minimum leave standard that was gravely needed in the United States (Radigan 1988, 2). Labor's approach to family policy was perhaps most clearly articulated in the Coalition of Labor Union Women's (CLUW's) American Family Celebration in 1988 and its subsequent efforts to promote a family bill of rights. CLUW attempted to incorporate issues of particular concern for working women, such as child care, family leave, and pay equity, into a traditional labor agenda for decent jobs, health care, housing, and other basic needs. Unions with large female membership became some of the main supporters of the FMLA. The American Federation of State, County, and Municipal Employees (AFSCME) and the Service Employees International Union (SEIU), which both had high numbers of women members, were key proponents of the FMLA.

These unions provided financial resources, interest group coordination, and staff for the lobbying drives (Dark 1999).

Businesses continued to oppose family leave policies, and they had more powerful lobbying groups than the women's movement or labor (Kaitin 1994, 109). Prior to the passage of the FMLA, thirty-four states, Puerto Rico, and the District of Columbia had already adopted some sort of family and medical leave laws (Women's Bureau, U.S. Department of Labor 1993). Likewise, over half of companies offered a leave option for employees, in large part out of fear of lawsuits, government intervention, unionization, or negative publicity (Kelly and Dobbin 1999; Friedman 1990; Auerbach 1990). The fact that many states and companies already provided some form of leave strengthened the business community's claim that a federal law was not necessary and was an unwelcome mandate (Rovner 1987). This opposition was a serious problem for family leave supporters because business had put together an anti-FMLA coalition of forty-three groups (Wisensale 2001, 144).

Republican leaders also grew increasingly unified in their opposition to what they saw as the expansion of the federal government, especially with regard to family policies. The administrations of both Ronald Reagan and George H. W. Bush gave low priority to labor issues and women's equality and named weak, inattentive administrators as directors of women's policy agencies (Stetson 1995, 259). Republicans consistently tried to block the passage of family leave laws, using tactics such as introducing controversial amendments and filibustering. Moreover, conservatives were more successful than WMAs at mobilizing constituent pressure to influence members of Congress (Sawyers and Meyer 1999, 199).

In 1990, the Democrats were able to pass a child care bill that President Bush grudgingly signed. The significance of this action on the fight for family leave should not be underestimated. Because child care and family leave advocates no longer had to divide their time between these two issues, they could turn greater attention to family leave. For example, Lenhoff says that the League of Women's Voters and the National Council of Jewish Women had both focused much of their attention on child care up to that point. Once the child care legislation passed, they were able to devote more of their time and resources to the fight for family leave.[41] The fact that the FMLA passed through Congress shortly after this legislative development bolsters the argument that the fragmentation of the women's movement and WMAs' low prioritization of family leave contributed to the passage of a relatively weak law. When the women's movement is united behind an issue and prioritizes it, WMAs are more likely to find legislative success.

Opponents of the legislation continued to claim that they were not against the idea of family leave, but they did not think that the federal government should mandate it. However, a 1989 survey reported that only 37 percent of women at companies with 100 or more employees were eligible for maternity leave; only 18 percent of men were eligible for paternity leave (Holmes 1990b). These numbers demonstrated to many that government intervention would indeed be necessary for family leave to become a reality.

On May 10, 1990, the House passed the family leave bill by a vote of 237 to 187, largely, but not completely, along party lines (Holmes 1990b). One month later, the Senate ratified the House bill with no further amendments. But on June 29, 1990, President Bush vetoed the bill. In a written statement, he reiterated his support for family leave, but only as long as businesses were allowed to provide it voluntarily (Holmes 1990a). The House tried to override the veto but fell fifty-three votes short.

When a new version of the bill with more stringent measures on leave authorization was introduced the following year, it passed the House on November 13. Realizing that they did not have enough votes to override the expected veto, the bill's proponents decided to cease legislative activity on the bill until 1992 so they could pressure Bush into signing it in hopes of gaining more electoral support from working families. However, their hopes were short-lived. After passing the House a third time (241 to 161) on September 10, 1992, the bill was ratified in the Senate by a voice vote before Bush vetoed it again. In another written statement, Bush again stressed his support for family leave in theory but also his belief that such a law would harm the economy and inhibit growth. He therefore appealed to Congress to "to establish an alternative, flexible family-leave plan that will encourage small- and medium-sized businesses to provide family leave for their employees" based on a refundable tax credit of up to $20 per day for up to sixty days of leave (Wines 1992, A1).

Knowing that his actions would not be well received by many voters, President Bush drew as little publicity to his veto as possible. On the other side, Bill Clinton made the FMLA part of his 1992 presidential campaign. In the end, Clinton won the presidency, and the Democrats gained a majority in both houses of Congress and made it clear that they were ready to support Clinton's legislative agenda (Clymer 1992a). When the new Congress convened in 1993, the FMLA took top priority. On February 5, 1993, it became the first major piece of legislation that Clinton signed into law (Koenig 1993).

In its final form, the FMLA guaranteed twelve weeks of unpaid job-protected leave for employees to care for a new child or sick spouse, parent, or child, as well as for the employee's own illness. During the leave, employers must continue providing health benefits for the employee. The coverage applies only to employees who have worked at the same company for at least 1,250 hours in the previous year. Only public agencies or private companies with fifty or more employees within a seventy-five-mile radius are required to provide leave, and employers may choose to exclude employees in the top 10 percent of the pay scale. All told, about 60 percent of workers are covered by the law (Ray, Gornick, and Schmitt 2009; Heymann and Earle 2010, 57).

Despite the FMLA's limited provisions, most family leave proponents saw it as a victory because Washington had finally acknowledged the need for government intervention to support families. At the same time, several were disappointed at what they perceived to be a watered-down version of the original legislation. Even Pat Schroeder "tended to pine for the purer bill she had introduced in 1985" (Elving 1995, 290). Some believed that activists had ultimately settled for a law that was much weaker than the original draft, and that with Clinton in the White House a stronger bill could have been advanced (Kaitin 1994, 112). Steven Wisensale asks an important question with regard to this viewpoint: "Why, especially during the honeymoon phase of [Clinton's] administration when his political influence was probably at its zenith, did the newly elected president choose to settle for the minimum, and thus provide the nation with one more example of what some may label as symbolic politics?" (2001, 151). Some suggest Clinton's decision was fueled by political opportunism: "rather than investing time and effort to force a stronger, more comprehensive law, Clinton expediently used the enactment of this compromised legislation as a pulpit from which to announce the end of gridlock in Washington" (Jacobs and Davies, 1994, 1). Others believe that "Clinton's support of the law appeared to be more a result of his election promises and his efforts to court the women's vote than of any direct pressure from feminists" (Mazur 2002, 113). By the time Clinton was elected, activists were convinced that he would sign the FMLA, and they felt no need to continue pressuring him. Many WMAs had already turned their attention to issues that were higher priorities for them, especially since some of them no longer supported the bill in its final form.

Conclusion

Major governmental action seldom occurs without significant interest group activity (Francia 2006, 120). Because a federal law granting family leave was seen as a great departure from the tendency of American policy makers to avoid regulating the so-called private sphere, interest groups had to launch a concerted effort to get such a policy passed. And although family leave advocates were eventually successful in getting the FMLA passed in 1993, the provisions of the bill were much less generous than leave benefits in the rest of the developed world. For this reason, some activists were disappointed with the bill that passed.

Support for family leave "began with feminists" (Elving 1995, 12) and then quickly branched out to labor communities. The FMLA also gained support from some conservative and religious activists, in large part because the coalition stressed that it was fighting to give workers more time with their families. Unlike government-sponsored child care, which relieves parents of the responsibility for full-time care, parental leave allows parents time off from their jobs to care for a child (Leira 2002, 75). Activists found a surprising ally in the Catholic Church. The U.S. Catholic Conference felt that the availability of family and medical leave might lower the number of abortions because women would not have to choose between family and career (Bernstein 2001, 9). AARP became a major advocate for the bill, primarily because it allowed employees time off to care for their elderly or sick relatives.

On the other side of the debate, business interests were staunchly opposed to the family leave bill. These opponents claimed that family leave would be too costly to implement and represented an unfunded mandate from the federal government. The business community in the United States is extremely powerful and during the campaign for the FMLA it had the resources to mobilize support for its cause; therefore, it was able to force family leave advocates to compromise on numerous occasions. The family leave coalition had substantially fewer financial resources than the business interests did, so politicians did not feel significant pressure to act in response to their demands.

In addition to strong opposition from business interests, family and medical leave suffered from a collective action problem. Because the proposed leave was a public good that would be available to all who qualified, rather than only those individuals who worked to pass it, it was difficult to inspire the public to fight for it (Olson 1965). Likewise, the leave would benefit only a small percentage of the population for a short amount of time, so it was hard to drum up steady support (Glass and Estes 1997, 307). There was also a fragmentation of interests in the United States: "Child advocates primarily focus[ed] on the neediest families; work-family advocates concentrate[d] on women who are trying to reconcile work and family; and feminists direct[ed] most of their efforts toward ensuring gender equality in the home and workplace" (Gornick and Meyers 2003, 300). Public sentiment was too weak to overcome conservative mobilization against expanded federal family leave policies (Morgan 2006, 137).

Many women's organizations, such as the Women's Legal Defense Fund, the National Women's Law Center, the Women's Equity Action League, the National Federation of Business and Professional Women, and the Association of Junior Leagues, participated in passing the FMLA in the United States. These WMAs cheered the bill for bringing work and family issues out of the shadows. Prior to this, such issues were considered to be part of the "private sphere" and therefore less deserving of policy attention—especially since the private sphere was associated with women. These activists hoped that the FMLA would be the beginning of greater governmental interest in issues surrounding work, gender, and the family.

Other women's organizations had a more complicated experience with the policy-making processes leading up to the passage of the FMLA. NOW and the Fund for a Feminist Majority ultimately withdrew their support for the FMLA coalition because they believed it had compromised on too many of women's initial demands. These groups saw the FMLA as a diluted version of the original family leave bill. The fact that the coalition asked for *unpaid* leave was especially problematic for these organizations. Many dissenters felt that coalition members started the legislative debate asking for less than they actually wanted, rather than asking for more than they wanted in anticipation of cuts and compromises that would need to be made in order to pass the bill (Bernstein 2001, 96–97). But during the drafting process, coalition members had felt little pressure from radical activists to ask for more generous leave benefits; therefore, they offered concessions early in hopes of passing the bill more easily (Sawyers and Meyer 1999, 198). Still, the opposition from NOW and Fund for a Feminist Majority was much different from that of the business community. Businesses were against the idea of any government law that guaranteed family leave to employees. Dissenters within the women's movement were strongly in favor of a family leave law; indeed, they wanted a law that was much more generous than the FMLA.

Historically the American women's movement has been large and strong. WMAs were successful in getting the PDA passed in 1978 (Gelb and Palley 1987) and were responsible for initially getting family leave on the agenda (Mazur 2002, 114). However, their influence then waned with regard to family leave policies. The women's movement as a whole lost some of its strength in the 1980s, but it was still able to sway the policy-making process when it set an issue as a priority, such as reproductive rights. But family leave was generally low on the movement's agenda. When the issue was first addressed, some WMAs were split between stressing either equality or difference. Divisions also emerged regarding whether the leave should be paid. Although these rifts did not cause significant damage to the women's movement, they did weaken the movement's bargaining power; therefore, legislators did not feel an urgency to address their demands. Indeed, even with a coalition that included segments of the women's movement, unions, AARP, children's defense organizations, disability rights groups, the Catholic Church, and critical actors in

Congress, it was still a difficult process to pass the FMLA. Moreover, the final bill was much weaker than family leave legislation in European countries and Canada.

Members of the coalition put forth two main arguments to explain why they fought until the end for a bill that was so far from what they had originally wanted. First, they felt that something was better than nothing. Knowing that a paid leave bill would not have passed in the political climate of the 1980s and early 1990s, advocates wanted to win at least the right for workers to take leave without the fear of losing their jobs. Beyond the direct positive effects on individuals eligible for FMLA leave and their families, the passage of the law fulfilled a symbolic purpose by showing that the federal government recognized the importance of work and family issues. Second, they viewed the FMLA as an important first step toward more comprehensive family leave legislation. Once family leave was mandated by the government, they hoped that both employees and employers would start to recognize it as an expected benefit of employment. Such a change in perception would open the door for expansion of the law (Selmi 2004).[42] Karen Nussbaum, executive director of 9to5, summarized the sentiments of the coalition:

> I'd be among the first to say this bill doesn't go far enough. Far too many working parents are excluded, and the burden of paying for their leaves remains squarely on the shoulders of the parents themselves. But . . . we need a minimum standard to be the law of the land. The FMLA is a symbol. If we pass it, we send the message that our government understands that working people need help balancing work and family. (1992, 6A)

Nussbaum, like most family leave advocates at the time, believed that after the mandated study of the FMLA's effects, a series of amendments would expand the law to become more responsive to employees' needs (Selmi 2004, 72). Additionally, some believed that the minimum standards required by the FMLA would become a "floor" of benefits that prompted employers to voluntarily create more generous policies in order to attract the best employees (80). As Chapter 3 demonstrates, these hopes have not materialized; fifteen years passed before the FMLA was amended for the first time.

3

From the FMLA to the FAMILY Act

Family Leave Policy at the National Level since 1993

A s described in Chapter 2, the Family and Medical Leave Act (FMLA) passed in 1993 after almost a decade of "conflict and compromise" in Washington (Elving 1995).[1] In its original form, the law guarantees twelve workweeks of unpaid, job-protected leave in a twelve-month period for eligible employees for three reasons: the birth, adoption, or foster care placement of a child; the care of an employee's spouse, child, or parent who has a serious health condition; or the employee's own serious illness.[2] All public agencies are covered by the FMLA regardless of the number of employees.[3] The law also covers private worksites that have employed at least fifty workers within seventy-five miles of the site for at least twenty weeks in the preceding or current calendar year. To qualify for leave under the FMLA, the employee must have worked for the same (covered) employer for at least twelve months. Although those twelve months do not have to be consecutive, the employee must have worked a minimum of 1,250 hours in the twelve months preceding the start of FMLA leave.

Employees are not entitled to receive wages during FMLA leave, although the employee may choose to substitute accrued paid leave, such as sick days or vacation time, for FMLA leave. The employer may also require such a substitution. During the employee's leave, the only benefit that the employer is obligated to maintain is health insurance coverage at the same level that would have been provided if the employee had been employed continuously for the duration of the leave. The law does not entitle employees to accrue benefits or seniority during leave; however, upon an employee's return, all benefits must be resumed at the level preceding leave. Likewise, employees generally have the right to return to either the same job or an equivalent position with identical pay, benefits, and other terms and conditions of employment. An employer can deny the restoration of an employee to his or her previous position if the employee is among the highest-paid 10 percent of employees and the denial would "prevent substantial and grievous economic injury to the operations of the employer" (U.S. Department of Labor 1993).[4]

The activists who fought for the passage of the FMLA saw the law as a starting point for moving family leave policies forward in the United States. Many believed—or at least hoped—that FMLA coverage would steadily expand to protect a greater number of workers and ultimately to include wage replacement. In reality, the FMLA remained virtually untouched until 2008, and the changes that have been made to the act have been minor compared to expectations. In this chapter, I examine family leave policy at the national level since the passage of the FMLA. I begin by discussing the handful of amendments to the FMLA that have been enacted to extend coverage to a greater proportion of the population, including families of military personnel and members of flight crews. I then address four Supreme Court cases that have directly involved or influenced FMLA provisions. After reporting on the results of the three sets of surveys commissioned by the Department of Labor since the passage of the FMLA, I analyze the extent to which the law has affected Americans' work-life balance and conclude that the statute has done little to address gender inequality, in large part because it provides leave that is unpaid. Examining proposals to expand the FMLA, I highlight the numerous arguments in favor of paid leave. In recent years, national-level efforts to increase family leave benefits in the United States have gained momentum and visibility. As a result, a growing number of politicians, including President Barack Obama, have publicly called for the United States to adopt more generous family leave policies. Policy makers have responded to the rising movement, as demonstrated by the introduction of the Family and Medical Insurance Leave (FAMILY) Act, a federal bill that would provide workers up to twelve weeks of paid family leave. After detailing these recent proposals, I conclude by considering the form that family leave policy in the United States will take in the future.

Amendments to the FMLA

For fifteen years, the FMLA remained virtually untouched. Although countless changes have been discussed, it was not until January 2008 that President George W. Bush signed into law the first amendments to the FMLA. Section 585 of the National Defense Authorization Act for Fiscal Year 2008 addresses "family leave in connection with injured members of the Armed Forces."[5] The amendments provide exigency leave if a spouse, son, daughter, or parent of an employee either is on active duty or has been notified of an impending call to active duty in the armed forces in support of a contingency operation. Qualifying exigencies include the following: short-notice deployment of seven days or fewer; time to arrange for child care, make financial or legal arrangements, or attend official ceremonies; and up to five days of leave for the employee to spend time with a deployed service member who is on temporary leave for rest and recuperation. The FMLA was also amended to allow employees who are the spouse, son, daughter, parent, or next of kin of a seriously injured service member to take up to twenty-six workweeks of leave during a twelve-month period for caregiving purposes.

In October 2009, President Barack Obama signed into law the National Defense Authorization Act for Fiscal Year 2010, which modified and expanded the military family leave provisions of 2008.[6] Under the new provisions, qualifying exigency leave would apply to employees with either family members serving in a regular component of the armed forces during deployment to a foreign country or family members in the National Guard or reserves who are deployed with the armed forces to a foreign country. The 2010 amendments also extended military caregiver leave for qualified veterans and expanded the definition of a "serious injury or illness" to include those that existed before the beginning of the member's active duty and were aggravated by service in the line of duty.

The FMLA was amended again in December 2009 with the Airline Flight Technical Corrections Act,[7] which declared that the FMLA has special rules that apply to airline pilots, flight attendants, and other airline crew members.[8] Specifically, a member of an airline flight crew fulfills the hours-of-service requirement for FMLA leave if he or she meets two conditions during the previous twelve-month period: the member has worked or been paid for at least 504 hours, and the member has worked or been paid for at least 60 percent of the minimum number of hours that he or she was scheduled to work in any given month. An employee in "reserve status" must have worked at least 60 percent of the hours for which he or she was paid for a given month. Shortly after these three laws were passed to amend the FMLA, the U.S. Department of Labor issued an Administrator's Interpretation in June 2010 to clarify the definition of "son or daughter" as it applies to an employee standing in loco parentis to a child. This interpretation made it clear that an employee may qualify for FMLA leave to care for the child of a same-sex partner (U.S. Department of Labor 2010).

The Supreme Court and the FMLA

In addition to the recent amendments to the FMLA, a number of U.S. Supreme Court cases have affected the coverage and enforcement of the law.[9] Four cases in particular warrant discussion because of their direct application to the FMLA. The first of these cases that made its way to the Supreme Court was *Ragsdale v. Wolverine World Wide, Inc.* in 2002.[10] Wolverine World Wide allowed its employees to take up to seven months of unpaid sick leave. After exhausting this leave, employee Tracy Ragsdale was still unable to return to work. When she requested additional time under the FMLA, she was denied. Ragsdale claimed that she was entitled to more job-protected leave because she had not been informed that the seven-month absence would count against her FMLA leave, which violated the U.S. Department of Labor's regulation that held an employer responsible for telling his or her employees when an absence would be considered FMLA leave.[11] According to a related regulation, if the employer failed to designate the leave under the FMLA, it would not count against the employee's twelve-week leave entitlement.[12] The U.S. Supreme Court sided with

Wolverine, ruling that the regulations issued by the U.S. Department of Labor were beyond the secretary of labor's authority; therefore, Ragsdale was entitled to no more leave.

In the 2003 case of *Nevada Department of Human Resources v. Hibbs*, the Supreme Court ruled that Congress intended for state workers to be covered under the FMLA when taking leave to care for a family member.[13] William Hibbs, an employee of the Nevada Department of Human Resources, requested and was granted twelve weeks of leave to care for his ailing wife. The department later informed Hibbs that he had exhausted his leave and had to return to work by a certain date. When Hibbs did not report to work, he was fired. He then sued the department in federal district court, alleging that he was denied his rights under the FMLA. The district court in Nevada found the state immune under the Eleventh Amendment. The Ninth Circuit reinstated the case and the state appealed to the Supreme Court. In a sharp departure from past rulings that had given precedent to the rights of state government over federal mandates, the Supreme Court ruled that state employees can sue in federal court for their FMLA rights (Pyle and Pelletier 2003). According to Chief Justice William Rehnquist, the FMLA was more "narrowly targeted" than previous similar lawsuits for age and disability discrimination. The Court declared that the law was meant to correct the long history of discrimination that women faced as a result of both the stereotypes about women's domestic roles and those that presumed that men lacked domestic responsibilities (Greenhouse 2003). This ruling ensured FMLA coverage for state employees; activists have continued to advocate for further expansions of family leave policies. The government relations director of NOW, Jan Erickson, applauded this decision, calling for even greater expansion of the FMLA with regard to eligibility, length of leave, and wage replacement (Erickson 2003, 11).

The 2012 case *Coleman v. Court of Appeals of Maryland* found that suits against the states under the self-care provision of the FMLA are barred by the immunity granted in the Eleventh Amendment.[14] Daniel Coleman had attempted to sue his employer, the Maryland Court of Appeals, for firing him after denying his request for ten days of medical leave to address his hypertension and diabetes. Although the case seemed similar to *Hibbs*, the Court found that there was no evidence of sex discrimination or stereotyping when it came to sick leave, and that Congress did not have such discrimination in mind when it enacted those protections in the FMLA. For that reason, the usual protections against suing a state should not be lifted.

The last of the four Supreme Court cases addressed here did not specifically target the FMLA, though the ruling directly affected the scope of the law's coverage. In the 2013 case of *United States v. Windsor*, the Court ruled that restricting federal interpretations of "marriage" and "spouse" to apply only to heterosexual unions was unconstitutional.[15] Edith Windsor and Thea Spyer, a same-sex couple living in New York, had been lawfully married in Canada in 2007. When Spyer died in 2009, she left her entire estate to Windsor, who was barred by the Defense of Marriage Act from claiming the federal estate tax exemption for surviving spouses.[16] When Windsor's case made it to the Supreme Court, the Defense of Marriage Act was declared unconstitutional under the due process clause of the Fifth Amendment. After the ruling, President Obama directed his cabinet to review all relevant federal statutes where the decision would need to be implemented. In February 2015, the Department of Labor issued a Final Rule that revised the definition of "spouse" under the FMLA so that eligible employees in a legal same-sex marriage are able to take FMLA leave to care for their spouse or family member, regardless of their state of residence (U.S. Department of Labor 2015c).

How Is FMLA Leave Used? Results from the 1995, 2000, and 2012 Surveys

February 5, 2015, marked the twenty-second anniversary of the signing of the FMLA, the only federal law that helps working men and women meet the demands of both work and family. Since its implementation, the law has allowed workers to take leave over 200 million times (National Partnership for Women and Families 2015c). However, not everyone has the same level of access to FMLA leave. The law's capacity to improve one's work-life balance often depends on the sex, class, and race of the individual.

Three years after the implementation of the FMLA, the Commission on Family and Medical Leave (1996) prepared a report for Congress detailing the ways in which employees were utilizing the nascent program.[17] It found that the law covered approximately 11 percent of all U.S. private-sector worksites; those sites employed 59.5 percent of the country's private-sector workers. Factoring in public-sector workers, all of whom are covered regardless of the size of their worksite, the proportion of all covered workers increased to 66 percent. Because not every employee in a covered worksite meets the eligibility requirements for FMLA leave, only 54.9 percent of all workers were both covered and eligible in 1995.

The utilization rate of FMLA leave among all private and public-sector employees was 2 percent, and there was a gender gap in leave usage: 20.0 percent of women took leave; 12.7 percent of men did. Of those who took leave, over 60 percent did so because of their own serious health problem. Approximately 20 percent used the time to care for an ill spouse, child, or parent, while 13.3 percent used it for the birth, adoption, or foster care placement of a child. Only 3.8 percent took leave for maternity disability. Most people (90 percent) took twelve weeks—the maximum amount allowed by the FMLA—or less. The median length of leave was ten days; the mean length was thirty-seven days. There was also a significant minority (3.1 percent) of employees who claimed that they needed leave but did not take it; almost 64 percent of those workers said that they could not afford to take unpaid leave. Others workers (34.9 percent) claimed that work was too important to warrant taking time off, and 29.9 percent worried about losing their jobs. Of the employees who took leave, 84 percent returned to work, and 10 percent were still on leave at the time of the surveys. Only 6 percent did not return to their employers after taking leave (Commission on Family and Medical Leave 1996).

To comply with the new law, approximately two-thirds of covered worksites reported that they changed some aspect of their family and medical leave policies. Covered establishments were much more likely to offer family and medical leave than noncovered establishments; however, there were still some problems with compliance. From August 1993 to September 1995, the Wage and Hour Division of the Department and Labor received almost four thousand complaints of noncompliance. Approximately 60 percent of the claims were deemed valid; most of them involved an employer's refusal to reinstate an employee to the same or equivalent position upon returning from leave. Still, from the employers' perspective, the experience with the FMLA was overall positive. Over 89 percent of employers at FMLA-covered worksites reported either a small increase or no increase in administrative costs, benefits, and hiring costs as a result of the FMLA. Fewer than 5 percent of them felt that the FMLA negatively affected any aspect of employee performance (Commission on Family and Medical Leave 1996).

For the most part, the FMLA went into effect without a hitch. In fact, many were surprised by the overall lack of commotion surrounding the new program. As Joseph Willis observed upon viewing the results of the surveys from 1995, "While still in its infancy, the Family and Medical Leave Act of 1993 has proved to be neither the godsend its proponents predicted nor the colossal burden its detractors anticipated. Instead, it seems to be an infrequently used program that is nowhere near as costly as first contemplated" (1997, 108).

In 2000, the Department of Labor commissioned another set of surveys to determine if FMLA usage had changed since 1995. David Cantor and colleagues (2001) analyzed the results in *Balancing the Needs of Families and Employers: Family and Medical Leave Surveys, 2000 Update: A Report.*[18] There was significant continuity from the previous report in many aspects of family and medical leave usage. For example, there was little difference in the proportion of employers and employees covered by the FMLA. In 2000, approximately 60 percent of all workers were both covered and eligible, a small decrease from 1995. About the same proportion (16.5 percent) of workers in 1995 and 2000 took leave for a family or medical reason in the eighteen months prior to the survey. There was also a similar gender gap: 13.5 percent of men took leave; 19.8 percent of women did. Of all leave takers, the 2000 surveys found that 58 percent of them were women. The median length of leave remained at ten days, and still 90 percent took twelve weeks or fewer (Cantor et al. 2001).

In addition to these similarities, there were a few new findings in the 2000 surveys. To begin, the reasons for taking leave differed from 1995, with significantly more workers taking leave for maternity disability (7.8 percent) or to care for a new child (17.9 percent). A little less than half (47.2 percent) took leave for their own health, and approximately 27.1 percent did so to care for an ill child, spouse, or parent. Although the number declined slightly, still 2.4 percent of those surveyed said they needed leave but could not take it; of those individuals, 77.6 percent cited financial reasons (Cantor et al. 2001).

Reactions from both employees and employers were again generally positive. Almost 79 percent of employees said that taking leave had positive effects on their ability to care for family members. Over 70 percent reported positive effects on their own or family members' emotional well-being; 63 percent said the leave had a positive impact on their own or their family members' physical health. A significant majority of employers (84 percent) said that the FMLA had either no effect or a positive effect on productivity. A full 90 percent of them reported either no effect or a positive effect on both profitability and growth. Approximately 8 percent of covered employers also cited cost savings due to the FMLA, primarily because of decreased turnover. This is not surprising since 98 percent of covered and eligible employees returned to work for the same employer after taking leave (Cantor et al. 2001).

In 2012, the Department of Labor commissioned a third set of surveys to determine employers' and employees' experiences with family and medical leave.[19] Jacob Alex Klerman, Kelly Daley, and Alyssa Pozniak (2014) describe the results in *Family and Medical Leave in 2012: Technical Report.* The proportion of covered and eligible workers remained steady at approximately 59 percent. About 13 percent of all employees took leave for a qualifying FMLA reason in the previous year, with FMLA-eligible workers more likely to do so. Women were 56 percent of leave takers. The share of men taking leave rose slightly from 13 percent in 1995 to 16 percent in 2012. Most leaves (70 percent) were still less than forty days; 42 percent of leaves lasted ten days or fewer. Longer leaves—those averaging fifty-eight days—were primarily taken by women who used the time to care for a new child. When men took leave for a new child, the average length of leave was twenty-two days.

Most leave (55 percent) was still taken for the employee's own illness. About one-fifth of leave was for pregnancy or a new child, and 18 percent was to care for a seriously ill relative. Leave for other qualifying reasons, including military reasons, which were not covered until 2008, was rare (2 percent). Employers continued to report a positive or neutral experience with the FMLA: 37 percent cited a positive effect on employee productivity, absenteeism, turnover, career advancement and morale, and the business's profitability. About half found no noticeable effect. Three-quarters of covered worksites also said that administering the law is easy. One of the more noteworthy findings from the 2012 surveys was the change in the proportion of workers who claimed they needed leave but could not take it; it increased to 5.0 percent of employees surveyed from 2.4 percent in 2000 (Klerman, Daley, and Pozniak 2014).

Approximately 18 million employees take family and medical leave each year (Jorgensen and Appelbaum 2014c). As noted earlier, many more need leave but cannot take it. Some of them do not meet the eligibility requirements for the job-protected leave that the FMLA provides, so they fear losing their job while on leave. Even those with job protection often worry that taking leave will cause them to fall behind or be seen as uncommitted to the job. Others simply cannot afford to take leave that is unpaid. Regardless of the reason, there is clearly unmet need for leave, yet it does not affect all groups equally. Of the workers in 2012 who said they needed leave but could not take it, 64 percent of them were women (Klerman, Daley, and Pozniak 2014; see also Gerstel and McGonagle 1999). Hispanic and nonwhite workers, as well as those earning below $34,000 per year, were also more likely than their counterparts to need leave but not take it (Klerman, Daley, and Pozniak 2014). There are clear inequalities based on sex, race, and class that are exposed by both FMLA eligibility requirements and the usage of leave. In addition, the effects of the FMLA are felt differently by various groups.

The Effects of the FMLA on Work-Life Balance

The FMLA was created to be a gender-neutral statute to promote equal employment opportunities for women and men (Greenhouse 2003). Yet, as the preceding survey results demonstrate, women are far more likely than men to take family leave, especially for the care of others, such as their children or their ailing parents. Men, on the other hand, are more likely to take leave as a result of their own illness (see also Armenia and Gerstel 2006; Glass and Estes 1997; Gerstel and McGonagle 1999). Overall, the FMLA has done little to alleviate women's caregiving responsibilities. If leave needs to be taken for caregiving purposes, it still generally falls on women to do so. This can be problematic because fewer women meet the FMLA eligibility requirements than men (Bardasi and Gornick 2000; Tilly 1996, 15), which means that they are more likely to have to take unprotected leave or exit the workforce completely in order to fulfill their caregiving duties.

The FMLA requires that an employee has worked at least 1,250 hours in the twelve months preceding the start of FMLA leave; this works out to approximately twenty-four hours a week. Women are more likely than men to work part time, which means that they are also more likely to fall short of the hourly requirement for FMLA leave. When women do work twenty-five or more hours per week, they are more likely to take longer leaves (Gerstel and McGonagle 1999). It seems that women can be hurt by working either part time or full time. If they work part time, they may not qualify for FMLA leave. If they work full time, they often must take longer leaves when the need arises because they do not have the greater schedule flexibility and "free" time that could be spent addressing the necessary caregiving while still working part time. Such leaves can hurt women in the long run.

When there is tension between an individual's work and family responsibilities, the worker's career often suffers in the form of lower productivity and greater turnover, which hurts the worker's potential career achievement (Glass and Estes 1997). Because women are more likely to have to address this "caregiver conundrum"—that is, the difficulty faced when trying to balance caregiving and work responsibilities—they continue to be disproportionately harmed by the current system of leave in the United States (Porter 2010, 356). When employees take leave, there is the chance that their employers will see them as less committed to the job, and therefore provide them with fewer opportunities for advancement (Padavic and Reskin 2002). Because women are more likely than men to take leave, they are more likely to be stigmatized in such a manner.

Female employees in the prime working ages of twenty-six to fifty-nine make only 38 percent of what their male counterparts earn. This gap can be ascribed in part to the greater amount of time that women devote to family responsibilities (Rose and Hartmann 2004).[20] The wage gap between mothers and women without children is telling: the first child generally reduces a woman's income by 7.5 percent; the second child reduces it another 8 percent (Butts 2004; see also Staff and Mortimer 2012; Budig and England 2001; Glauber 2007). Because the FMLA is partly responsible for women's greater time at home, the argument can be made that the FMLA has helped undermine women's earning potential in the United States while doing little to alleviate their responsibilities in the so-called private sphere.

In 1965, women performed approximately six times the amount of housework that men did. Although this gender gap has narrowed over time, women are still estimated to do 1.6 times the amount of housework as men (Bianchi et al. 2012; see also Sayer 2005). Even when women take leave from paid work outside the home, they still perform the "second shift" of housework and child care (Hochschild 1989). In many cases, women have also adopted the "third shift" of caring for family outside the home (Gerstel 2000; Gerstel and McGonagle 1999).

Leave policies influence the choices that women make regarding leave. For example, Wen-Jui Han and Jane Waldfogel (2003) found a positive correlation between the length of time a state allowed for leave and the likelihood that a woman would take leave within the three months following the birth of a child. When states provided more leave time, women were more likely to take leave. They found no such effect on men's leave taking (see also Waldfogel 1999; Han, Ruhm, and Waldfogel 2009). Whether women are eligible for FMLA leave also has a direct effect on their childbearing decisions. Compared with women who are not eligible for FMLA leave, eligible women increase the probability of having a first and second birth by about 1.5 percent and 0.6 percent each year, respectively. In comparison to other women, women who are eligible for FMLA leave are also giving birth earlier. Among eligible women, the implementation of the FMLA affected the probability of giving birth, increasing it by about five percentage points for a first birth and three percentage points for a second birth (Cannonier 2014).

Public policy clearly has an impact on leave decisions. As noted earlier, the FMLA allows an employer to refuse to reinstate a worker who is among the highest-paid 10 percent of employees. The effects of this provision can be wide-ranging. Management's usage of leave often sets an example for the rest of the workforce. If management does not take leave, lower-level employees may be more hesitant to make use of available leave as well. Moreover, there can be gendered consequences of this proviso of the FMLA. Because men are more likely to be employees at this income level, there is a greater chance that they will be denied leave based on the "key employee" exception. In this way, men are discouraged from fulfilling their familial obligations at home, and the notion of the "ideal (male) worker" (J. Williams 2000) is reinforced.

In an examination of care leave policies in Western Europe, Kimberly J. Morgan and Kathrin Zippel (2003) argue that most countries only appear to offer a gender-neutral choice to parents. Because of the existing structural gender inequalities and dominant gender norms in society, the gender-neutral language of the laws actually reinforces women's status as full-time caregivers. Ariane Prohaska and John F. Zipp (2011) came to a similar conclusion after analyzing the ways in which the FMLA affects how Americans divide leave between mothers and fathers—a choice that has a significant impact on gender equality both at work and in the home. According to the authors, the decision to take leave is made in the context of the household, the workplace, and the state. Although it is the individuals and their families who ultimately decide who will take leave and for how long, that decision is heavily influenced by both workplace options that are shaped by state policies and cultural expectations about gender roles. Using feminist theories of the state (MacKinnon 1989; Orloff 1993), the authors determined that the FMLA has had relatively little impact on gender inequality, despite the fact that feminists fought to ensure that ideas of gender equality were thoroughly incorporated into the law (Prohaska and Zipp 2011).

According to Catharine MacKinnon (1989), laws can never actually be gender neutral if there is a significant gender hierarchy in society. Therefore, even laws that profess gender neutrality, such as the FMLA, are not gender neutral. Deborah J. Anthony says that the FMLA, which primarily deals with pregnancy, childbearing, and caregiving, was created from an outside, male perspective, rather than from the viewpoint of those who are largely doing the work. She asserts that "creating gender-neutral laws does not erase socially imposed roles; such laws actually tend to reinforce norms as they obscure the social forces that naturalize gender difference and pressure women in the home" (2008, 488). Therefore, the FMLA—as the governmental policy that has the greatest influence on leave decisions in the United States—ultimately bolsters women's position as primary caregiver (Prohaska and Zipp 2011, 1429–1430).

Amy Armenia and Naomi Gerstel (2006) also find that unpaid leaves mandated by the FMLA may sustain gender inequality. Women take significantly longer leaves than men, especially when that leave is for the care of a newborn. Noting that leave to care for newborns is the only type where women extend the twelve-week allowance of the FMLA, the authors claim that it is in the length of leaves where the FMLA most clearly fails to achieve gender neutrality—let alone gender equality. The fact that the length of leaves to care for a sick spouse, parent, or child are similar for men and women demonstrates that men generally use leave for family crises, while women are still held primarily responsible for the routine care of family members, especially newborns (Armenia and Gerstel 2006; see also Coltrane 1996; Gallagher and Gerstel 2001; Gerstel and Gallagher 1994).

To explain the continued gender inequalities in spite of the seemingly gender-neutral FMLA, Armenia and Gerstel (2006) point to both policy layering and cultural expectations. First, they suggest that employees rely heavily on the old system that is primarily aimed at women and their physical disabilities during pregnancy and childbirth. Since the passage of the Pregnancy Discrimination Act, most leaves for pregnancy and childbirth are covered in the same manner as leaves for disabilities, which means that they are usually paid. Because leave mandated by the FMLA is unpaid, it is more rational for women to take leave than men—at least from an economic viewpoint. This decision is often reinforced by the fact that men typically earn higher incomes than their women partners. Second, gender inequalities may remain pervasive because of cultural expectations about gender roles. In the workplace, employers and coworkers are more likely to support women's need to take leave for family responsibilities in informal ways, while not doing the same for men. Likewise, in the home there is still the expectation that women will provide greater nurturance and care (Armenia and Gerstel 2006, 888).

In addition to perpetuating gender inequalities, the FMLA may affect some racial groups more than others. Stressing the intersectionality of race and gender, Armenia and Gerstel (2006) find that white men are significantly less likely to take family leaves than white women or men and women of color. There is clearly a class component at work here. Because there is a larger wage gap between white spouses than between African American, Hispanic, or Asian spouses (Wallace 2014; Glynn and Powers 2012), it is often less economically practical for white men to take unpaid FMLA leave than it is for their partners. This is not to say that taking leave is easy for people of color. Because they generally have fewer resources (Oliver and Shapiro 2006), people of color often cannot take the leave that they need (Armenia and Gerstel 2006). The FMLA has primarily become a job security statute for middle- and upper-class workers who can afford to take unpaid leave (Palazzari 2007). Yet because of structural gender inequality and cultural gender norms, it is the women in those classes who predominantly use FMLA leave.

Many workplaces still promote—either directly or indirectly— policies designed for the "ideal worker" who can put in long hours and does not require time off for family responsibilities (J. Williams 2000). Such a model assumes that the worker is supported by a stay-at-home partner who will provide the necessary caregiving; the FMLA has largely reinforced this model. The provisions of the FMLA have done little to improve the work-life balance for most workers and have primarily strengthened stereotypical gender roles. As a result, both women and men are marginalized: "Women continue to struggle to reconcile work with their traditional caregiver role, while men struggle to reconcile family with their traditional provider role" (Palazzari 2007, 432).

Fathers are expected to be the successful breadwinners in the family, as dictated by the principles of "hegemonic masculinity" (Catlett and McHenry 2004). At the same time, the so-called new fatherhood requires that fathers are actively involved with daily family life (McDonald and Almeida 2004). Kari Palazzari (2007) refers to this situation as the "daddy double-bind," leaving fathers with no real way to fulfill both roles successfully. In theory, the FMLA should help fathers alleviate some of their work-life conflict. However, as noted earlier, the law largely maintains the status quo with regard to gender roles. Employers continue to expect that women will take the bulk of leave, especially after the birth or adoption of a child. Men, on the other hand, are largely encouraged to take only a few days off work after the arrival of a new child. Thus, the caretaking patterns established from the beginning typically put fathers in the position of secondary caregivers. Over time these patterns become difficult to break and ultimately perpetuate the myth that mothers are better suited to be parents, which reinforces the idea of women as primary caretakers (Palazzari 2007, 457–458).

Fathers typically have little power to tip the balance more favorably toward their family lives. Employers are less likely to encourage men to take family leave than women, and many fathers worry that they will be seen as less ambitious or committed to work if they attempt to play a greater familial role. Fearing employer retribution, men often use a small number of paid vacation and sick days upon the arrival of a new child instead of FMLA leave. Although employer discrimination is prohibited by the FMLA, it can be difficult to prove and courts have been hesitant to get involved in the issue. Overall, the limited provisions of the FMLA, coupled with weak enforcement policies and judicial outcomes, have allowed employers to remain hostile toward employees—especially men—who seek to break from the "ideal worker" mold (Palazzari 2007). This has the effect of simultaneously reinforcing the idea that women belong in the home.

Ultimately, most scholars agree that the FMLA has done little to improve the work-life balance for both men and women. However, because women often start at a greater disadvantage because of cultural expectations that they are primarily responsible for caregiving and homemaking—even when working outside the house as well—they continue to suffer disproportionately as a result of the FMLA's limited provisions. Because of its gender-neutral language, some consider the FMLA a success by liberal feminist standards. But the law does not actually address gender inequality, so many consider the FMLA feminist only in its "symbolic purposes" (Fine 2006, 63; see also Grossman 2004).

Proposals to Expand the FMLA

The FMLA has been criticized by numerous scholars for its limited ability to help individuals reconcile their work lives with their family obligations. Because of the stringent employer coverage and employee eligibility requirements, no more than 60 percent of the workforce actually has access to FMLA leave (Ray, Gornick, and Schmitt 2009; Heymann and Earle 2010, 57). To the dismay of many, the law has remained largely unchanged since its passage, despite continuous calls by activists, legislators, and scholars for its expansion. Even Patricia Schroeder, the congresswoman who sponsored the first version of the FMLA and has been one of the strongest advocates for family leave, has become disheartened by the stagnation:

> We thought if we could just get it [the FMLA] passed, in a couple of years it could be expanded. But that didn't happen. Two years ago, I was asked to go to the celebration of FMLA's 20th anniversary. I said, "Are you kidding? I'm so embarrassed you haven't expanded this. What are we celebrating? It's still unpaid." (Quoted in Voss 2015, 166)

There have been numerous proposals to expand coverage to a greater number of workers. One way to achieve this would be to apply the FMLA to businesses with fewer than fifty employees (Jorgensen and Appelbaum 2014c; L. Levine 2010; Mayer 2013). In fact, in every Congress since the passage of the FMLA in 1993, a bill has been introduced to lower the threshold for coverage of private-sector employers from fifty to twenty-five employees (O'Leary 2007, 59; see also Porter 2014; National Partnership for Women and Families 2013). Some have suggested lowering the threshold even further. After analyzing the results of the 2012 Department of Labor surveys on the usage of FMLA leave, Jacob Alex Klerman, Kelly Daley, and Alyssa Pozniak (2014) recommended a threshold of twenty employees. A 2009 bill defined an FMLA-covered employer as one that had two or more employees (Porter 2014). Palazzari (2007) argues that extending FMLA leave to all employees would make the law more effective and relevant to workers' lives. Helene Jorgensen and Eileen Appelbaum (2014b) found that expanding the FMLA to cover small firms with fewer than fifty employees would not pose an undue financial hardship for the businesses.

In addition to lowering the employee threshold for employer coverage, many recommend adjusting the number of hours that an employee is required to work before becoming eligible for leave (L. Levine 2010). The Family Leave Insurance Act of 2009 would have changed the requisite number of hours from 1,250 in the previous year to 625 hours in the previous six months (Porter 2014).[21] Some call for a decrease in the total number of hours in the previous year, from 1,250 to 780 (Klerman, Daley, and Pozniak 2014). The Part-Time Worker Bill of Rights Act of 2013 would have eliminated the hours-worked requirement altogether so that more part-time workers could gain FMLA protections (National Partnership for Women and Families 2013). Jorgensen and Appelbaum (2014c) estimate that expanding FMLA coverage in this way—by including smaller businesses and employees who have worked fewer hours—would increase access to job-protected leave for between 1.4 and 8.3 million more employees in the private sector, depending on the extent of the changes to the current law.

A number of proposals have sought to expand the definition of "family member" to allow employees to care for individuals beyond just their immediate family (Armenia and Gerstel 2006; Bornstein 2000; Mayer 2013). For example, the Family and Medical Inclusion Act of 2013 would have allowed employees to take FMLA leave to care for a domestic partner, parent-in-law, adult child, sibling, grandchild, or grandparent (National Partnership for Women and Families 2013).[22] There have also been calls to increase the number of reasons that an employee can take leave, such as attending children's extracurricular activities or caring for a child's minor illness (Wisensale 2003; Porter 2010). In 1996, President Clinton proposed allowing workers twenty-four hours of unpaid leave each year to fulfill certain family obligations, such as attending children's educational activities or taking children or elderly relatives to medical appointments (Anthony 2008). The Violence against Women Act of 1999 would have permitted employees to take leave to address domestic violence issues (Jordan 1999). The Parental Bereavement Act of 2013 proposed an amendment to the FMLA that would entitle an eligible employee to up to twelve weeks of leave to grieve the death of a son or daughter (National Partnership for Women and Families 2013).

Some have proposed more unconventional ways to address the failings of the FMLA. To correct the fact that the FMLA in its current form reinforces outdated gender roles, Palazzari (2007) suggests a bonus number of weeks if mothers and fathers take equal amounts of leave. Nicole B. Porter (2014) proposes severing the FMLA coverage for the care of others from the care of oneself and very short-term absences to care for others. In her plan, the FMLA would still cover leave for the birth or adoption of a child and leave to care for family members, but only when that leave is expected to last longer than ten days. A separate statute would be enacted to cover short-term absences for both self-care and the care of others. Longer self-care issues would fall under the purview of the Americans with Disabilities Act. The goal of her plan is to limit the abuse—or the potential for abuse—of the FMLA and decrease the complexity of the law.[23] Porter believes that these changes would lead to less hostility toward the FMLA from employers, which would have positive spillover effects for employees. For example, she suggests that employers might limit their opposition to reforms calling for increased coverage or some type of income replacement.

One of the principal sponsors of the FMLA, Senator Christopher Dodd (D-CT), became one of the biggest advocates for its expansion. Understanding that the FMLA was meant to be merely a starting point for paid leave in the United States, Dodd worked to amend the statute in a variety of ways from the moment it was enacted. For example, after the FMLA passed in the 103rd Congress, Dodd introduced an amendment in the 104th Congress to extend coverage to worksites with at least twenty-five employees and to allow employees time to attend their children's educational extracurricular activities.[24] In 2002, Dodd sponsored the Family and Medical Leave Expansion Act, which would direct the secretary of labor to provide grants to assist states that wanted to provide paid family leave.[25] It would also expand coverage of the FMLA by including worksites with twenty-five or fewer employees and permitting employees to take leave to address the effects of domestic violence. Most recently, in the Family Leave Insurance Act of 2007, Dodd called for eight weeks of partially paid leave at the national level.[26] Dodd left politics a few years later, ending his thirty-year Senate career. In his absence, the number of politicians who have vocalized their support for paid family leave has only continued to grow. Since the passage of the FMLA, the most common suggestion to improve family leave has been to include wage replacement (Hayes 2001; Palazzari 2007; Porter 2014; O'Leary 2007). The next section describes the positive effects that paid leave can have on women, men, children, seniors, and businesses, elucidating the expanding support for such policies.

The Need for Paid Family Leave

As discussed earlier, a significant portion of the workforce does not meet the eligibility requirements for leave under the FMLA because they either work for a company with fifty or fewer employees or they have not worked for the company for 1,250 hours or more in the previous year. Of those covered, many cannot afford to take unpaid time from work because they do not have access to some form of income support during leave (Lerner 2015; Jacobs and Gerson 2004; Heymann 2005). Currently, only 13 percent of workers in the United States have access to paid family leave through their employer; less than 40 percent have paid medical leave through an employer-provided disability program (National Partnership for Women and Families 2015b). The lack of paid leave hurts all workers, but low-income employees, women, and minorities are especially affected. Expanding family leave to include wage replacement would enhance the economic security of families, increase gender equity in the workplace and home, improve the physical and emotional well-being of mothers and children, and boost employee retention rates.

Increased Economic Security for Low-Income Workers

Although family leave helps individuals balance their responsibilities at work and at home, without paid benefits it can have severe economic repercussions. Indeed, one-quarter of all poverty spells in the United States begin with the birth of a new child (Waldfogel 2001, 100). Low-income workers have the greatest need for financial support when a new child arrives or a family member is seriously ill, but they are the least likely to have access to paid leave. Of the workers in the bottom quarter of private-sector wage earners, only 5 percent receive paid leave; 21 percent of the top quarter of earners have access to paid leave (U.S. Department of Labor 2014b; see also Fass 2009). Likewise, employees in managerial or professional occupations or who work for a company with at least one hundred employees are more likely to have access to paid leave (Hegewisch and Hara 2013).

Employees with higher salaries are more likely to take time off because they can afford to; approximately 73 percent of American workers who take leave under the FMLA make over $30,000 a year (Cantor et al. 2001; see also Han and Waldfogel 2003). Fathers in middle- and high-occupational-prestige jobs have 41 percent and 78 percent, respectively, higher odds of taking leave than those in low-prestige jobs (Nepomnyaschy and Waldfogel 2007, 437–439). Because individuals with higher levels of education are more likely to hold these types of jobs, education also helps predict the use of leave. Although 60 percent of new mothers with at least a bachelor's degree receive paid maternity leave, only 22 percent of those will less than a high school degree do (T. Johnson 2008, 10).

Among workers who are eligible for unpaid leave, many cannot afford to take it. In a nationally representative survey in 2000, almost 88 percent of workers who said they needed leave but did not take it cited financial reasons (Cantor et al. 2001). New research shows that nearly one in four employed mothers returns to work within two weeks of childbirth because of a lack of wage replacement during leave (Lerner 2015). In 2012, 62 percent of employees who took leave with partial or no pay reported that it was difficult to make ends meet; 30 percent said it was "very difficult" (Klerman, Daley, and Pozniak 2014). Moreover, approximately 14 percent of workers who take unpaid leave apply for some sort of public assistance during that time (Jorgensen and Appelbaum 2014a; see also Grant, Hatcher, and Patel 2005). In a study of new mothers who entered Wisconsin's Temporary Assistance for Needy Families (TANF) programs, Marci Ybarra (2013) finds that a significant minority of them use the program as a short-term resource during unpaid maternity leave from work. In other words, many of these new mothers use TANF in the same way that other mothers use paid family leave. When women take family leave that is paid, they are 39 percent less likely to receive public assistance or food stamps (Bakst 2016).

Low-income workers are disproportionately affected by the lack of paid family leave in the United States. But it is difficult to separate these class issues from issues of race and sex. For example, African Americans and Latinos/Latinas are less likely to receive paid leave when a new child arrives than white workers (Glynn and Farrell 2012). Based on a nationwide telephone survey, Naomi Gerstel and Katherine

McGonagle found that even though African Americans are more likely to report needing leaves, they are less likely than any other racial group to take them, primarily because they cannot afford to miss work (1999, 520). Similarly, Lenna Nepomnyaschy and Jane Waldfogel found that non-Hispanic black and Hispanic fathers both have approximately 40 percent lower odds of taking leave than non-Hispanic white fathers (2007, 437). With regard to gender, women are more likely to be in low-wage, part-time jobs, which means that they are less likely to have access to pregnancy and family leave than their professional counterparts (O'Leary 2007). Indeed, full-time workers are three times more likely to receive paid family leave than part-time workers (U.S. Department of Labor 2014b). When they do receive family leave, women from lower-income households take less time off after childbirth than women from higher-income households (McGovern et al. 2000).

There are 5.4 million lesbian, gay, bisexual, and transgender (LGBT) workers in the United States. Recent figures show that approximately 37 percent of LGBT adults in the United States have had a child, so a growing number of LGBT workers are encountering the need for family leave (A Better Balance 2015, 16). As of result of the 2013 decision in *United States v. Windsor*, eligible employees in legal same-sex marriages can take FMLA leave to care for their spouse or family member. However, before same-sex marriage became legal in all parts of the United States, many same-sex couples were not able to take advantage of such leave policies, even if they met all of the other eligibility requirements. On June 26, 2015, the U.S. Supreme Court ruled in *Obergefell v. Hodges* that state-level bans on same-sex marriage are unconstitutional. The decision makes it much easier for same-sex couples to obtain a legal marriage, as well as to use FMLA benefits for which they are eligible.[27] For many LGBT workers, the Court's decision also signifies that their families can now be included in employer-offered leave policies that apply only to legally married couples. Overall, the legalization of same-sex marriage throughout the United States means that millions of LGBT workers who might have been excluded from family leave policies in the past will now have a greater opportunity to use them. Access to family leave that is paid is especially important for same-sex couples raising children because those couples are more likely than the population as a whole to live in poverty (A Better Balance 2015, 16).

Adding wage replacement to family leave policies would lessen the financial burden on all workers. If leave were paid, a greater number of single-earner families and two-earner families of more income strata would be able to make use of leave time (Pyle and Pelletier 2003). Low- and middle-income families would benefit most directly from paid family leave because they typically cannot afford a reduction in family income, especially during the "life-cycle squeeze" (Palazzari 2007, 464).[28]

Gender Equality in the Home

The FMLA has had little effect on the division of unpaid labor in the home, as women continue to do most care work and domestic labor and are more likely than men to take family leave (Bianchi et al. 2012; Sayer 2005; Lester 2005; B. Smith 2002; Gerstel and McGonagle 1999). Since women who take unpaid leave do not contribute to the family income, they are often seen as second-class members of the family; this reinforces the male breadwinner model. Indeed, in the United States, attention is focused on the paid workforce, and little consideration is given to activities in the "private sphere" such as care work. Paid family leave would demonstrate a higher social value put on care work. Since women are overwhelmingly the primary caregivers, this would positively affect them. Moreover, wage replacement would increase the number of men who would take family leave (Appelbaum and Milkman 2011).

If more men took leave after the arrival of a new child, gender equality in the home would increase as families came to resemble the dual earner-carer model (Selmi 2000, 755). Countries that have the greatest number of dual earner-carer families have implemented policies that provide incentives to maximize the likelihood that men will take advantage of the benefits offered them (Gornick and Meyers 2003, 101). Because men typically have higher salaries than women, they are more likely to take advantage of leave policies that include wage replacement. As a result of California's paid family leave program, the average father's leave-taking increased by almost a week (Baum and Ruhm 2013). The program has also contributed to an increase in the duration of leaves taken by male caregivers (Appelbaum and Milkman 2011). Fathers' use of leave is highest when it is well paid and is specifically designated for the father and cannot be transferred to the mother (O'Brien 2009). For example, out of all of the provinces in Canada, only Quebec offers nontransferable paid paternity leave; the rest provide gender-neutral leave that can be shared between the mother and father. Consequently, 82 percent of fathers in Quebec take leave, but only 12 percent of fathers in the rest of the provinces do (McKay and Doucet 2010).

Fathers who take paternity leave for longer than two weeks are more likely to be involved in a range of child care tasks and ultimately spend more time caring for their children. Fathers who took less than two weeks often have no greater level of involvement than fathers who take no leave at all (Nepomnyaschy and Waldfogel 2007; see also Huerta et al. 2013; Tanaka and Waldfogel 2007; O'Brien, Brandth, and Kvande 2007; Malin 1994, 1998). Not only does this benefit women (in heterosexual relationships) by dividing the amount of care work between partners, but children also benefit from having two parents who are active in their lives. For example, Maria del Carmen Huerta and colleagues (2013) found evidence that children who have highly involved fathers tend to perform better on cognitive tests.

As more men take family leave, women will no longer be viewed as the primary caregivers and will begin to lose the stigma as the most frequent leave-takers (Ayanna 2007; Grossman 2004; Selmi 2004). Scott Coltrane, speaking to Claire Cain Miller (2014), claims that if more women become breadwinners and more men ask for and use paid family leave, it will become increasingly difficult for employers to treat them differently on the basis of gender roles. Moreover, when "men are committing to do tag-team parenting and they're willing to sacrifice some of their wage potential, it's very helpful for the women and also for the long-term wages of the family" (C. Miller 2014).

Gender Equality in the Workforce

In addition to the negative effects unpaid leaves have on gender inequality in the home, they contribute to lower levels of women's participation and earnings in the workforce. Women comprise 46.8 percent of the American labor force (U.S. Department of Labor, n.d., "Labor Force by Sex"). Their participation rate in the paid workforce has been steadily increasing since World War II, peaking at 59.9 percent in 2000; it currently stands at 57 percent. Mothers make up a significant portion of these numbers: 70 percent of women with children under age eighteen participate in the labor force. Looking only at women with children under age one, still 57.3 percent are part of the labor force (U.S. Department of Labor, n.d., "Women in the Labor Force"). But women in the workforce are disproportionately hurt by limited access to paid family leave.

Lack of family leave often has a negative effect on women's participation in the workforce. Without access to at least job-protected leave, many women exit the labor force when the need for leave arises. As Francine D. Blau and Lawrence M. Kahn (2013) indicate in their study of twenty-two Organisation for Economic Co-operation and Development (OECD) countries, in 1990 the United States had the sixth-highest female labor force participation rate among them. Over the next two decades, its relative position gradually fell; in 2010 the United States ranked seventeenth on the list. The authors point to the expansion of family-friendly policies in other OECD countries, such as paid parental leave, to explain 29 percent of the decrease in U.S. women's labor force participation rates relative to the other countries.[29]

Because women are typically responsible for caregiving, they are more likely to spend time away from work, decreasing their lifetime earnings (Rose and Hartmann 2004, iv). Indeed, unpaid leave is a significant factor in the long-term earnings gap between men and women. Moreover, there is an earnings gap between mothers and other women. Women with one child face a 4 percent penalty in wages; women who have two or more children suffer a 12 percent penalty (Waldfogel 1997, 1998). To ensure that at least some of their leave is paid, women who take maternity leave often use a combination of vacation days, sick days, personal days, and short-term disability time if available. But this piecemeal approach is problematic because women have few vacation or sick days available when they return to work. Furthermore, many working women do not have this option to coordinate maternity leave (Vahratian and Johnson 2009, 178).

Paid leave would help bring about more gender equality in the labor market. In the year after giving birth, new mothers who take paid leave are more likely than those who do not to stay in the workforce. Mothers with paid leave are also 54 percent more likely to report wage increases (Houser and Vartanian 2012; see also Baum and Ruhm 2013). California's paid leave program has contributed to an increase in the working hours of mothers with children between ages one and three; this likely leads to an increase in their earnings (Rossin-Slater, Ruhm, and Waldfogel 2013).

According to Robert Drago, "Given the current concentration of maternity leave provisions among coupled mothers with privilege, such an expansion [of paid leave] would disproportionately help the working poor, women with lower levels of education and lower status jobs, and women of color" (2011, 626). Indeed, California's paid leave program has had a significant effect on the ability of non-college-educated, unmarried, and nonwhite mothers. Prior to the program, those mothers averaged one to two weeks of leave. Since the enactment of paid family leave, they average between four and six weeks of leave, which is similar to more advantaged mothers (Rossin-Slater, Ruhm, and Waldfogel 2013, 242–243).

As discussed in the previous section, the inclusion of wage replacement has a significant effect on men's use of family leave. As a greater number of men take leave for longer amounts of time, a more equitable division of labor in the home develops. Moreover, men's increased use of family leave benefits women in the workforce as well: Sweden's Institute for Labor Market Policy Evaluation observed that a mother's future earnings rose an average of 7 percent for every month of leave that the father took (C. Miller 2014).

Increased Mother and Child Well-Being

Family leave provides parents time to bond with a new child; however, workers who receive only unpaid leave are more likely to return to work early. Indeed, women who had paid leave took approximately four more weeks off work than women without paid leave (McGovern et al. 2000). Mothers facing financial strain are twice as likely to return to work within twelve weeks as mothers who are not (Guendelman et al. 2014). When mothers take short leaves after the arrival of a child, it negatively affects both mother and child.

The World Health Organization and the American Academy of Pediatrics tout the benefits of breast-feeding and recommend that babies be exclusively breast-fed for the first six months of life.

In addition to the benefits that babies receive, breast-feeding may also provide health benefits for mothers, including possible protection against cardiovascular disease, diabetes, and breast cancer (Schwarz et al. 2009; Stuebe et al. 2009). But breast-feeding for six months is difficult when women return to work shortly after giving birth. With access only to unpaid leave, many women—especially poor mothers—return to their jobs within a few weeks after giving birth, which greatly reduces the likelihood that they will continue to breast-feed (Crittenden 2001, 258–259; see also Lerner 2015).[30] Since California implemented its Paid Family Leave (PFL) program in 2004, the median duration of breast-feeding has doubled for all new mothers who used it, from five to eleven weeks for mothers in high-quality jobs, and from five to nine weeks for those in low-quality jobs (Appelbaum and Milkman 2011, 5). Rui Huang and Muzhe Yang (2015) found that as a result of California's program, exclusive breast-feeding increased between three and five percentage points through the first three and six months, and breast-feeding through the first three, six, and nine months increased by ten to twenty percentage points.

Women who have access to paid maternity leave are less likely to have low-birth-weight babies (Stearns 2015). Job-protected paid leave also significantly decreases infant mortality; other forms of leave, such as unpaid leave or non-job-protected paid leave, have no significant effect (Tanaka 2005; Ruhm 1998; Human Rights Watch 2011). Moreover, children are more likely to experience health and developmental problems if their mothers return to work within twelve weeks of giving birth, for they are less likely to receive regular medical checkups, breast-feeding, and up-to-date immunizations in the first year of life (Berger, Hill, and Waldfogel 2005; Daku, Raub, and Heymann 2012; Human Rights Watch 2011). Paid leave also benefits women's health: mothers with at least eight weeks of paid leave are less likely to experience postpartum depression and more likely to report better overall health than women with fewer than eight weeks leave (Chatterji and Markowitz 2012). Paid leave can improve emotional outcomes and strengthen families as well. The bonding time that paid family leave provides for adoptive parents can help with the transition and the needs of the child (Human Rights Watch 2011).

Benefits to Businesses

Paid family leave clearly helps employees and their families, but businesses also benefit from paid leave (Bartel et al. 2014). In a competitive economy, family-friendly workplace policies can attract top talent (A Better Balance 2015). Businesses that provide paid family leave face reduced turnover rates and increased employee productivity (Center for State Innovation 2008). Indeed, 94 percent of workers who receive their full wages while on job-protected leave return to their same employer; only 76 percent of workers taking job-protected unpaid leave return to the same job (Bell and Newman 2003, 4). In 2007, when Google increased paid maternity leave from twelve weeks to eighteen weeks, the rate at which new mothers left the company fell by 50 percent (Wojcicki 2014). The costs of turnover—including recruitment, replacement, and training—are high. It costs businesses about 150 percent of a salaried employee's yearly pay to replace him or her; for hourly workers, turnover costs are between 50 and 70 percent of the employee's annual pay (A Better Balance 2015). Although critics claim that paid leave will reduce company profits, the fact that all other developed countries have paid leave demonstrates that such policies do not undermine economic growth and competitiveness (Damme 2011, 1).[31]

Ruth Milkman and Eileen Appelbaum recently surveyed companies and their employees about their experiences with California's PFL program to determine how well it is working. Most employers stated that PFL has either a "positive effect" or "no noticeable effect" on productivity (88.6 percent), profitability/performance (91.1 percent), turnover rates (92.8 percent), and employee morale (98.5 percent) (2013, 68). Eighty-seven percent reported that there are no cost increases associated with the program, and 9 percent stated that they actually save money as a result of lower turnover rates or reduced benefit costs (78). Most employers reported that they coordinate their own benefits with the state's PFL program. Companies save money when employees use PFL instead of—or in combination with—employer-provided paid sick leave, vacation, or disability benefits (78–79; see also A Better Balance 2015).

Opponents of paid family leave often claim that small businesses will be disproportionately harmed by such policies, but Milkman and

Appelbaum did not find this to be the case in California. To cover the work of leave-takers, most businesses temporarily assigned their work to other employees. When employees were surveyed about the effects of their coworkers taking leave, 93.6 reported either a positive or neutral impact. Although small businesses may face greater challenges because of the size of their available workforce, they adjust by implementing a combination of methods to compensate for employees on leave. For example, almost 40 percent of small businesses reported that they hire temporary workers to cover leave takers' absences (2013, 72–73). Notably, the employer can pay a temp worker with the money that would have gone to the employee on leave. Because the leave-taker is simultaneously receiving wage replacement through the state's insurance program, neither the employer nor the employee loses money. Most small businesses cannot afford to provide the same benefits as larger companies. The PFL helps make small businesses more competitive by facilitating their ability to retain or attract valuable workers (A Better Balance 2015).

Beyond the FMLA

Since the passage of the FMLA in 1993, actors at both the federal and state levels have attempted to amend the act. With few exceptions, these efforts have failed, in part because Republicans controlled Congress for the decade after the passage of the FMLA and because business interests continue to oppose government regulations (Wisensale 2003, 140). Moreover, many advocates for family leave turned their focus to other issues after passage of the FMLA. In recent years, there has been a resurgence of attention on family leave as a growing number of individuals are confronted with the considerable limitations of the FMLA.

The FMLA was always meant to be the first step on a path toward a family-friendly nation (National Partnership for Women and Families 2015c). Changes to the statute are necessary to address the realities of current caregiving responsibilities (Anthony 2008). As written, the FMLA primarily benefits middle- and upper-class workers and does little to improve gender inequalities. Expanding coverage to part-time employees who work fewer than twenty-four hours a week and employees at small businesses, as well as broadening the definition of "family member," would significantly increase the number of protected workers. But most research asserts that the inclusion of wage replacement would have the greatest equalizing effect on the law. Although this could be achieved by amending the FMLA, many advocates have proffered solutions that would work outside the existing statute. For example, there have been calls for offering tax subsidies to businesses to encourage them to provide replacement pay during leave (Palazzari 2007). Lori Auray (1994) proposes a cost-sharing solution for parental leave that would apply to families in which both partners are employed. In this scenario, each partner's employer would pay half the cost of providing leave after the birth or adoption of a new child, including all medical costs related to pregnancy. As a result of this practice, "employers would view the cost of pregnancy as a cost of employment, rather than as a cost of employing women" (Auray 1994, 414).

The proposal that has most recently garnered considerable attention originated in the U.S. Congress. In March 2015,[32] Senator Kirsten Gillibrand (D-NY) and Representative Rosa DeLauro (D-CT) sought to address the shortcomings of national-level family leave policy in the United States by introducing the Family and Medical Insurance Leave (FAMILY) Act.[33] The FAMILY Act enables workers to receive 66 percent of their wages (capped at $1,000 per week) for up to twelve weeks for the same reasons covered by the FMLA: the birth or adoption of a child; the serious illness of a child, parent, spouse, or domestic partner; the employee's own serious illness; and certain military leave and caregiving purposes. It does not provide job protection, but all workers who pay into and are eligible for Social Security benefits for at least one year are eligible for wage replacement benefits. The plan is funded by employer and employee contributions of 0.2 percent of wages, or two cents for every ten dollars in wages. The amount would be capped at $4.36 per week for each of the highest earners, and the average worker would contribute $1.38 per week. The act would establish the Office of Paid Family and Medical Leave within the Social Security Administration (SSA) to administer the program. Payments would be made from the newly created Federal Family and Medical Leave Insurance Trust Fund in the Treasury (Office of Senator Kirsten Gillibrand, n.d.). After being read in the legislature on March 18, 2015, the FAMILY Act was referred to the

Finance Committee in the Senate and the Ways and Means Committee in the House. No further action has been taken on the bill.

Coverage of the issue of paid family leave continues to grow. In 2015, President Obama did something that no other president has done: he called for paid family leave in the State of the Union address (Obama 2015). He followed this action with a presidential memorandum instructing agencies to allow federal employees to take up to six weeks of paid sick leave—even if they have not yet accrued that much—for the birth or adoption of a child or to take care of family members with serious health conditions (Executive Office of the President 2015). Although employees have to "repay" this advance leave with the sick days that they accrue in the future, it gives them greater flexibility to balance work and family.[34] Still, because the change came in the form of a presidential memorandum, a subsequent administration could reverse course. A law passed by Congress would carry more weight.

Representative Carolyn Maloney (D-NY) has been working toward such a law since 2000. In every subsequent session of Congress, Representative Maloney has introduced paid leave legislation for federal employees; however, it has not made much progress. The Democratic-controlled House passed her proposal in 2008 and 2009, but the Senate did not act. Most recently, on January 26, 2015, she sponsored the Federal Employees Paid Parental Leave Act of 2015, which would provide six weeks of paid parental leave for federal employees after the birth, adoption, or foster placement of a child.[35] It was referred to the House Committee on Oversight and Government Reform, where it has remained. On September 15, 2015, Senators Brian Schatz (D-HI) and Barbara Mikulski (D-MD) introduced a companion bill in the Senate; it was referred to the Senate Homeland Security and Governmental Affairs Committee.[36] The proposed legislation would not require federal employees to use their accrued sick or annual leave in order to receive their wages while caring for a new child; instead, they would receive paid administrative leave. President Obama has urged Congress to pass the bill. Ultimately, "between the memo and the proposed legislation, Obama is advocating for 12 weeks total of paid leave for federal workers from two different leave banks—sick and administrative" (Lunney 2015). However, the Federal Employees Paid Parental Leave Act of 2015 would not provide paid leave for employees to care for a sick or injured family member or for an employee's own serious illness or injury.

President Obama's calls for paid leave legislation have been met with resistance, especially from Republicans. Business-minded Republicans worry that not all companies are equally equipped to cover the costs of government-mandated paid leave. Representative Charlie Dent (R-PA) says, "I certainly encourage employers to provide paid family leave, but not all employers are the same. Some are better positioned to do so than others. It's that simple" (quoted in Marcos 2015). There is particular concern for small businesses, as House Small Business Committee chairperson Steve Chabot (R-OH) articulates:

> The American families going without paid sick leave or maternity care do so because Washington makes our small businesses choose between providing those benefits or paying the price of overregulation and higher taxes. We won't make these jobs any more secure by handing employers another federal mandate, we'll make them better and more stable by reducing the uncertainty and frustration that happens when Washington is in the way. (Quoted in Marcos 2015)

As the campaign for the 2016 presidential election has progressed, paid family leave has emerged as a prominent issue. In April 2015, at the Women in the World Summit in New York, Democratic presidential hopeful Hillary Clinton called for paid family leave in the first major speech of her presidential campaign. Paid leave has not been a significant priority for Clinton in the past, but as momentum on the issue has grown across the country, she has further incorporated it into her platform. On Mother's Day in 2015, her campaign released a video clip full of nostalgic images of her mother with messaging about her support for the issue. Moreover, she hired paid leave expert Ann O'Leary as one of her top three advisors (Sandler 2015). In the Democratic presidential debate on October 13, 2015, Clinton said "I believe in equal pay for equal work for women, but I also believe it's about time we had paid family leave for American families and join the rest of the world" (quoted in Wooldridge 2015). Clinton has spoken out against the FAMILY Act because it relies on an increase to the payroll tax. Her plan would provide twelve weeks of paid family and medical leave and a minimum two-thirds wage replacement rate, but it would be funded by increased taxes on the wealthy (Sussman and Meckler 2016).

Clinton's main rival for the Democratic nomination, Vermont senator Bernie Sanders, has been even more vocal about the issue, calling the lack of paid leave "an embarrassment" for the United States (Wooldridge 2015). At a breakfast with reporters in June 2015, Sanders asserted that he wants to take back "family values" from the Republican Party: "My concept of what family values is about is that the United States should not be the only major country that does not guarantee paid family and medical leave when a woman has a baby" (quoted in Shiner 2015). A cosponsor of the FAMILY Act, Sanders supports a tax increase on all workers so that everyone would have access to paid leave.

The one-time third Democratic candidate, former Maryland governor Martin O'Malley, has also spoken out in favor of paid family leave, noting that the lack of paid leave is partially responsible for the persistent gender pay gap:

> Part of the reason women are paid less than men for doing the same work is that many are forced to leave the workforce in order to raise their families, or penalized for doing so. . . . If women decide to have families, they shouldn't have to choose between their career and taking care of their children. All parents—both men and women, gay or straight, married or single—should be able to take at least 12 weeks of leave, with pay, in order to care for newborn children or other loved ones. (O'Malley 2015)

On the Republican side of the aisle, only former presidential candidate Marco Rubio came out in favor of paid family leave: "One of the greatest threats to family today is that too many Americans have to choose between being there for their children in times of great need, or meeting the basic financial needs of their families" (quoted in C. Miller 2015b). However, as Claire Cain Miller (2015b) pointed out in her aptly titled piece "Marco Rubio's Plan for Paid Leave Does Not Require Paid Leave," Rubio did not think that the federal government should require paid leave. Instead, he proposed a 25 percent tax credit to employers who voluntarily offer their employees at least four weeks of paid family leave. Employers would be capped at $4,000 in credits per employee per year, and the length of covered leave would be limited to twelve weeks within that year. No other Republican candidate has proposed any type of plan to increase the availability of paid family leave (Covert 2015b; Jordan 2015).

Representative Paul Ryan (R-WI) made headlines in October 2015 when he said that if he became Speaker of the House, he would not give up his family time. Family leave advocates applauded his message, noting that it will help change traditional assumptions about gender roles and caregiving (Levs 2015). At the same time, many have called Ryan a hypocrite because he has voted against federal legislation requiring paid family leave. In his hometown of Janesville, Wisconsin, a national women's advocacy group, UltraViolet, has put up two billboards criticizing Ryan for blocking benefits for others that he is able to enjoy (Crow 2015). Although Ryan is a cosponsor of the Working Families Flexibility Act, it would not create a paid leave system.[37] Instead, the act allows workers to choose paid time off as compensation for working more than forty hours in one week.[38] As Josh Levs (2015) observes, "[Ryan's] own legislation begins with a demand that workers give up family time in order to earn any." The National Partnership for Women and Families (2015a) says that the act "sets up a dangerous false choice between time and money, when working families urgently need both."

As coverage of paid family leave continues to grow, it raises questions about the best way to implement such a program. This chapter focuses primarily on the national level and the possible strategies for either FMLA expansion or the creation of a new federal policy that would address the lack of paid leave in the United States. In the absence of such a program, a variety of actors have taken it upon themselves to implement paid family leave to fill the gaps left by the FMLA. Headlines have been filled with stories of major corporations that have either adopted or expanded parental leave. In addition to private businesses, a number of local governments have recently adopted paid family leave policies. These developments are covered in greater detail in Chapter 6. The next two chapters examine efforts to pass paid leave at the state level.

4

Success in the States

*Paid Family Leave in California, New Jersey,
Rhode Island, and New York*

The passage of the Family and Medical Leave Act (FMLA) in 1993 was a major accomplishment in forcing employers to recognize that workers have family needs (Vogel 1995, 118). The bill's symbolic impact was significant; this was the first piece of federal legislation that guaranteed family leave to many workers in the United States. But since its passage, the FMLA has come under considerable criticism. Not only does the program exclude about 40 percent of all workers because they do not meet the stringent eligibility requirements, but there is also no wage replacement provided during leave (Ray, Gornick, and Schmitt 2009; Heymann and Earle 2010, 57). In a May 2015 survey of 1,022 adults across the United States, 80 percent said that they favor "requiring employers to offer paid leave to parents of new children and employees caring for sick family members" ("Americans' Views" 2015). The Institute for Women's Policy Research (2010) found that 76 percent of likely voters support expanding the FMLA to include paid leave. However, there has been little progress at the national level in the last two decades.

In the United States, innovations in family policies often arise at the subnational level. In the American federal system, states have the freedom to decide social policies that are not addressed by the federal government. Prior to the passage of the FMLA, numerous states had already passed some type of family leave policy, although there was much variation among them (Women's Bureau 1993). Since 1993, most states have introduced a paid family leave bill. In this chapter, after providing a brief background on the devolution of family leave policy making in the United States, I examine the four state campaigns that have passed paid family leave: California, New Jersey, Rhode Island, and New York.[1] I trace the development of the policies and analyze the factors that played the greatest role in their passage, paying particular attention to the actions of women's movement actors (WMAs), labor unions, and organizations that focus on children and seniors. I also highlight the role that critical actors in the government have played in the policy-making process. Finally, I examine the composition of the executive and legislative branches of each case to determine the effects of partisanship.

The Origins of Family Leave Policy at the State Level

Even before the passage of the FMLA in 1993, many states were trying to pass their own family leave laws. In 1987, two years after Pat Schroeder introduced the first federal-level family leave bill, four states (Connecticut, Minnesota, Oregon, and Rhode Island) adopted some type of unpaid family leave policy (Wisensale 2001, 123–124). In the six years that followed, most states introduced family leave legislation. By the time the FMLA became law, thirty-four states, Puerto Rico, and the District of Columbia had enacted a family leave policy, though there was significant variation among the laws. Some of them only provided time off for pregnancy and childbirth; others allowed both women and men to care for infants, parents, or other family members with serious health conditions. Most of them required employees to have worked for an employer for a certain length of time, and companies below a certain size were often exempt from coverage. Perhaps the greatest variation concerned length of leave; it fluctuated from sixteen hours to one year (Women's Bureau 1993).[2]

After the passage of the FMLA, focus shifted to the federal level as legislators sought to build on the new initiative. However, the national legislature was not receptive to the idea of expanding the FMLA, especially since both congressional houses were dominated by Republicans. Between 1993 and 1999, legislators introduced almost twenty bills that would expand the FMLA; none of them passed (Wisensale 2003, 140). After all of those failed attempts, advocates—including President Clinton—turned their attention back to the states.

On May 24, 1999, President Clinton showed his support for the devolution of paid family leave by issuing a memo that directed the Department of Labor to develop regulations that would allow states to use the Unemployment Insurance (UI) system to fund leave for new parents.[3] In this way, FMLA leave could become paid leave.[4] Moreover, Clinton ordered the secretary of labor to develop model legislation that the states could use to follow these regulations (Clinton 1999). With the exception of three states (Alaska, New Jersey, and Pennsylvania) that require negligible employee payments, the UI system is funded wholly through employers' federal and state payroll taxes. Therefore, employers would assume primary responsibility for financing parental leave for employees. The administration estimated that this strategy would provide an additional six million people with paid leave. Although job protection would not be included in the program, the Clinton administration was largely working under the assumption that these benefits would go to employees who were on FMLA leave.

The directive had an immediate effect. Between May 24, 1999, and July 2000, thirteen states introduced legislation that included a provision for paid family leave (Wisensale 2003, 142). On July 31, 2000, the Massachusetts legislature became the first in the nation to pass a paid family leave bill; it was vetoed by Republican governor Paul Cellucci on August 10 (Bernstein 2001, 127). Four days later, the U.S. Department of Labor issued a Final Rule that officially established the Birth and Adoption Unemployment Compensation (BAA-UC) experiment that would allow states to tap into their UI funds to provide partial wage replacement to employees who take leave following the birth of adoption of a child (U.S. Department of Labor 2000). In 2001 and 2002, over a dozen states introduced bills that would extend UI benefits to new parents on leave.

Many advocates supported funding family leave through the UI system because the administrative mechanisms were already in place and the cost per covered employee was relatively low (Pyle and Pelletier 2003). However, an analysis completed by the Employment Policy Foundation (EPF) excoriated Clinton's plan. In a letter and statement that EPF president Edward E. Potter submitted to the U.S. House's Subcommittee hearing on the issue, the EPF claimed that funding family leave through the UI system would cost up to $28.4 billion annually—one and a half times the current cost of the system. The report also stated that the plan would push as many as forty-nine states and the District of Columbia below recommended solvency levels and require employers' tax rates to rise by as much as eightfold (U.S. House Committee on Ways and Means 2000).

The EPF's analysis was based on the assumption that all states would choose to fund FMLA leave through UI (Pyle and Pelletier 2003). In reality, only about fifteen states were considering the program when it was repealed. Nonetheless, in a move partly fueled by the EPF's report, the Bush administration repealed the BAA-UC regulations in October 2003 (Brown 2010, 196). The administration declared that UI is for individuals who are unemployed because of a lack of suitable work, not parents who initiated their own separation from the workforce and are not available to work (U.S. Department of Labor 2003). Many felt that this "contradict[ed] Bush's earlier portrayal of his White House as 'family friendly,' and indicate[d] a lack of understanding of a struggle that many people face daily in balancing their work and family lives" (Pyle and Pelletier 2003, 379). The National Organization for Women (NOW) harshly criticized this decision, calling for the reinstatement and expansion of the program in the short term, followed by the passage of comprehensive paid family leave (National Organization for Women 2003). NOW's response demonstrated the new momentum in the fight for family leave in the early 2000s, which took shape primarily at the state level. In 2001 alone, twenty-six states proposed paid leave legislation (Wisensale 2003, 143–144). The following year, California became the first state to adopt paid family leave.

Paid Family Leave in the States

Because Congress has been reluctant to expand the FMLA or adopt a new federal-level paid family leave law, efforts to increase family leave coverage have largely been concentrated at the state and municipal levels, where the campaigns have earned laudable success (Bernstein 2001; Bruinius 2016). For example, six states and the District of

Columbia have extended unpaid family leave coverage to employees working in companies with fewer than fifty employees, and seven states and the District of Columbia have expanded unpaid family leave to workers with less than one year of job tenure or fewer than 1,250 hours worked in the previous year. Four states and the District of Columbia provide more than the twelve weeks of job-protected leave mandated by the FMLA, and laws in nine states and the District of Columbia have expanded the definition of covered family members (National Partnership for Women and Families 2014). Currently, five states, twenty-four cities, and one county have passed paid sick time laws that workers can use to address their own short-term illness or to seek medical care for a family member (National Partnership for Women and Families 2016; Covert 2016). However, these policies typically only allow employees to accumulate about five paid sick days per year; there is still significant unmet need for longer-term paid family leave.

As described earlier, one (short-lived) attempt to bring workers paid family leave was through the use of unemployment compensation funds. A second way to fund paid leave has been the use of Temporary Disability Insurance (TDI). However, as detailed in Chapter 1, TDI only provides women with leave for pregnancy and childbirth; it does not cover other forms of family leave. The third approach is to provide paid leave in the states (Palazzari 2007). Almost every state has proposed some type of paid family leave bill, yet most of them have stalled in the legislature. Many states have made significant progress in the fight for paid leave but have ultimately failed to garner enough legislative support to make it a reality. Three states (Illinois, Ohio, and Virginia) have passed legislation that provides paid family leave to state employees. But only four states have been able to pass paid family leave laws that cover virtually all workers in the state: California, New Jersey, Rhode Island, and New York. Table 4.1 presents the details of each policy. California, New Jersey, and Rhode Island have successfully implemented their programs, and New York's plan is scheduled to take effect in 2018. Although Washington State enacted paid parental leave in 2007, policy implementation has been postponed indefinitely, and most activists have organized behind a new, more comprehensive family leave bill that has yet to pass. For that reason, Washington's experience is examined in Chapter 5. The remainder of this chapter explores the policy-making process in the other four states that have enacted paid family leave.

California

A coalition of women's movement actors, labor unions, and groups representing the interests of seniors, children, and people with disabilities led the grassroots effort to pass the nation's first paid family leave bill in California (Milkman and Appelbaum 2004, 51). On September 23, 2002, less than a year after the bill's introduction, Governor Gray Davis signed the Paid Family Leave (PFL) insurance program into law, making California the first state in the country to offer such benefits. Beginning on July 1, 2004, this leave became available to workers who are covered by the State Disability Insurance (SDI) program, which includes all private-sector employees, regardless of the size of the organization they work for, and most part-time workers and others who are unlikely to have access to paid leave benefits through their employers (48). Although public-sector employees are typically not eligible for paid leave under the California program, approximately 80 percent of the state's workforce is covered (Brown 2010, 195).

To implement the program, California essentially just expanded its existing SDI program, allowing workers to take leave not just for their own disabilities, but also to care for family members (Brown 2010, 196). The bill was viewed as especially valuable to women, who make up the majority of low-wage workers (Milkman and Appelbaum 2004, 45). PFL offers up to six weeks of benefits during a twelve-month period to care for a child, parent, spouse, registered domestic partner (including same-sex partners), grandparent, grandchild, sibling, or parent-in-law who is seriously ill, or to bond with a new child after birth, adoption, or foster care placement.[5] After a one-week waiting period, employees receive approximately 55 percent of their lost wages during this time, up to a weekly maximum of $1,129 (in 2016).[6] Administered by the California Employment Development Department, the PFL program is funded by a payroll tax on employees, rather than employers, through the SDI program. The contribution rate for employees who are covered by SDI, which includes both disability insurance and PFL, is 0.9 percent; an employee's maximum

	California	New Jersey	Rhode Island	New York
Status	Adopted 2002; effective 2004	Adopted 2008; effective 2009	Adopted 2013; effective 2014	Adopted 2016; scheduled to start in 2018 and be fully implemented by 2021
Reasons for leave	(1) Care for a child after birth, adoption, or foster care placement; (2) care for a seriously ill child, parent, spouse, domestic partner, grandparent, grandchild, sibling, or parent-in-law; (3) care for own disability, including pregnancy	(1) Care for a child after birth, adoption, or foster care placement; (2) care for a seriously ill child, parent, spouse, domestic partner, or civil union partner; (3) care for own disability, including pregnancy	(1) Care for a child after birth, adoption, or foster care placement; (2) care for a seriously ill child, parent, parent-in-law, spouse, domestic partner, or grandparent; (3) care for own disability, including pregnancy	(1) Care for a child after birth, adoption, or foster care placement; (2) care for a seriously ill child, parent, parent-in-law, spouse, domestic partner, grandchild, or grandparent; (3) address certain military family needs
Duration of leave	Six weeks for family care; fifty-two weeks for own disability	Six weeks for family care; twenty-six weeks for own disability	Four weeks for family care; thirty weeks for own disability (but no more than thirty weeks per year for combined family and own disability care)	In 2018, eight weeks; in 2019 and 2020, ten weeks; in 2021 and following years, twelve weeks
Job protection	Not more than FMLA and CFRA	Not more than FMLA and NJFLA	Job and health benefits protection	Job and health benefits protection
Eligibility	Earned at least $300 from which SDI deductions were withheld during any quarter in the base period	(1) Worked at least twenty calendar weeks of New Jersey–covered employment; (2) earned either at least $168 during each of the twenty weeks or at least $8,400 during the base year	Earned at least $11,520 from which TDI/TCI deductions were withheld during the twelve-month base period or alternate base period†	Part-time and full-time employees who have worked for their employers for at least twenty-six consecutive weeks

TABLE 4.1 PAID FAMILY LEAVE PROGRAMS IN CALIFORNIA, NEW JERSEY, RHODE ISLAND, AND NEW YORK, 2016

Wage replacement level	55 percent of an employee's weekly earnings, up to $1,129 per week*	66 percent of an employee's weekly earnings, up to $615 per week	4.62 percent of an employee's wages paid in the highest quarter of the base period; minimum is $84 per week; maximum is $795 per week‡	In 2018, 50 percent of employee's weekly earnings, up to cap equal to 50 percent of the statewide average weekly wage (capped at $648 at 2015 levels); by 2021, rate will increase to 67 percent (capped at $868 at 2015 levels)
Funding mechanism	Employee-funded through SDI program; contribution rate is 0.9 percent of wages for both disability and family care combined	TDI program is jointly financed by employers (between 0.10 and 0.75 percent contribution rate) and employees (0.25 contribution rate); family care is funded entirely by employees (0.08 percent contribution rate)	Employee-funded through TDI program; contribution rate is 1.2 percent of an employee's first $64,200 in wages for both disability and family care combined	Employee-funded through TDI program; contribution rate will begin at approximately $0.70 per week and increase to approximately $1.47 per week by 2021

Sources: A Better Balance 2016; California Employment Development Department, n.d.; Katz et al. 2016; New Jersey Department of Labor and Workforce Development, n.d.; Rhode Island Department of Labor and Training, n.d., "Temporary Disability Insurance."

* Beginning in 2018, weekly benefits will increase from 55 percent of an employee's lost wages to either 60 percent or 70 percent, depending on income (Family Values @ Work 2016).

† If this amount has not been met, an employee may still be eligible for benefits if he or she earned at least $1,920 in one of the base period quarters, the total base period taxable wages are at least one and one-half times the employee's highest quarter of earnings, and the base period taxable wages are at least $3,840.

‡ An employee may also be entitled to a dependency allowance if he or she has dependent children under age eighteen or over age eighteen and incapacitated. This allowance is limited to five dependents and is equal to the greater of $10 or 7 percent of the benefit rate.

yearly contribution is $960.68 (in 2016) (California Employment Development Department, n.d.). The program does not protect the employee's job during leave, but many workers are covered under the FMLA and the California Family Rights Act (CFRA).[7]

California's SDI system had already proven to be an effective way to distribute benefits before paid family leave legislation had even been introduced. In 1999, following a period of economic growth that generated large budget surpluses for the state, organized labor, which was at the peak of its political power in California, successfully lobbied for an increase in SDI benefits (Milkman and Appelbaum 2004, 51). At the same time, California enacted a new law that allowed workers to use up to half of their annual sick leave to care for ill family members. Following these changes, activists began lobbying lawmakers for paid family leave benefits (Labor Project for Working Families 2003).

Paid family leave was supported by a broad coalition across California. The Labor Project for Working Families started an education campaign in 1992 to inform labor unions about ways in which work-life conflicts could be reconciled. In 1999, the organization created the Work and Family Coalition, which brought together state and local labor groups and advocacy and community groups to work on issues affecting families and the workplace. A number of prominent women's organizations were outspoken members of the coalition, including 9to5 National Association of Working Women, American Association of University Women, California Commission on the Status of Women, California National Organization for Women, California Women's Law Center, Coalition of Labor Union Women, Equal Rights Advocates, National Partnership for Women and Families, and Older Women's League (Labor Project for Working Families 2003). The California Labor Federation, which is the state-level American Federation of Labor and Congress of Industrial Organizations (AFL-CIO), has also historically been a strong advocate of state safety net benefits and rights for workers. In early 2001, the Labor Project for Working Families received a planning grant and a two-year program grant from the David and Lucille Packard Foundation to commence the campaign for paid family leave. At that time, the Coalition for Paid Family Leave/Share the Care was formed.

State senator Sheila Kuehl, an influential Los Angeles Democrat, agreed to be the lead author of the bill. She had earned respect from her peers across ideological lines and had a strong relationship with the governor. Jenya Cassidy, the education and training coordinator for the Labor Project for Working Families, claims that Kuehl made paid family leave one of her main priorities.[8] Introduced on February 20, 2002, SB1661 originally called for twelve weeks of paid family leave, with the costs evenly split between employees and employers. The bill passed the Senate and went to the Assembly in June.

After this initial success in the Senate, the coalition gained more members and increased its activities. At the grassroots level, workers distributed postcards at union meetings, and coalition members staffed tables at conferences. The American Civil Liberties Union (ACLU) of Southern California also created a website that allowed supporters to send faxes directly to their Assembly members (Labor Project for Working Families 2003). At the same time, opposition was growing rapidly.

As the California Chamber of Commerce grew increasingly worried about the passage of paid leave, it began a widespread campaign against the original bill, in large part because it called for an employer contribution. The chamber claimed that businesses—especially small businesses—would suffer by having to pay for the leave, possibly driving them to other states (Dorfman and Lingas 2003; Milkman and Appelbaum 2004). Chamber members sent out thousands of letters and faxes to legislators opposing the bill. Because the economy was suffering at the time, people were more inclined to take these warnings seriously.

While the bill was in committee in the Assembly, moderate, business-oriented Democrats started pushing for changes, such as removing the employer contribution (Labor Project for Working Families 2003). They believed that putting the entire burden for funding on employees would lessen opposition from businesses; moreover, they did not want to risk alienating business interests. On August 23, 2002, the bill was amended to remove the employer contribution and then changed from twelve to six weeks of leave, since employees were going to be paying for all of it. An amendment was also added that allowed employers to require employees to use up to two weeks of vacation time before receiving PFL benefits (California State Legislature, n.d., "Complete Bill History"). Despite these changes, business interests' opposition was still strong.

Although the leave would be funded exclusively through employee contributions, business interests continued to claim that it would cost companies more in the long run because they would have to pay overtime or train workers to cover for employees on leave. Moreover, businesses feared that they would have little control over the process because it would be administered by the state (Valenti 2003). Julianne Broyles, director of employee relations and small business for the California Chamber of Commerce, said that "leaves are unpaid for a very good reason—to prevent abuse of the system" (quoted in Valenti 2003).

At the time of the paid family leave debate, Democrats were in control of California's Assembly and Senate and the governor's office, which made for a more receptive political environment. A 2002 analysis of the costs and benefits of implementing paid family leave in California concluded that companies in the state could save up to $89 million because of increased employee retention and decreased turnover. The study claimed that a paid leave program could also save California $25 million annually because of decreased reliance on state assistance programs such as Temporary Assistance for Needy Families and Food Stamps (Dube and Kaplan 2002, 5; see also Koss 2003).

The bill passed the Assembly on August 27, 2002; it passed the Senate three days later and was sent to the governor's desk (California State Legislature, n.d., "Complete Bill History"). By this point, the coalition had grown to more than seven hundred unions, organizations, and individual members, and it had the ability to influence the governor's decision. Davis had recently shown his support for workers' rights by signing several major labor bills, so the coalition reminded him that the PFL bill would protect workers as well. Knowing that Davis was concerned with the electoral gender gap, advocates also highlighted women's interests in paid family leave (Labor Project for Working Families 2003). The Labor Federation convinced national political figures, celebrities, and the head of the AFL-CIO to call and send letters to Governor Davis. Likewise, women's movement actors and union members produced thousands of postcards, faxes, e-mails, and letters to the governor asking for his support for the bill. Less than a month after the Assembly passed the bill, Governor Davis signed paid family leave into law.

The activists were unified on the issue and made it a priority. Maggie Cook, president of the Los Angeles chapter of the Coalition of Labor Union Women (CLUW) since 2000, affirms that the fight for paid family leave in California was a "solidarity effort across the boards."[9] Claiming that lawmakers would pass the legislation only if advocates worked to get it, Cook says that paid leave was a priority for both the local chapters of CLUW throughout California and the national organization, which sent out "marching orders" to the chapters about different tactics to use in the effort to pass paid leave. Carol Rosenblatt, executive director of CLUW's national office, confirms this, stating that paid family leave is very important to the organization.[10] She asserts that although it is critical for all employees, working women are especially burdened when paid leave is unavailable because they are often the ones who have to take off work to care for a child. Mary Bergan, president of the East Bay chapter of CLUW, states that her office prioritized paid family leave as well.[11] According to Bergan, the East Bay chapter primarily reacted to the directives of Netsy Firestein, the founder and director of the Labor Project for Working Families.

The San Jose chapter of 9to5 California was also an active participant in the fight for paid family leave. According to Cathy Deppe, California lead organizer for 9to5, legislation designed to balance work and family life is a major priority for the organization.[12] Although it has only approximately one hundred members, it boasts a much wider range of contacts and is able "to put out a lot of street heat." For example, prior to the passage of paid family leave, 9to5 members made themselves available to the media and for legislative meetings. They went to Sacramento every year that the issue was part of the legislative agenda in order to testify in favor of it. They also worked to collect petition signatures and participated in the rallies calling for paid leave that were spearheaded by the Labor Project for Working Families.

National organizations such as NOW, whose support for the FMLA waned through the policy process because the bill did not include wage replacement, stood firmly behind California's paid leave bill. NOW's president at the time, Kim Gandy, applauded California's passage of the bill, stating that "no one should have to choose between family and paycheck. I hope other states will follow California's lead in making workplaces more family friendly" (National Organization for Women 2002). Judith Lichtman, president of the National Partnership for Women and Families, said that it would allow workers "to both live up to their family needs and be a dedicated worker" (quoted in Edds 2002, A03). John Sweeney, president of the AFL-CIO, called the California leave law "a significant step forward for the state of California and workers struggling to balance the demands of careers and families" (Sweeney 2002).

The public also supported the passage of the bill. A 2003 survey found that 84.9 percent of Californians favored a law that guaranteed paid family leave. Support was highest among women, African Americans, Latinos, Asian-Pacific Islanders, and individuals with lower levels of education (Milkman and Appelbaum 2004, 52–53; see also Weir 2002). This confirms that family leave is especially important to women and that the demographic groups that have the greatest support for paid leave are typically the ones who need it most.

State business groups criticized the governor's decision. Allan Zaremberg, president and chief executive of the California Chamber of Commerce, maintained that California businesses were already struggling with the high costs of energy and worker compensation claims, as well as overtime payments calculated on an eight-hour workday instead of a forty-hour workweek. According to Zaremberg, paid family leave would continue to make it more difficult for California to attract and retain businesses, in part because employers would "have no control over their workforce or the hidden costs associated with replacing an absent worker" (quoted in Edds 2002, A03). Deanna R. Gelak, executive director of the National FMLA Technical Corrections Coalition, which is composed of employers working to change FMLA requirements, expressed similar fears about the effects that a paid family leave law would have on businesses in the state. She claimed that California's "controversial" approach raises "a host of privacy concerns, not to mention the monstrous bureaucracy that will be required to track this leave" (quoted in Shuit 2002).

California made history when it became the first state to implement paid family leave. Jenya Cassidy of the Labor Project for Working Families says that the law would not have been possible if the coalition had not made it such a priority. She claims that since there was no policy in the United States like it at the time, it was "like a dream to get it passed," and there was little dissent within the coalition.[13] However, as Steven Wisensale explains, California's model will be difficult to replicate in states that do not have an existing TDI program. Moreover, as economies suffer throughout the country, states are more likely to focus on paid leave only for the care of a new child, excluding care for spouses, parents, and other family members (2006, 189–190). Washington, a state without a TDI program, exemplifies Wisensale's claim, for although it passed paid leave in 2007, it covered only leave to care for a new child. Moreover, financial issues have delayed the implementation of the law indefinitely (see Chapter 5).

New Jersey

On May 2, 2008, Democratic governor Jon Corzine signed a bill to provide workers in New Jersey six weeks of paid leave during a twelve-month period to care for newborns and newly adopted or foster children, or for a seriously ill family member, including a child, parent, spouse, domestic partner, or civil union partner. Under the Family Leave Insurance provision of the New Jersey Temporary Disability Benefits Law, workers taking leave may receive up to two-thirds of their average weekly wage, with a maximum of $615 (in 2016). To qualify for benefits, an employee must work for a New Jersey covered employer for at least twenty weeks and earn at least $168 per week or $8,400 or more during the base year, which is the fifty-two weeks preceding the beginning of leave. Although New Jersey's TDI is funded by both employers and employees, the family leave program is financed only by employees through a 0.08 percent payroll tax. The maximum yearly deduction for Family Leave Insurance is $26.08 (in 2016) (New Jersey Department of Labor and Workforce Development, n.d.). As in California, the law does not guarantee the employee's reinstatement upon return from leave; only employees covered by either the FMLA or the New Jersey Family Leave Act (NJFLA) receive job protection.[14]

The New Jersey Time to Care Coalition fought tirelessly to pass paid family leave. This coalition included many prominent women's organizations, labor groups, and organizations focused on the rights of families, children, and seniors, such as the American Association of University Women–New Jersey, Association for Children of New Jersey, Center for Women and Work, Mothers and More–New Jersey, National Organization for Women–New Jersey, New Jersey Foundation for Aging, New Jersey League of Women Voters, New Jersey Women Lawyers Association, Older Women's League, Partnership for Working Families, SEIU 1199–New Jersey, and United Steelworkers 4-149 (New Jersey Time to Care, n.d.). In 2002, the Institute for Women's Policy Research sponsored a study to determine the fiscal viability of a paid family leave program in New Jersey. Since the program would cost between $113 and $134 million per year, and the government would allocate $128 million in revenue to cover expenses, the authors of the study concluded that such a plan was viable (Naples and Frank 2001, 6).

In 2006, the New Jersey chapter of NOW sent letters to women business owners asking for their support in the fight for paid family leave, asserting that "feminist small business owners understand the unique challenges all women face in the workforce." Because paid family leave is a "feminist issue," the letter went on to reiterate the organization's commitment to it, stating that "paid family leave insurance legislation fits with NOW's mission by helping to bring all women into full and equal partnership with men" (National Organization for Women 2006, 3). As during the fight for national legislation on family leave during the 1980s and 1990s, NOW remained a staunch advocate of equal treatment, rather than special treatment.

In 2007, Laurie Pettine, chair of NOW-NJ Mothers' and Caregivers' Economic Rights Task Force, sent a message to all NOW-NJ chapters asking them to travel to the Senate Budget and Appropriations hearing on the Family Leave Insurance bill so they could testify in support of the legislation. She repeated the earlier call to feminist business owners who would be willing to speak publicly in favor of paid family leave (National Organization for Women 2007a). At the hearing, Maretta Short, president of NOW-NJ, gave a personal testimony in favor of the bill, citing the benefits that the legislation would bring to workers, families, and businesses (National Organization for Women 2007b). Local branches of NOW in New Jersey also prioritized paid family leave. According to Susan Waldman of Morris

County NOW, the chapter wrote letters to the editor, circulated petitions, drew up press releases, wrote to legislators, and participated in lobby days to convince lawmakers to adopt paid family leave.[15]

The activism of MomsRising was crucial to the passage of paid leave. Members sent over sixty-three thousand letters to legislators, made hundreds of phone calls, and decorated and displayed onesies in front of the New Jersey Statehouse Annex. They spent hours directly lobbying legislators and testifying to committees in the Assembly and Senate. In addition, the organization delivered a letter to the legislature that contained the signatures of numerous small-business owners who believed that paid family leave would have a positive impact on business (MomsRising 2008). The organization continued its "Power of the ONEsie" campaign in New Jersey, hanging a long chain of decorated onesies around the capitol building to represent family members who would benefit from paid family leave (MomsRising, n.d.).

An October 2006 poll found that 78 percent of New Jersey residents favored the idea of a paid family leave bill. As in California, the groups who would benefit most from the bill—women, minorities, and low-income individuals—reported the highest levels of support (Eagleton Institute of Politics 2006). The Chamber of Commerce in New Jersey vehemently opposed the passage of paid family leave. Jim Leonard, senior vice president of the chamber, said that "legislators and the governor seem to think our residents and employers have deep pockets and unlimited resources to fund their bloated bureaucracy, when that is far from the case. This madness has to end" (quoted in Livio 2008a). During the debate, Republican state senator Christopher Bateman claimed that "this is the wrong time to pass this bill that will send more businesses out of New Jersey. Maybe at the right time, in the right economy, this would be the right bill" (Livio 2008a). Strong business opposition ultimately affected the provisions of the bill. The version (S2249/A3812) introduced in 2006 provided up to twelve weeks of benefits (New Jersey Legislature, n.d., "Senate, No. 2249"). The bill (A873) introduced in the Assembly in the 2008 legislative session originally provided twelve weeks of benefits as well; however, the Assembly labor committee shortened it to six weeks (New Jersey Legislature, n.d., "Assembly, No. 873"; New Jersey Legislature, n.d., "Assembly Committee Substitute"). The corresponding

Senate bill (S786), which was introduced two weeks after A873, had already amended the duration of benefits to six weeks, largely in response to ongoing pressure from business interests (New Jersey Legislature, n.d., "Senate, No. 786"). As opposition grew, women's movement actors intensified their grassroots campaign, holding numerous lobbying events, press conferences, and seminars to raise awareness of the need for paid family leave. Adrienne Lesser, public policy director of the New Jersey chapter of the American Association of University Women (AAUW-NJ) from 2005 to 2011, stated that the organization worked to increase the publicity that the issue of paid family leave received by writing letters to the editor and contacting legislators.[16] She stressed the importance of keeping in contact with lawmakers to let them know that organizations such as the AAUW-NJ are supporting them and want them to back these issues in the legislature. Her claims reinforce the significance of grassroots activism in the fight for paid family leave.

The National Partnership for Women and Families (NPWF) has consistently advocated paid family leave; in fact, the organization has an entire department dedicated to work and family issues. In an interview with Work/Family and Fairness Program Assistant Marion Johnson, she reiterated that paid family leave is a major priority for the NPWF.[17] She reported that the organization has worked on various state-level campaigns for paid family leave, and although there may have initially been some dissent in New Jersey and California regarding the level of benefits, NPWF has always presented a united front. Overall, the coalition in New Jersey was cohesive in its support for paid family leave. Moreover, as demonstrated by the level of activism within the state, the issue was a top priority for many organizations.

As in California, New Jersey's executive and legislative branches were controlled by Democrats when paid family leave was adopted. In New Jersey, Governor Jon Corzine's support for the legislation went beyond partisanship. A year before the bill passed, Corzine was in a near-fatal car accident. His children were able to spend weeks helping him recover, but the experience helped him realize that most people do not have the financial resources to allow them to take unpaid time from work to care for their families (Associated Press 2008). Reflecting on his own experience, he said, "I believe the daily reality of the lives of New Jersey families makes this historic law a necessity. . . .

I am confident this self-funded family insurance program will improve family life, fill a gap in our social contract with our citizens and attract workers to this state" (quoted in Livio 2008b).

Rhode Island

Passed on July 23, 2013, Rhode Island's Temporary Caregiver Insurance (TCI) program took effect on January 5, 2014. The law provides workers with up to four weeks of job-protected[18] paid leave during a twelve-month period to bond with a new child or care for a seriously ill child, parent, parent-in-law, spouse, domestic partner, or grandparent.[19] While on leave, employees receive 4.62 percent of the wages paid to them in the highest quarter of their base period. The minimum benefit is $84 per week; the maximum benefit is $795 per week (in 2016). Like its TDI program, Rhode Island's TCI is financed entirely by employee payroll deductions. Employees in Rhode Island are eligible for benefits if they have earned at least $11,520 in either the base period or an alternative base period. The base period refers to the first four of the last five completed calendar quarters before the starting date of a new claim. Employees who do not earn at least $11,520 during the base period or an alternative base period may still be eligible for benefits if they meet the following three conditions: (1) they earned at least $1,920 in one of the base period quarters, (2) their total base period taxable wages are at least one and one-half times their highest quarter of earnings, and (3) their base period taxable wages equal at least $3,840 (Rhode Island Department of Labor and Training, n.d., "Temporary Disability Insurance").

After the policy success in New Jersey in 2008, the paid family leave movement appeared to lose momentum throughout much of the country, primarily as a result of the recession. Retrenchment became the norm, so any programs that were perceived to cost the state money or hurt businesses were potential targets to be dismantled. In this environment, the campaigns for paid family leave knew that they had little chance of success; therefore, many of them temporarily turned their attention to other issues. As the economy began to rebound, activists in Rhode Island resumed their efforts. Within the legislature, state senator Gayle Goldin was one of the strongest supporters of paid family leave.

As is the case for many individuals, Senator Goldin's advocacy began as a result of her personal experiences.[20] In 2001—over a decade before she became a senator—she broke her back when the balcony she was standing on collapsed. Because Rhode Island had TDI, she was able to take paid disability leave from her job. However, TDI did not allow her husband to take paid leave to act as caregiver for her. After Goldin recovered, she was again faced with the limitations of the TDI program when she became a parent through adoption. TDI covered only pregnancy and disability leave, so as an adoptive mother, she could not receive paid leave to bond with her new child. This reality was especially harsh in light of the fact that Goldin's sister, who had also just become a mother, could take almost a year of paid leave because she lived in Canada. Thus, even before she joined Rhode Island's Senate, Goldin began to work for the passage of paid family leave in Rhode Island.

Goldin initially directed her efforts toward legislation that would expand TDI to allow for parental leave. That policy goal was not achieved, but she was a part of the effort that passed a tax credit law that would help to offset the costs of unpaid leave taken by adoptive parents. Although this law signified progress, Senator Goldin said that it did not really address the heart of the problems caused by a lack of paid family leave. Therefore, she continued to work on this issue when she took part in the Women's Policy Institute run by the Women's Fund of Rhode Island (WFRI). Jenn Steinfeld, executive director of WFRI, describes the Women's Policy Institute as a nine-month fellowship program in which women learn how to understand and draft legislation, as well as how to organize and advocate for policies that will help to improve gender equality in Rhode Island.[21] As a participant, Goldin worked with others at the Policy Institute on how to design the best paid family leave policy, and she was able to bring together a coalition of advocates on the issue. Indeed, Steinfeld says that the institute consistently provides a pool of women who are ready to engage in the policy process and effect change. After graduating from the Women's Policy Institute with invaluable hands-on experience in the policy-making process, Goldin became the strategic initiatives officer at WFRI. In 2012, she won her campaign for Rhode Island State Senate.

Senator Goldin said that she went into office determined to pass paid family leave.[22] Therefore, she did a lot of "internal advocacy" in which she spoke with her colleagues about the benefits of paid family leave. Because she was a policy analyst, she was able to discuss the issue from various angles to demonstrate the ways paid family leave would help individuals, families, and businesses across Rhode Island. It is not surprising that Goldin became the primary sponsor of the 2013 paid family leave bill. Other key actors in the legislature also supported the bill, which was crucial to its passage. In particular, Senate president Teresa Paiva Weed (D-District 13) made paid family leave legislation a priority and signed on as a cosponsor of the Senate bill. Representative Elaine Coderre (D-District 60) agreed to sponsor the companion bill in the House, which was significant because she was the highest-ranking and longest-serving woman in the House. The Senate bill was introduced on February 6, 2013; the House bill was introduced on March 19, 2013. The original legislation provided eight weeks of paid family leave per year. As the bills progressed through the Senate Labor Committee, the Senate Finance Committee, and the House Finance Committee, the period of benefits was reduced to four weeks. The bill was also amended to ensure that workers could not file concurrently for both TCI benefits and TDI benefits (Rhode Island General Assembly, n.d., "2013—H 5889"; n.d., "2013—H 5889 Substitute A"; n.d., "2013—S 0231"; n.d., "2013—S 0231 Substitute A"; n.d., "2013—S 0231 Substitute B"). Democratic governor Lincoln Chafee signed the bill into law on July 11, 2013.[23]

As in California and New Jersey, paid family leave in Rhode Island was passed by a Democratic legislature. On paper, Rhode Island's General Assembly is overwhelmingly Democratic. However, Shanna Pearson-Merkowitz, associate professor of political science at the University of Rhode Island (URI), says that party politics in Rhode Island are complicated.[24] According to Pearson-Merkowitz, party identification is often meaningless in Rhode Island. Half of voters are registered as independents, which allows them to vote in either party's primary elections. The number of people who identify as Democrats dwarfs the number of declared Republicans. Pearson-Merkowitz claims that there is a general aversion to the Republican label in Rhode Island; however, the state and its legislators are more conservative than party identification numbers suggest. This distinction helps explain why paid family leave did not sail through the General Assembly without opposition. Helen Mederer, who is a professor of sociology and a member of the URI Work-Life Committee, added to this explanation. According to Mederer, many legislators—especially those who were more conservative—worried about the perception that they were too generous.[25] In an attempt to avoid such characterization, some lawmakers took a tougher stance against paid family leave benefits.

The main opponents of Rhode Island's paid family leave bill were business interests. According to Goldin, the National Federation of Independent Business, the Providence Chamber of Commerce, and the Northern Rhode Island Chamber of Commerce were especially hostile to the legislation.[26] But opponents of paid family leave were not always easy to spot. Rachel-Lyn Longo, who conducted research on paid family leave under Professor Pearson-Merkowitz at URI, found that the Rhode Island Department of Children, Youth and Families spoke out against the bill because of the anticipated administrative burdens the law would cause for them.[27]

According to Pearson-Merkowitz, the legislative leadership in Rhode Island is extremely strong.[28] Consequently, when leaders put their name on a bill, the chances of it passing increase significantly. In the case of paid family leave, Pearson-Merkowitz said that the support of Senator Teresa Paiva Weed was central to its passage. As president of the Senate, Paiva Weed was able to bring more attention to the bill and ensure that it stayed on the agenda. Representative Elaine Coderre played a similar role in the House. As the highest-ranking and longest-serving woman in the House, Coderre had significant influence over the policy-making process. After extensive research on Rhode Island's experience, which included interviews with numerous policy makers, Rachel-Lyn Longo concluded that "the bill was passed because important people wanted it to pass."[29] Sherry Leiwant, cofounder and copresident of the work and family legal center A Better Balance, also stressed the importance of critical actors in the passage of paid family leave.[30] Because A Better Balance helped with the drafting of Rhode Island's bill, Leiwant was able to observe the progression of the legislation from the beginning. According to Leiwant, women legislators were crucial to the bill's passage in Rhode

Island, especially Senator Goldin, Senator Paiva Weed, and Representative Coderre.

Coupled with the advocacy within the legislature, the activism of the We Care Rhode Island Coalition played a vital role in the passage of paid family leave. Senator Goldin affirmed that the American Association of Retired Persons (AARP) made it a top priority for 2013, and the state-based organization Senior Agenda Coalition had a lobbyist to work on the issue. Rhode Island Parent Information Network, which has more than one hundred employees, not only advocated for the issue, but many of the parents from the network shared their own personal stories of why paid family leave is necessary. Service Employees International Union also played a significant role in the fight for paid leave, seeing it as an issue of workplace equality. Moreover, the organization represents health care workers, such as certified nursing assistants and home health workers, who are often the ones asked to stay home and care for elderly or ailing parents.[31]

In addition to labor groups and organizations focused on seniors, families, and individuals with disabilities, Leiwant emphasized the importance of women's movement actors in the campaign.[32] Rhode Island NOW, Women's Center of Rhode Island, and the Women's Fund of Rhode Island were all active in the campaign. WFRI took a leadership role in the movement, and Steinfeld said that the TCI program was "absolutely a priority prior to passage."[33] WFRI "recognized that this [paid family leave] is an issue for all workers, but especially for women who still bear the biggest responsibility for family care" (Leiwant 2013). Marcia Coné, who was head of WFRI when the law was passed, noted the importance of the policy for workers: "Our workforce has changed and our economy has changed. Temporary Caregiver Insurance will enable working people to care for their children, their parents, their loved ones, without fear of falling behind on their bills or losing their jobs" (quoted in Bravo 2013). The URI Work-Life Committee made a point to contact Senator Goldin and the WFRI to volunteer their social science background and lend support to the movement. Committee members Barbara Silver and Helen Mederer said that they often took part in the events to promote paid family leave and had testified at the State House in support of the issue.[34] For example, in

June 2013, Silver provided the following testimony before the Senate Finance Committee:

> The TCI bill does not just make good economic sense for Rhode Island. It is a class equity issue as lower income workers have less access to flexible work schedules, less job security and fewer options when faced with caregiving challenges. It is [a] gender equity issue, as women are still the predominant caregivers, and caregiving challenges can disproportionately impact their job security or advancement. It is a race/ethnicity issue, as white people are much less likely to assume care for an elderly relative compared to Asians, Hispanics, and African Americans. (Silver 2013)

Paid family leave had a strong advocacy group behind it in Rhode Island, both in and out of the legislature. Key legislators worked to keep the issue on the agenda while promoting the merits of paid family leave to their colleagues. The coalition worked to increase awareness of the issue and public support while pressuring politicians to back legislative changes. Coalition members represented a diverse group of interests, including women, labor, families, children, seniors, and individuals with disabilities. Surprisingly, many Rhode Island business owners also played an activist role in the movement. For example, an owner of a manufacturing company in Rhode Island who was a part of the coalition wrote an op-ed piece explaining the reasons that he supported paid family leave. Senator Goldin says that the piece helped give legislators a narrative that was different from the one that they typically heard from business interests that were opposed to paid family leave.[35]

Ultimately, the strength and unity of the coalition and the efforts of critical actors in the legislature were vital to the passage of paid family leave in Rhode Island. Interestingly, many people I spoke with also pointed to the size of the state to help explain the bill's success. As Jenn Steinfeld observed, in a state as small as Rhode Island, every legislator goes home at the end of the workday.[36] Consequently, constituents have "good physical access" to their representatives and can make their views known to them more easily than in larger states.

New York

On April 4, 2016, Democratic governor Andrew Cuomo signed into law a bill establishing paid family leave in New York State. The policy will provide employees eight weeks of job-protected paid leave beginning in 2018; this will increase to ten weeks in 2019 and 2020 and to twelve weeks starting in 2021. Workers will be able to take leave to bond with a child after birth, adoption, or foster care placement; to care for a seriously ill child, parent, parent-in-law, spouse, domestic partner, grandchild, or grandparent; or to address certain military family needs. Both part-time and full-time employees who have worked for their employer for at least six months will qualify for leave, regardless of the size of the business. Employees on leave in 2018 will receive 50 percent of their weekly earnings, up to a cap that is equal to 50 percent of the statewide average weekly wage. Based on the 2015 average weekly wage of $1,296, benefits would be capped at $648. Gradually increasing over three years, the wage replacement rate will be 67 percent in 2021 (capped at $868 at 2015 levels). As in California, New Jersey, and Rhode Island, New York will provide paid family leave through its existing TDI system, which means that businesses will not be affected by administrative changes. Although New York's TDI program is financed by both employers and employees, only employees will contribute to the paid family leave fund. The contribution rate will begin at approximately $0.70 per week and increase to approximately $1.47 per week by 2021 (A Better Balance 2016; Katz et al. 2016).

When New York's law takes effect in 2018, it will be the country's most generous paid family leave program to date. But policy provisions are not the only thing that sets New York's experience apart from that of California, New Jersey, and Rhode Island. After attempts to pass paid leave in the New York legislature failed for almost fifteen years, the paid family leave program became a reality as part of the state's budget bill. To understand how the process unfolded, it is necessary to examine the state's previous legislative efforts.

Activists in New York had a long and arduous battle to enact paid family leave. A paid leave bill first passed the New York State Assembly in June 2005 but then stalled in the Senate. A 2007 bill suffered a similar fate. At that time, many activists began to shift their focus to other issues. Although they continued to campaign for the bill, the movement did not have the same force of previous years. When a paid family leave bill was introduced in the Assembly and Senate in 2009, it did not even make it out of committee (New York State Assembly, n.d., "Bill No. A08742").

The New York Paid Family Leave Insurance Campaign has led the fight for paid family leave. Often referred to as the "Time to Care New York" coalition, it comprises over one hundred organizations and businesses, such as Children's Defense Fund–New York, Coalition of Labor Union Women, Long Island Women's Agenda, Ms. Foundation, National Association of Women Business Owners–NYC, National Council on Jewish Women–NY State, Nontraditional Employment for Women, NOW-NYS, Older Women's League–Brooklyn, United Federation of Teachers, United Food and Commercial Workers Women's Network, Women Builders Council, and Women's City Club of NY (Time to Care, n.d.). In a 2011 interview, Donna Dolan, executive director of Time to Care, discussed the formation of the coalition.[37] She stated that the initial members were primarily unions, which included paid family leave on their agendas but did not prioritize it. Women's groups and organizations centered on children's issues joined the coalition fairly early, and although other concerns were higher on their agendas than paid leave, many of these organizations said that they would give the issue equal attention. Senior groups were the last to join the coalition. The coalition members used a variety of tactics to win support for family leave, including sending postcards to legislators and holding themed press conferences, such as "Mother's Day," in which they invited legislators who were mothers to speak on the issue.

Dolan said there was still momentum in the movement during the 2007 campaign. On June 5, representatives of numerous coalition organizations testified at the public hearing of the Senate Labor Committee on Paid Family Leave. Dolan's testimony described the paucity of options for the ever-increasing number of dual-earner families with children, as well as the growing support for paid family leave in New York. Specifically, she pointed to a Community Service Society poll that found that 70 percent of New Yorkers supported extending the state's TDI system to provide paid family leave (Dolan 2007). Marcia Pappas, president of NOW-NYS at the time, addressed the ways in which paid leave would help parents: "By giving working families a limited benefit and a few months of guaranteed time off to care for their newborns, new mothers or fathers would have the opportunity to stay at home with their babies for a little while longer, without risking economic hardship" (Pappas 2007). Carolyn Sevos of the National Association of Women Business Owners–New York City reported that the three hundred thousand businesses owned by women in New York City generate $65 billion in sales annually. She then pledged the organization's strong support for the bill, pointing out that California businesses have been positively affected by the state's paid leave law (Sevos 2007).

Business interests also testified at this Senate committee hearing. Thomas Minnick, who was vice president of the Business Council of New York, claimed that paid family leave would add to the "already heavy burden of employer mandates" on businesses in New York and hinder long-term job growth (Minnick 2007). In 2008, the Business Council launched an electronic advocacy campaign to give business interests the ability to voice opposition to paid family leave. The program allowed opponents of the bill to send letters to legislators through the Business Council's Grassroots Action Center (Business Council of New York State 2008). Before taking office on January 1, 2011, Governor Andrew Cuomo made it clear that he would not pass any bills that be believed would raise the cost of doing business in New York (Cuomo 2010).

As the coalition was coming together in the early 2000s, there was some internal dissent about the generosity of the bill that continued for much of that decade. Dolan stated that many activists believed that raising TDI benefits, which have remained the same since 1989, would have to be a part of any paid family leave bill.[38] They worried that if the increase was not included in the legislation, the government would wait another fifteen years before addressing the issue. On the other hand, some paid leave advocates thought that the priority should be to get paid leave on the books first and negotiate for higher TDI benefits later. Ultimately, legislation introduced in 2005 and 2007 did not include an increase in TDI benefits, but the 2009 legislation did. This division over benefits may have contributed to the loss of momentum in the fight for paid family leave in New York in the second half of the decade.

Since San Francisco passed the nation's first paid sick time law in 2006, momentum for that issue has grown throughout the United States, and many activists have turned their attention away from paid family leave to devote more time to the paid sick days campaign. In 2011, Dolan stated that the coalition was still working on paid family leave but in a more "behind the scenes" capacity.[39] In part this was because there was a fear that it would be confusing to put forth bills on both family leave and sick days in the same legislative session, as many people might not recognize the difference between them.[40] Sherry Leiwant of A Better Balance, which is a national-level organization based in New York, also shed light on the ostensible loss of momentum behind paid family leave, stating that the issue had been a priority for the organization when it was first introduced but that the legislative setbacks from 2005 to 2009 were demoralizing.[41]

In 2011, Marge Ives, chair of the Women's Issue Committee and vice president of public policy for the Women's City Club of New York, asserted that the organization had been involved in the campaign for paid family leave for many years.[42] However, she said that other issues had topped its agenda in recent years, in part because activists were focusing on legislation they believed had a greater chance of being adopted. For example, in the aftermath of the Lilly Ledbetter Fair Pay Act of 2009, the organization made it a priority to pass legislation to make it illegal for companies to prohibit employees from discussing their salaries. Paid sick days also moved to the top of the agenda, in part because those bills were often introduced at the city level, making it easier to pass and administer such legislation more quickly.

Some organizations, such as the New York Section of the National Council of Jewish Women (NCJW-NY), have consistently prioritized issues other than paid family leave, such as child care, reproductive choice, domestic violence, and religious issues (National Council of Jewish Women–New York Section, n.d.). In 2011, Hannah Golden of the NCJW-NY confirmed this, stating that paid family leave was not one of the organization's major issues at the time.[43] Karen DeCrow, former vice president of the Greater Syracuse chapter of NOW in New York and the president of the National Organization for Women from 1974 to 1977, said that paid family leave was not a high priority for the organization in New York in 2011, primarily because of the economic climate.[44] She said that Governor Cuomo was working to keep businesses in New York, making it unlikely that he would support a paid family leave bill that had attracted considerable opposition from business interests. Moreover, the fact that the state's union movement had been losing strength made it more difficult to pressure legislators to pass such a bill. Referring to NOW at the national level, DeCrow said that although issues such as paid family leave and child care have consistently been high on the organization's agenda, they have never been at the top; issues like reproductive rights, equal pay, and domestic violence have typically gotten more attention.

In recent years, momentum began to swing back toward paid family leave in New York, as demonstrated by the passage of a paid family leave bill in the Assembly in both 2014 and 2015. The 2015 bill (AB 3870/SB 3004) would have expanded the existing TDI program to provide twelve weeks of job-protected paid leave to care for a new child or a seriously ill family member. The bill also would have increased the benefit cap for TDI for the first time since 1989 from the current level of $170 to $600 over a four-year period.[45] Employees would have financed the paid family leave fund (New York State Assembly, n.d., "Bill No. A03870"). The passage of the bill in 2015 was the fourth time the Assembly has passed such legislation (A Better Balance 2015, 24). However, as in previous legislative sessions, it was not able to get through the Republican-controlled Senate.

I revisited the issue with Donna Dolan in 2015 to gain a better understanding of the revival in activism. Part of it, she said, can be attributed to the passage of legislation for paid sick days in New York City in June 2013.[46] Once paid sick time passed, it allowed activists to turn their attention back more fully to paid family leave. Since our 2011 conversation, Dolan said there had also been significant movement in unions for paid family and sick leave, which helped reinvigorate the coalition. However, business interests have continued to put up strong resistance to paid family leave. According to Dolan, some of them have a misunderstanding of what the bill would provide, believing that workers could take twelve weeks of paid leave on top of twelve weeks of FMLA. Others are simply against any type of government intervention in business.

Unshackle Upstate, a business advocacy group based in Rochester, has continued to spread the message that paid leave would likely increase the burden on local businesses. In 2015, executive director Greg Biryla said, "There are a bunch of different proposals out there, but some of them are one-size-fits-all models. Trying to put a mandated expense onto mom-and-pop shops the same you would a Walmart simply isn't palatable to the upstate business community" (quoted in Clausen 2015). Kenneth Pokalsky, vice president of the Business Council of New York State, recently testified to a state committee on the issue: "It really does put—particularly smaller businesses—in a bind. . . . We believe it is important to allow employers to fashion their overall leave policies based on their own circumstances and capabilities, and within the context of company-specific compensation plans" (quoted in Clausen 2015). Yet Dolan has found that many small businesses have told the coalition that they would prefer a government-sponsored paid leave program so that they could provide their employees with the paid family leave that they need without having to pay for it themselves.[47] Indeed, a 2013 survey showed that 83 percent of New York small-business owners supported expanding the state's TDI program through a small employee contribution that would cover the costs of family leave (A Better Balance 2015, 5).

Paid family leave became primarily a partisan issue in the New York legislature. Generally, Democrats have favored paid leave, and Republicans have opposed it. For example, in the 2015 legislative session, Republican state assemblyman Bill Nojay expressed his concern that paid family leave will simply turn into "extra vacation days": "If it is a tough family medical leave policy that requires doctor's verification and other safeguards against abuse, it may become the law in New York. Without those adequate safeguards, I hope the legislature would not pass it, and I would vote against it" (quoted in Clausen 2015). Attitudes like this meant that there was little chance of passing a paid family leave bill in the Republican-controlled Senate. Donna Seymour, public policy vice president of the American Association of University Women–New York State (AAUW-NYS), expanded on this idea in 2015. According to Seymour, the leadership in the legislature has a significant amount of power to move the process forward or to ensure that bills do not make it to the floor.[48] She said that the supermajority of Democrats in the Assembly has "always been very friendly to these kinds of issues, so moving legislation the majority wants is easy." In the Assembly, the leadership has facilitated the passage of paid family leave legislation. However, the (Republican) Senate leadership has consistently kept such legislation from the Senate floor.

In February 2015, Governor Cuomo seemed decidedly against paid family leave, stating that there was little "appetite" for such legislation in Albany (Swarns 2015). Yet less than a year later, he had completely reversed his position. During his State of the State address on January 13, 2016, Cuomo made an impassioned plea for paid family leave:

> At the end of the day, family matters. Intimate relationships matter. And in this 24/7 world, let this state make a statement about what's really important. And those relations are important. And we should be there for one another, especially in a family environment. . . . Let's pass family leave this session. (Quoted in S. Levine 2016)

Cuomo's about-face on paid leave was fueled by events in his own life. His father passed away on January, 1, 2015, hours after Cuomo was sworn in for a second term as governor. Reflecting on the experience, Cuomo said, "I have kicked myself every day that I didn't spend more time with my father at that end period. . . . I'm lucky; I could've taken off work, I could've cut days in half, I could've spent more time with him" (quoted in S. Levine 2016). In May 2015, Cuomo's long-time partner Sandra Lee underwent a double mastectomy after being diagnosed with breast cancer. As he helped her during her recovery, Cuomo again recognized the importance of spending time with loved ones during such difficult experiences. Understanding that many New Yorkers do not have the resources to take unpaid time from work to care for a family member, Cuomo became a staunch advocate of paid family leave legislation.

Although Cuomo's sponsorship of paid family leave was primarily the result of his own life experiences, he also saw that support for the issue was growing rapidly throughout New York. Cuomo himself was partly responsible for this surge. As Seymour described, Cuomo's comment about a lack of appetite for paid family leave helped reinvigorate the coalition because it "gave us something to push back against."[49] Many activists wrote op-ed pieces refuting Cuomo's statement, and constituents called their legislators to endorse paid leave legislation. Because 2016 is an election year for the New York State legislature, politicians are keenly aware of the issues their constituents advocate. Dolan said that the coalition worked closely with small businesses and business associations representing tens of thousands of workers across New York State to promote paid leave.[50] They organized a small-business press conference, got business owners to write op-ed pieces in favor of paid leave legislation, and held three breakfasts for minority and female small-business owners to inform them of the benefits of paid family leave.

Several factors influenced the passage of paid family leave in New York. The grassroots activism led by the Time to Care New York coalition was essential for educating and mobilizing the population about the issue and pressuring lawmakers to champion legislative change. Seymour said that organizations such as the AAUW-NYS, New York Women's Equality Coalition, and Planned Parenthood prioritized the issue and worked hard to achieve legislative success.[51] Senior citizen groups played an important role in advocacy as well. Seymour also highlighted the recent efforts of Citizen Action of New York, especially because it had paid organizers. Since many of the groups in the coalition are volunteer-based, she said it was significant to have an organization with money to spend on campaigning.

Activists laid the groundwork for paid family leave in New York. However, Governor Cuomo's commitment to the issue gave it the momentum necessary to become law in 2016. Dolan, who has been working for paid family leave in New York for over a decade, confirmed this: "If the governor hadn't made it [family leave] a priority, it wouldn't have passed."[52] He traveled the state and held rallies to get people excited about paid family leave and an increase in the state's minimum wage, which Dolan said were his two main priorities in the 2016 budget. Vice President Joe Biden, who lost his son Beau to brain cancer in 2015, joined Cuomo at a rally for paid family leave in January 2016. U.S. Secretary of Labor Tom Perez was in Buffalo in March 2016 to endorse New York's bill. Such events brought national attention to New York's campaign.

Finally, Seymour pointed to the importance of timing, saying that the larger discussion on paid family leave across the country at the time helped put the movement over the top in New York.[53] Paid family leave has become an issue in the 2016 presidential debates, and President Obama has called for expanded access to paid family leave on numerous occasions.[54] The passage of paid parental leave for city employees in New York City in December 2015 also brought statewide attention to the issue. Within New York State, recent changes in legislative leadership may have helped the paid leave campaign as well. In 2015, both Speaker of the Assembly Sheldon Silver and Senate Majority Leader Dean Skelos were arrested on corruption charges and replaced in office. Seymour said that although the new leader in the Republican-controlled Senate was not much more receptive to the issue of paid leave, he did not have the "entrenched opposition" of Skelos. Moreover, both new leaders were eager to achieve legislative victories to help them consolidate their leadership.

Conclusion

Although the passage of the FMLA in 1993 gave families some relief, it was only a first step. Approximately 40 percent of the labor force is not covered by the FMLA, and many workers who have coverage cannot afford to take unpaid leave. Moreover, without wage replacement, family leave generally reinforces traditional gender roles. In this way, the lack of paid leave disproportionately harms women in both the home and the workplace.

The benefits of paid family leave are wide ranging. Not only do they improve women's status, but they also help release men from the pressure of being the sole breadwinner in the family. Parents are able to spend more time with their children, workers can more easily take time for family caregiving, and low-income and minority groups have greater access to the leave that they need. Even businesses benefit from paid family leave policies in the form of increased productivity and employee morale, as well as decreased turnover rates.

Activists have been trying to expand family leave policies since the passage of the FMLA. Such efforts have largely devolved from the federal level to the state level, making it imperative to examine state campaigns. This chapter traces the policy-making process in the four states that have passed paid family leave, finding in each of them a cohesive coalition made of women's movement actors, labor unions, and advocacy organizations for families, children, individuals who are disabled, and seniors. In addition, the presence of critical actors in the legislature has often helped overcome the opposition of business interests and conservative policy makers who resist what they see as government interference in business. As this chapter demonstrates, policy environment also has a considerable effect on legislative outcomes. In California, New Jersey, and Rhode Island, Democrats were in control of both the legislative and executive branches when paid leave was adopted. In New York, lawmakers passed paid family leave as part of the budget, which meant that it did not have to go through the Republican-controlled Senate as a stand-alone issue. The Senate had blocked the progression of paid family leave on the four occasions since 2005 that the Democrat-controlled Assembly passed such a bill. Therefore, without a change in party composition, it was unlikely that the Senate would have passed paid family leave in the near future. As Chapter 5 describes, partisan issues have affected the policy-making process in a number of states that are currently struggling to pass paid family leave. Moreover, the importance of an existing TDI system cannot be overstated. Each of the states in this chapter had a government-run funding mechanism in place before adopting paid family leave. The lack of such a mechanism has significantly hampered efforts both to enact and—in the case of Washington State—implement paid family leave.

5

When Paid Family Leave Fails to Pass
in the States

Washington, Oregon, Massachusetts, and Hawaii

As Chapter 4 discusses, California, New Jersey, Rhode Island, and New York have adopted paid family leave policies. Many other states have introduced similar policies but have not been able to gain enough legislative support for their passage. In this chapter, I follow the progression of paid family leave legislation in four such states: Washington,[1] Oregon, Hawaii, and Massachusetts. The details of each state's bill are listed in Table 5.1. For each case, I again speak with activists to understand the role that they have played in the campaign. I also look for critical actors who have influenced the policy-making process and examine the political environment to determine the effects of partisanship.

Washington

After the passage of paid family leave in California, activists around the United States increased pressure on their own state governments to enact similar legislation. In Washington on May 8, 2007, Democratic governor Christine Gregoire signed into law SB 5659, which mandated five weeks of paid leave to parents of newborn and newly

TABLE 5.1 PAID FAMILY LEAVE BILLS IN HAWAII, MASSACHUSETTS, OREGON, AND WASHINGTON

	Hawaii (HB 2128/SB 2961)	Massachusetts (H 1718/S 1008)	Oregon (SB 966)	Washington (HB 1273/SB 5459)
Date introduced	1/25/16 in House; 1/27/16 in Senate	1/20/15 in House; 4/15/15 in Senate	3/18/09	1/16/15 in House; 1/22/15 in Senate
Existing state TDI program	Enacted in 1969*	None	None	None
Eligibility	All employees	Worked 1,250 hours for the employer	Work in firm with at least twenty-five employees; optional for smaller employers	Worked 680 hours during "qualifying year" (first four of the last five completed calendar quarters)
Qualifying reasons for benefits	(1) Care for a child after birth, adoption, or foster care placement; (2) care for a seriously ill child, spouse, parent, or reciprocal beneficiary (which may include a same-sex partner)	(1) Care for a child after birth, adoption, or foster care placement; (2) care for a seriously ill spouse, child, parent, parent of spouse, grandparent, or grandchild; (3) care for own disability or serious illness	(1) Care for a child after birth, adoption, or foster care placement; (2) care for a seriously ill child, parent, grandparent, grandchild, parent-in-law, or a person with whom the employee is acting in loco parentis	(1) Care for a child after birth, adoption, or foster care placement; (2) care for a seriously ill child, parent, spouse, or state-registered domestic partner; (3) care for own disability or serious illness

Length of benefits	Twelve weeks	Twelve weeks for family care and twenty-six weeks for care for own disability or serious illness	Six weeks	Twelve weeks for family care and twelve weeks for care for own disability or serious illness
Amount of benefits	58 percent of the employee's weekly earnings, up to $570 per week	Sliding scale based on income level, from 66 to 95 percent of weekly wages, up to $1,000 per week	Flat rate of $300 a week to full-time workers; part-time workers would receive a prorated amount	5.2 percent of average quarterly wages (approximately two-thirds of weekly wages), up to $1,000 per week
Source of funding	Employee payroll deduction, averaging $0.43 weekly	Employer contribution; level to be determined	Flat tax of $0.02 an hour paid by employees	0.2 percent premium on employees' wages that is matched by employers
Job protection for workers eligible for benefits	Not more than FMLA and HFLL	Yes (for up to twelve weeks)	Not more than FMLA and OFLA	Not more than FMLA and FLA

Sources: Hawaii State Legislature, n.d., "SB2961"; Massachusetts State Legislature, n.d., "Bill H.1718"; Oregon State Legislature, n.d., "SB 966 A"; Washington State Legislature, n.d., "HB 1273"

Note: I include the most recent paid family leave bill (in its original form) proposed to each state legislature.

*Although Hawaii has a TDI program, it has largely been privatized.

adopted children (Washington State Legislature, n.d., "Family Leave Insurance"). However, this law has not been implemented because of a lack of a funding mechanism. After a number of failed attempts to fund the program, most advocates have abandoned the 2007 law in favor of a more comprehensive paid family leave bill. To understand the status of the current legislation, it is necessary to examine the earlier efforts in the policy-making process.

Paid family leave was introduced in both the 2001 and the 2005 legislative sessions before it passed in 2007. Democratic senator Karen Keiser was the primary sponsor of the legislation in the state Senate in 2007, and Democratic representative Mary Lou Dickerson introduced the bill in the state House. Senate majority leader Lisa Brown (a Democrat) was also a major champion of the bill (Washington State Legislature, n.d., "SB 5659"). Paid family leave had high public support as well. In March 2007, a poll of Washington voters found that 73 percent supported the creation of a family leave insurance fund through either a small deduction from workers' paychecks or a combination of employee and employer payments (Economic Opportunity Institute 2007).

The Washington Family Leave Coalition,[2] administered by the Economic Opportunity Institute, led the fight for paid leave. This coalition includes a number of women's organizations, such as the American Association of University Women of Washington State, MomsRising, the National Organization for Women (NOW), and Northwest Women's Law Center (Washington Work and Family Coalition, n.d.). Labor organizations like the Amalgamated Transit Union and the Washington State Labor Council AFL-CIO belong to the coalition, as do groups that represent seniors and children, such as AARP Washington and Children's Alliance, respectively. Marilyn Watkins, policy director at the Economic Opportunity Institute, reported that the coalition took part in traditional legislative lobbying but also launched a major grassroots effort, sending individual letters and e-mails to legislators.[3]

The League of Women Voters of Washington (LWVWA) took an active role in the passage of paid family leave. Lonnie Johns-Brown, lobbyist for the organization, stated that the LWVWA sent alerts to its members asking them to call and e-mail their legislators in support of the bill, to contact the Speaker of the House to persuade him to allow the bill to come up for a vote, and to sign in to support the bill at key hearings.[4] As one of the organization's lobbyists, Johns-Brown took part in important meetings with legislators, as well as vote counting and strategy sessions with the leadership of the Paid Family Leave Coalition. According to Johns-Brown, the LWVWA primarily saw paid family leave as an issue of family support and early childhood education. Indeed, the organization's policy leads on early learning issues first put the issue on the league's agenda. Although the organization supported a number of issue areas, within early childhood education, paid family leave quickly became a priority. Moreover, once the policy leads presented their ideas on paid leave to the league board, the organization united behind the issue. Margie Reeves, another member of the LWVWA lobby team, echoed these sentiments. She asserted that "paid family leave was one of our priorities from the beginning . . . mostly for the health and safety of the newborn and the support for families."[5]

MomsRising, an activist women's organization founded in 2003 that focuses primarily on issues affecting mothers, played a crucial role in the passage of paid family leave in Washington. The organization flooded legislators with over fourteen thousand e-mailed letters, thousands of phone calls, more than six hundred "mom made" cookies, and numerous Polaroid photos of parents and children who would benefit from paid family leave. Moreover, these women's movement actors (WMAs) led an extensive campaign to educate the community about the need for addressing family-friendly issues (MomsRising 2007c). Referring to the fact that 75 percent of mothers are in the workforce today, Kristin Rowe-Finkbeiner, executive director of MomsRising, claimed that "Washington's workplace policies need to respond to these dramatic shifts, otherwise we're punishing mothers simply for being mothers, forcing them to mortgage their futures to take care of their babies" (quoted in Economic Opportunity Institute 2007).

On February 6, 2007, Rowe-Finkbeiner testified before the Washington State House Commerce and Labor Committee, urging it to pass paid family leave (MomsRising 2007a). MomsRising also first employed its "Power of ONEsie" display in Washington. Activists decorated hundreds of baby onesies to stretch around the state capital as a visual representation of people who need and support paid family leave. They claimed that "each onesie signifies one person—mother, father, child, grandmother, grandfather, aunt, uncle, or other—who cares deeply about building a family-friendly America, but can't take the time off work, or away from kids, to actually be at the capital" (MomsRising, n.d.).

The chief sponsor of the bill, Senator Keiser, acknowledged the vital role that MomsRising played in the passage of paid family leave in Washington, stating that the bill "would not have passed without the great work of MomsRising. Being able to mobilize thousands of constituents to e-mail our governor and individual lawmakers made all the difference. It's a great model for an authentic political movement made up of people who are unable to attend rallies or raise huge amounts of campaign donations. It's a way for real people to make a real difference" (quoted in MomsRising 2007c; see also MomsRising 2007b).

According to Watkins, businesses had a "strong ideological opposition" to any government involvement; therefore, they launched a countermovement to stop the passage of paid family leave.[6] Don Brunell, president of Washington State's chamber of commerce, the Association of Washington Business, wrote an editorial in the *Puget Sound Business Journal* in which he described the ways that paid family leave threatened employers. Calling paid family leave "another costly and complex mandate," Brunell decried "the costs associated with lost productivity, overtime, and increased hassle in the scramble to replace key employees on paid leave." He claimed that paid leave would also increase the "hidden cost" in unemployment insurance taxes (Brunell 2007).

The original bill proposed benefits for workers taking leave to bond with a new child, to care for a seriously ill family member, or to recover from their own serious illness. However, partly in response to opposition from business, on April 20, advocates reduced the scope of coverage, removing the provisions that provided benefits for the employee's own illness or to care for a sick family member (Washington State Legislature, n.d., "SB 5659"). The fact that Washington, unlike California, did not already have a well-established system for delivering paid medical leave via a disability program also contributed to this revision.

Watkins said that the coalition worked well together and "found consensus pretty easily" on issues.[7] Moreover, she stated that paid family leave was high on the Economic Opportunity Institute's agenda since its founding in 1998. Therefore, the organization served as leader of the coalition, rallying the other members to prioritize family leave as well. This strategy had the desired effect: in 2007 Washington became the second state to pass paid family leave legislation. Originally the law was scheduled to take effect in October 2009; however, because of the lack of a solid funding plan, Washington has continually postponed implementation of paid family leave.[8]

In the years following the passage of paid family leave in Washington, legislators have tried to expand the law while working to realize its implementation. On February 1, 2012, Senator Keiser—the sponsor of Washington's 2007 law—introduced SB 6570, which would amend the family leave law to include care for a family member and care for the employee's own serious illness. This bill also increased the length of leave and the amount of benefits and called for the program to be funded exclusively by employee contributions. The legislation was referred to the Senate Committee on Labor, Commerce, and Consumer Protection, where it failed (Washington State Legislature, n.d., "SB 6570"). The following year, a similar bill (HB 1457/SB 5292) was introduced. Although it made progress in the House, it did not make it out of the Senate Commerce and Labor Committee (Washington State Legislature, n.d., "HB 1457").

At the same time that the legislature was considering revisions to the 2007 family leave law, SB 5159 was introduced to repeal it (Washington State Legislature, n.d., "SB 5159"). The sponsor of SB 5159, Republican senator John Braun, said of the paid leave law, "It may have seemed like a good idea, but we don't have the money to do it. We need to face the reality and deal with it" (quoted in La Corte 2013). Like the family leave expansion bill, it did not pass. Instead, HB 2044 was enacted, which delayed the implementation of the 2007 family leave bill until funding and payment of benefits are authorized. Prior to this, the legislature had passed bills in 2009 and 2011 that pushed the enactment of family leave back two years; the 2013 legislation eliminated a deadline for implementation (Washington State Legislature, n.d., "HB 2044").

After numerous failed attempts to amend and implement the 2007 law, most paid family leave supporters in Washington have decided to abandon it and start anew with a more comprehensive paid family leave bill. In January 2015, Democratic representative June Robinson and Senator Keiser concurrently introduced HB 1273 and SB 5459, respectively. Although it does not include job protection, this bill would provide twelve weeks of partial wage replacement for employees on leave to care for a new child or a seriously ill or injured child, parent, spouse, or state-registered domestic partner. In addition, an employee could receive benefits for up twelve weeks while on leave to care for his or her own serious illness or injury. Wage replacement rates would be 5.2 percent of the employee's average quarterly wages—approximately two-thirds of weekly wages—up to $1,000 per week. To be eligible for these benefits, the employee must have accrued at least 680 hours during the previous qualifying year. The program would be funded by a 0.2 percent premium on workers that would be matched by employers. The House Labor Committee passed the bill and referred it to Appropriations in February 2015; the Senate bill has been stuck in the Commerce and Law Committee since January 2015. The bill has stayed alive by five resolutions passed in 2015 and 2016 to reintroduce and retain it in its present status. Most recently, such a resolution was passed on March 20, 2016 (Washington State Legislature, n.d., "HB 1273").

As discussed earlier, the Washington Family Leave Coalition was instrumental in the passage of the 2007 paid leave law. This coalition—now known as the Washington Work and Family Coalition—is leading the current campaign for paid family leave in Washington. The coalition members are primarily women's organizations, labor unions, and groups that focus on the well-being of children and the elderly (Washington Work and Family Coalition, n.d.). To understand the progression of paid family leave in Washington since 2007, I spoke again with Watkins. She highlighted the influence that the 2008 recession had on paid family leave in Washington, noting that the 2008 legislative session had appropriated funds for the implementation of the paid leave law in 2009.[9] However, the governor froze all nonessential funding shortly after that. The speaker of the House and the Senate majority leader said that they would make it a priority in 2009 to revive and revise the

2007 law so that it more closely resembled the original bill that provided both family and medical leave. But when the legislative session began in 2009 and everyone realized the extent of the budget shortfall, the coalition decided to pull the bill from the schedule because it knew that it would not pass in the middle of the massive program cuts that were occurring.

Stymied at the state level, the coalition began exploring the possibility of moving legislation forward on paid sick days at the municipal level. In 2011, Seattle followed San Francisco to become the second city in the country to adopt paid sick days. In 2012, the Washington Family Leave Coalition changed its name to the Washington Work and Family Coalition to reflect the broader focus of the coalition beyond just paid family leave. But that is not to say that paid family leave was forgotten in Washington.

Since the 2011 legislature had postponed the implementation of the 2007 paid family leave law until 2015, the coalition knew that it needed to get its expanded bill passed in the 2013 session to be a part of the plans for 2015. Therefore, as Watkins recounted, it convened a working group to draft a whole new bill and decided that paid family leave at the state level would be the coalition's legislative priority for 2013.[10] But as Seattle's paid sick days law went into effect in September 2012, workers throughout the state clamored for similar legislation. Therefore, instead of prioritizing paid family leave, the issue ended up sharing the 2013 legislative agenda with paid sick days, which was garnering more attention at the time. Unfortunately for the coalition, the Republicans had taken control of the Senate when some of the Democrats decided to caucus with them after the 2012 elections. As the coalition expected, both paid family leave and paid sick days progressed through the House in 2014 and 2015 but could not make it through the Senate. According to Watkins, paid sick days have taken precedence for the coalition, but paid family leave is still on its agenda. The fact that activists have prioritized paid sick days helps in part explain the adoption of paid sick days legislation in Tacoma in 2015 and in Spokane in 2016. As a lower priority, expanded paid family leave policies have not yet passed in Washington. For the time being, the only option available to workers in Washington is unpaid, job-protected leave under the FMLA or the Washington State Family Leave Act (FLA).[11]

Oregon

In 2007, with Democrats the majority in both the Oregon House of Representatives and Senate, activists believed that the paid family leave bill introduced by Democratic representative Diane Rosenbaum could become a reality. But after narrowly passing the House along party lines, the measure failed by two votes in the Senate, as five Democrats joined the opposition (Walsh 2007). The Democrats who voted against the bill were known as moderate, business-friendly legislators (Steves 2007). Representative Rosenbaum reintroduced the bill as SB 966 in the 2009 legislative session. Although the Democrats still maintained a legislative majority, the bill did not make it out of committee (Oregon State Legislature, n.d.).

The Oregon Family Leave Act (OFLA) provides workers twelve weeks of unpaid, job-protected leave.[12] The 2009 proposed legislation would have created Oregon Family Leave Insurance, which would give employees six weeks of paid leave to care for a new child or a seriously ill child, parent, grandparent, grandchild, parent-in-law, or person with whom the employee is acting in loco parentis. All workers in firms with at least twenty-five employees would be eligible for benefits. Part-time workers would receive a prorated amount, and smaller employers could opt in to the program if they chose. The plan would be funded by employee contributions of $0.02 per hour—about $42 per year—and workers would be eligible for $300 a week in benefits. Although Oregon does not have a TDI program, funds for Family Leave Insurance would be collected through existing payroll reporting methods that collect for the Workers' Benefit Fund and the Tri-County Metropolitan Transportation District of Oregon (TriMet) (Oregon State Legislature, n.d.; Time to Care for Oregon Families, n.d.). Regan Gray, policy director of Children First for Oregon at the time, stressed the importance of this collection method because it meant that a new administrative system would not have to be created, which would keep costs low.[13] The Institute for Women's Policy Research and the Oregon Center for Public Policy conducted forecasts for the program, estimating that annually, workers would pay about $30 million into the plan, but it would only pay out about $20 million in benefits. Administrative costs were estimated at about 5 percent of the total (Langlois 2009).

The Time to Care for Oregon Families coalition was the primary advocate for paid family leave in Oregon leading up to the 2009 legislative initiative. It was made up of over one hundred organizations and businesses, including the American Association of Retired Persons Oregon, American Association of University Women of Oregon, Children First for Oregon, Family Forward Oregon, League of Women Voters of Oregon, MomsRising, National Council of Jewish Women–Oregon Section, National Partnership for Women and Families, Nursing Mothers Counsel of Oregon, and Oregon AFL-CIO.

On April 8, 2009, supporters of the bill flocked to a hearing on the proposed legislation. Chief sponsor Diane Rosenbaum, who had been elected state senator in 2008, spoke in favor of the bill, pointing out that many workers cannot afford to take unpaid leave. The committee also heard from individuals who had suffered financial hardship because they did not have access to paid leave, health care professionals who touted the importance of family care, and businesses that wanted to provide their employees with paid family leave (Oregon State Legislature 2009). The main opposition came from business interests. J. L. Wilson, a lobbyist for Associated Oregon Industries, questioned whether employees would actually be able to fund the plan, stating that "we believe the future demands of the program can only be funded through increased taxes on workers or new taxes on businesses" (quoted in Mapes 2009). The Oregon branch of the National Federation of Independent Businesses also decried the legislation, stating that it would put an administrative burden on smaller employers (Langlois 2009). Christina Martin of Cascade Policy Institute claimed that the program would tax many workers who would receive little direct benefit from it (Mapes 2009). However, a number of employers spoke out in favor of the bill. For example, Gretchen Peterson, a vice president of Hanna Andersson clothing, asserted that paid family leave would lower stress levels and lead to happier workers. To support her claims, she pointed to the fact that Hanna Andersson operates in California and New Jersey and "has not experienced any negative impacts" (quoted in Langlois 2009).

Although paid family leave had considerable support from WMAs, labor groups, and organizations representing the interests of children and seniors, there was some disagreement within the coalition about the bill itself. In particular, many WMAs—especially mothers—wanted a much more generous program than the proposed legislation offered. Family Forward Oregon advocated a full year of paid leave that was completely funded by employers. According to Regan Gray, these WMAs hoped to pass "an ideal package, rather than what would be viable."[14] Gray stated that there was also some disagreement about the way in which the issue should be framed. Many members of the coalition did not want to portray paid family leave as a women's issue because there was a stigma in Oregon about "welfare moms" who only had children to receive money. Therefore, the coalition stressed the fact that the program would allow workers to care for a sick family member. Indeed, many mothers—especially those who were advocating much more generous benefits—were discouraged by the coalition from testifying for fear that the bill would lose support.

Although there were disagreements among activists regarding the scope of the legislation and frame of the issue, they did not lead to major rifts within the coalition. However, the fact that other issues were higher priorities for the organizations within the coalition weakened the chances of passing paid leave legislation. During the 2009 legislative session, a budget shortfall plagued most groups; therefore, they were pushing for tax increases. According to Gray, since it was highly unlikely that the Assembly would pass two bills that would raise taxes—especially over opposition from businesses—most paid leave advocates put their support behind the tax bill to resolve the budget shortfall.[15] This turned out to be a watershed moment for the movement in Oregon; paid family leave legislation has not been introduced since 2009.

In 2015, I spoke with Regan Gray again to get a better understanding of why paid family leave has largely fallen off the radar in Oregon. Currently with Okulitch and Associates, a government relations firm specializing in state-level legislative advocacy and issue management, Gray summed up the issue by saying that legislation for paid sick days is getting the bulk of the attention. After coming close in 2007, and then making little progress in 2009, the coalition began to lose steam. Children First for Oregon's funding to work toward paid family leave ran out at this time, and the newly formed Family Forward Oregon felt that they would have a better chance of success with paid sick days at the local level.[16]

In a recent interview, Lisa Frack, communications director for Family Forward Oregon, said that the organization formed specifically around the issue of paid family leave about six years ago.[17] It began as a group of moms who were fed up with the fact that there were few programs to provide parents with help to balance work and family. Stating that Family Forward Oregon sees itself as a feminist organization, Frack noted that women are often disproportionately hurt by the lack of such policies.

Andrea Paluso, cofounder and executive director of Family Forward Oregon, turned her attention to paid sick days after the 2009 paid family leave bill stalled. After the 2010 elections led to a 30-30 split of Democrats and Republicans in the Assembly and only a two-seat Democratic lead in the Senate, the prospects dimmed for the passage of a paid family leave bill. Therefore, Paluso decided to work locally for something more basic: "There's this huge section of the workforce that doesn't have a single paid day off. Paid maternity leave seems unrealistic when you can't even take a sick day" (quoted in McIntosh 2013). Evidence of Family Forward Oregon's efforts can be seen in the passage of paid sick days in Portland in 2013, Eugene in 2014, and then the entire state of Oregon in 2015. Frack said that once the state passed a paid sick time bill, paid family leave would again become the top priority of Family Forward Oregon.[18] With Democratic control of the legislative and executive branches, as well as the revived attention of activists, Oregon looks poised to adopt paid family leave legislation in the near future.

Massachusetts

During the 1980s, numerous states proposed some type of family leave legislation. It is not surprising that Massachusetts—a historically liberal state—was among them. Massachusetts was one of the first states to ratify the Equal Rights Amendment, and it had maternity disability laws dating back to the 1970s (Bernstein 2001). In the mid-1980s, an independent Parental Leave Commission in Massachusetts studied the issue for two years before introducing fourteen separate bills during the 1987 legislative session. Most of the bills applied only to parents and excluded companies with fewer than six employees. However, unlike all of the other state-level family leave bills at the time, the proposals in Massachusetts called for wage replacement (Wisensale 1989b). Anya Bernstein asserts that the decision to call for paid leave "reflected the advocates' identities as feminist organizers who believed that they needed to represent the concerns of all women, not just the high-income women who can afford to take time off from their jobs without pay" (2001, 56).

None of the bills introduced in 1987 made it out of the Joint Committee on Commerce and Labor (Wisensale 1989b). Realizing that a paid parental leave bill would not pass at the time, activists turned their attention to the possibility of developing a Temporary Disability Insurance (TDI) program that would cover both disability and dependent care. They believed that such a program, which would ensure wage replacement during family leave, would also garner enough support from various interest groups to enable them to form a coalition large enough to influence the policy-making process more strongly (Bernstein 2001). The plan ultimately failed, but Massachusetts again made history as the only state—outside of the five that have adopted it—to attempt to create a TDI program. Currently, workers in Massachusetts have only the leave available to them through either the FMLA or Massachusetts Maternity and Adoption Leave, which provides up to eight weeks of unpaid leave for new parents who work for an employer with at least six employees (Guerin, n.d.).

The most recent paid family leave bill (H 1718/S 1008) introduced in Massachusetts is as progressive as the proposals in the 1980s had been at the time. As its name implies, The Family and Medical Leave and Temporary Disability Insurance Program Act will establish a family and medical leave program as well as a temporary disability insurance program for employees. The proposed legislation provides workers up to twelve weeks of job-protected leave to care for a new child or a seriously ill or injured family member, or to recover from the employee's own serious illness or injury. Monetary benefits will last up to twelve weeks for family care and up to twenty-six weeks for the employee's own non-work-related disability or serious illness. The proposed legislation applies to employees who have worked for their employer for 1,250 hours and will provide benefits on a sliding scale based on income. Workers who earn minimum wage will receive 95 percent of their weekly salary; the highest earners will receive 66 percent of their weekly salary. Benefits will be capped at $1,000 per week for all employees. Notably, this plan is completely funded by employers. Contributions will go to the new Family and Employment Security Trust Fund, which will be administered by the Division of Family and Medical Leave in the Executive Office of Labor and Workforce Development; the Treasurer of the Commonwealth will manage the fund (Massachusetts State Legislature, n.d., "Bill H.1718"). In addition to this bill, Representative Antonio Cabral has introduced similar legislation (H 809). The bills differ in the amount of benefits: H 809 provides 66 percent of weekly wages, up to $1,000, for all employees (Massachusetts State Legislature, n.d., "Bill H.809").

The bills were referred to the Joint Committee on Labor and Workforce Development on April 15, 2015. Since that time, there has been little legislative movement on the issue. On October 27, 2015, advocates for H 1718/S 1008 testified at a legislative hearing at the Massachusetts State House. In total, twenty-eight elected representatives, activists, and individuals who have been personally affected by a lack of paid leave spoke in favor of the bill; not a single person spoke in opposition (Farnitano 2015). On March 16, 2016, the committee reporting date for each of the bills was extended to May 16, 2016 (Massachusetts State Legislature, n.d., "Bill H.1718"; Massachusetts State Legislature, n.d., "Bill H.809").

To understand why paid family leave has not yet passed in Massachusetts, it is necessary to look at previous legislative attempts. Deb Fastino is the executive director of the Coalition for Social Justice (CSJ), the leading organization in the fight for paid family leave in Massachusetts. In a recent interview, she said that in the decade before 2015, a new paid family leave bill was introduced each year but never made any progress.[19] To explain the lack of action, she pointed to the fact that those proposals included employee-funded leave. As an organization that fights for the economic security of individuals and families, the CSJ, which works closely with labor groups, would not support such a bill. Therefore, it primarily focused on other issues, such as paid sick time.

Activists in Massachusetts fought for paid sick days for over a decade before the legislation passed in 2014. According to Fastino, the Massachusetts Paid Leave Coalition had primarily targeted the legislature during that time—with little success. When Fastino and the CSJ got involved in the campaign, they implemented a new strategy "to take it [paid sick days] back in our hands." Rather than focusing only on the legislature, the activists ran both a legislative and a ballot campaign. They gathered over 350,000 signatures—more than any other campaign in Massachusetts history—to get paid sick days on the ballot. In November 2014, the measure passed with almost 60 percent of the votes; the law took effect on July 1, 2015.

According to Fastino, paid family and medical leave was the "next logical step" after paid sick days passed, for they both send the values message that workers should not have to choose between their jobs and their loved ones or their health. Therefore, the CSJ has put its considerable weight behind H 1718/S 1008. Because all of the previous bills called for employee-funded leave, Fastino says that the 2015 bill marked the beginning of a new effort. In the short amount of time that the CSJ has prioritized paid family leave, there has already been significant grassroots activity. The campaign has made nearly twenty-two thousand calls to targeted voters asking them to contact their legislators about supporting paid family and medical leave; thus far, this has resulted in over eight hundred calls to legislators. The campaign also helped to get over seventy-seven cosponsors on the bill, and it is working to collect five hundred personal stories about the need for paid leave. Fastino is also a cochair of Raise Up Massachusetts, a coalition of more than one hundred labor, faith, and community organizations working to improve economic and social justice in Massachusetts. This coalition has marked paid family leave as one of its three priorities for 2016 (Raise Up Massachusetts, n.d.). On March 26, 2016, Raise Up Massachusetts hosted a community forum so that constituents could talk with state legislators about the importance of passing paid family leave (Mei 2016).

As paid leave legislation gains attention throughout Massachusetts, more organizations are joining the debate. For example, Massachusetts National Organization for Women (Mass. NOW) has marked paid family leave as one of its priorities. According to vice president of communications Katie Prisco-Buxbaum, Mass. NOW will become more involved in the campaign as the bill moves forward.[20] She said that the national discussion on paid family leave has brought more attention to the issue in Massachusetts, making the passage of a bill more likely. Patricia Comfort, executive director of the Women's Bar Association (WBA) in Massachusetts, said that her organization was starting to pay more attention to the issue as well.[21] Although the WBA supported paid sick days before its passage in 2014, paid family leave has not been one of its priorities. However, in 2015, Comfort said that it seems likely it will become a priority issue in the near future.

As in other paid family leave campaigns, many business interests in Massachusetts are opposed to the legislation. According to Fastino, there has not been major action against the issue yet, in part because paid family leave has just started to gain statewide attention.[22] Moreover, until recently, business interests have been focused on delaying the implementation of paid sick days. As paid family leave gains momentum, Fastino expects to see increased opposition from organizations such as the National Federation of Independent Business in Massachusetts, Retailers Association of Massachusetts, Associated Industries of Massachusetts, and Massachusetts Restaurant Association.

In September 2014, Massachusetts was a recipient of one of the U.S. Department of Labor's grants to study the costs of paid family leave implementation. The Massachusetts Department of Labor Standards received $117,651 to conduct research about the costs of implementing a family and medical leave program. The preliminary results of the simulation model estimate that the number of people taking leave in Massachusetts will increase by 3.6 percent when leave is paid. The average length of leave will increase from 6.4 weeks to 7.2 weeks (based on a five-day week), and the median length of leave will increase from 3 weeks to 4 weeks. The average weekly replacement wage for workers will be $665; the average weekly cost per employee will be just over $3.00 (Albelda and Clayton-Matthews 2015, 3). The coalition will use the results of the simulation to gain a better understanding of how to proceed with the campaign. In addition, it continues to inform the population about paid family and medical leave and encourages individuals to pressure their legislators to support the bill. There has also been more localized action in Massachusetts on the issue. In May 2015, Boston city councilors unanimously passed a law to give Boston's nonunion employees paid parental leave (Bartlett 2015). Following that vote, attorney general Maura Healey announced that she will grant six weeks of paid parental leave to employees in her office (Levenson 2015).

In a recent survey of likely 2016 presidential election voters in Massachusetts, 72.5 percent of respondents supported a paid family and medical leave plan that would provide workers with twenty-six weeks for their own illness and twelve weeks for the birth of a child or the care of a spouse, child, or parent (Coalition for Social Justice, n.d.). Clearly there is growing momentum for paid family leave in Massachusetts, and it will be interesting to see how the issue progresses now that the CSJ has made it a priority.

Hawaii

In addition to the FMLA, Hawaii is covered by the Hawaii Family Leave Law (HFLL), which allows employees to take four weeks of unpaid, job-protected leave. Although the law only covers companies with at least one hundred employees within the state, its eligibility requirements are less stringent than those of the FMLA. To qualify, an employee only has to work at a covered company for at least six consecutive months; there are no restrictions based on the number of hours worked (Hawaii Department of Labor and Industrial Relations, Wage Standards Division, n.d.). However, that still leaves a significant proportion of the workforce unprotected. This is especially problematic for Hawaii's family caregivers because the state has one of the fastest-growing populations over age sixty-five in the country (Hawaii Department of Health 2013). Even when an employee qualifies for leave under the FMLA or the HFLL, there is no mandate for wage replacement. Therefore, activists in Hawaii are working on paid family leave legislation.

In 2015, a paid family leave bill made significant progress through the Hawaiian legislature, but it did not make it out of the conference committee. In its original form, the 2015 bill (SB 965/HB 496) provided relatively generous benefits. Although it did not include job protection, employees would receive twelve weeks of benefits, up to $552 per week (in 2015), for the care of a new child or a seriously ill child, spouse, parent, or reciprocal beneficiary, which may include a same-sex partner. The program would be funded by employees through a separate mechanism set up in the Department of Labor to collect contributions into a trust fund. The contributions would be based on the employee's average weekly salary, taxed in accordance with the employee contribution rate to the temporary disability fund, and estimated to average around $0.43 per week (Hawaii State Legislature, n.d., "HB496"). As one of the five states with an existing TDI program, Hawaii seemingly has the opportunity to avoid the problems that have plagued other states, such as Washington, that have to build a completely new mechanism through which to fund paid family leave. However, Hawaii's TDI system differs significantly from the programs in California, New Jersey, Rhode Island, and New York, because it has largely been privatized. Employers in Hawaii choose from three methods of providing TDI benefits: purchasing an insured plan from an authorized insurance carrier; adopting a self-insured plan in which the employer pays benefits directly to employees; or approving a collective bargaining agreement that contains TDI benefits at least as favorable as required by law (Hawaii Department of Labor and Industrial Relations, Disability Compensation Division, n.d.). Most employers choose to buy a TDI plan from an authorized (private) carrier, and penalties for employers who do not provide TDI for their employees are rarely enforced. Overall, the government plays little role in the distribution of TDI benefits. Therefore, the TDI system at the governmental level in Hawaii is not currently equipped to easily expand benefits for the purposes of family leave.

After being introduced in the Senate and House, the 2015 bill moved quickly through various committees, picking up a number of amendments along the way. On April 14, 2015, the bill passed the Senate and went to the House. However, the House disagreed with the Senate's amendments, so the bill did not progress before the end of the legislative session in May (Hawaii State Legislature, n.d., "HB496"). Cathy Betts is executive director of the women's policy agency the Hawaii State Commission on the Status of Women. Because she helped draft the bill, she was able to witness its dismantling during the legislative process.[23] As it went through the Senate, it was amended to exclude businesses with fewer than fifty employees, and the implementation date was pushed back so that there would be time to facilitate further discussion on the issue.

Because a bill for the provision of paid sick days (HB 1047/SB 1025) was introduced the same week as the paid family leave bill, there was some confusion in the legislature and the public over the differences between the issues. Moreover, the paid sick days bill provided weak protections for employees, especially in small businesses, so most family leave advocates did not support it. Yet during the amendment process, the sick time bill was actually attached to the paid family leave bill, which dramatically lowered the chances of the final product passing. Ultimately, the bill was so far removed from what Betts had originally helped draft that she decided to change the bill into primarily a proposal for an actuarial study to determine the costs of implementing a paid family leave. She said that since she knew the bill was headed for failure, she hoped that she could salvage something from the process.

In the end, the paid family leave bill could not garner enough support in the legislature to pass, even in its dismembered form. Betts said that the main reason it failed is that there was a lack of political will or political focus on the issue for legislators. For some legislators, paid family leave is still seen as only a "mom thing," which means that it will not be a high-priority issue. She also pointed to the ability of chambers of commerce to impede the policy-making process. Hawaii is an island state that relies heavily on the in-state economy, especially in the tourism and service industries. Fearing the fragility of Hawaii's economy, legislators are often wary of angering business interests—especially the chambers of commerce, which are very powerful in Hawaii.

Lisa Kimura, executive director of Healthy Mothers, Healthy Babies, which was one of the main organizations fighting for paid family leave, echoed Betts's sentiments.[24] In her experience, she has encountered a number of women legislators who are hesitant to advocate paid family leave because they worry about appearing to support only "women's issues." In 2015, it was not the Women's Legislative Caucus that put paid family leave on the legislative agenda in Hawaii. Rather, the Keiki Caucus and the Kupuna Caucus, which represent the interests of children and elders, respectively, were the biggest supporters to help introduce paid leave legislation. Like Betts, Kimura identified chambers of commerce as the issue's biggest opponents, regardless of the fact that the bill would be completely funded by employees.

According to Kimura, paid family leave has really only gained attention in Hawaii in the last few years. This may be partly explained by Hawaii's recent struggle for marriage equality. Often the types of organizations that support marriage equality—especially those that are feminist—are also in favor of family-friendly legislation. During the fight to legalize same-sex marriage, many activists, deciding to give their full attention to one issue, prioritized marriage equality. From that perspective, it is not surprising that the movement for paid family leave is still in its beginning stages. But with the legalization of same-sex marriage in Hawaii in 2013, more activist organizations in the state have turned their attention to paid family leave, and Kimura said that she felt encouraged by the progress made on the issue in 2015.

Kimura asserted that paid family leave is a top priority for her organization because it benefits families in so many ways, including reducing infant mortality rates and increasing opportunities for breast-feeding and family bonding. In the 2015 campaign for paid leave, Healthy Mothers, Healthy Babies took part in a variety of outreach efforts, such as speaking to groups like PHOCUSED (Protecting Hawaii's Ohana, Children, Under-Served, Elderly and Disabled) about the ways in which paid leave will help vulnerable populations in Hawaii. The organization also met with actors in the government, such as the Hawaii State Commission on the Status of Women and the Women's Legislative Caucus, to discuss the issue and attempt to move legislation forward. Kimura said that she is working to continue to expand the coalition of paid family leave supporters and to incorporate more voices into the policy-making process.

In 2016, Hawaii began its third attempt to pass paid family leave in as many years. In its original form, the 2016 bill (SB 2961/HB 2128) closely resembled the legislation introduced in 2015. It would provide virtually all employees twelve weeks of paid leave, up to $570 per week (in 2016), for the care of a new child or a seriously ill child, spouse, parent, or reciprocal beneficiary. The program would be financed by employee contributions into a trust fund set up by the Department of Labor. Although the bill survived four Senate committees and two House committees, it was significantly altered. The duration of benefits was first reduced from twelve weeks to four weeks. More damaging was the subsequent elimination of a family leave provision in the bill in favor of a funded actuarial study on the cost of implementing paid leave in Hawaii (Hawaii State Legislature, n.d., "SB2961"). In April 2016, the bill died in the House Finance Committee.

At first glance, the current legislation appears to follow a path similar to the 2015 bill. But Shay Chan Hodges, community activist and author of *Lean On and Lead: Mothering and Work in the 21st Century Economy*, said that there are important differences between the two legislative experiences.[25] According to Hodges, paid family leave was "not really on [legislators'] radar" in 2015. When she asked members of the Women's Legislative Caucus why they did not push the issue in that legislative session, many said that their focus was on moving domestic violence legislation forward. In contrast, Hodges found a number of legislators who were "really committed to paid family leave" in 2016. For example, she pointed to the work that Jill Tokuda, Gil Keith-Agaran, and Roz Baker did to ensure that the bill made it out of the Senate committees. Hodges also claimed that the amendment that changed the bill from providing paid leave benefits to mandating an actuarial study was not the defeat that has been described. Because TDI in Hawaii has essentially been privatized, a public system for funds must be established before paid leave can be implemented. Therefore, an actuarial study is a necessary first step. According to Hodges, Senator Keith-Agaran also suggested to her that a study might be better than a paid leave policy at this point because it will show the chambers of commerce that the program will not devastate the Hawaiian economy. With such evidence in hand, advocates could push for a more generous policy than would likely pass.

Hawaii's executive and legislative branches are controlled by Democrats. In fact, there is only one Republican in the twenty-five-seat Senate; seven Republicans are in the fifty-one-seat House. Although this suggests that paid family leave would face relatively less opposition from lawmakers, partisanship in Hawaii is complicated. Most Hawaiian voters have an aversion to the Republican label, so politicians are unlikely to identify with that party, regardless of their ideological beliefs. Betts explained that there is no real partisan line in Hawaii because almost all politicians identify as Democrats.[26] However, Democrats who are closer to business are less likely to support paid leave. Kimura said that a number of politicians are Democrats "in name only," holding conservative views on many issues.[27] Therefore, the seemingly ideal political environment for a paid family leave bill may actually hinder its advancement. Moreover, as Hodges pointed out in a 2015 interview, there "hasn't really been an outspoken champion [of paid family leave] in the state government or governor's office."[28] Without a critical actor to rally support for the issue, it may be difficult to gain legislative momentum. Still, in 2016 Hodges said that she is optimistic moving forward because the commitment from legislators this year looks different from that of last year.[29] As support for paid family leave continues to grow within both the legislature and the activist community, Hawaii comes closer to joining the list of states with paid leave.

Conclusion

Paid family leave at the state level has gained an increasing amount of attention since California adopted the first paid leave law in 2002. Numerous states have attempted to replicate California's experience, with little success. This chapter examines four such cases to gain a better understanding of the issues that prevent paid leave legislation from passing. While there was initially disagreement within some of the coalitions regarding the generosity of benefits as well as the framing of the issue, it has largely dissipated at this point. It now seems that activists in these cases are mostly on the same page with regard to their demands. However, in the face of budget cuts and legislative setbacks, many campaigns temporarily turned their attention to other issues—especially paid sick days. Although this shift may have stalled progress on paid family leave in the short term, it could benefit the paid family leave movement in the long run. As more cities and states pass paid sick days, the victorious coalitions are relaunching their campaigns for paid family leave, often in concert with a public that is more informed and supportive of the issue than in the past. If activists can successfully mobilize this public support, they have a greater chance of overcoming opposition in the legislature.

6

The Future of Family Leave in the United States

The Enduring Need for Policy Change

Americans work more hours per employee each year than workers in any other industrialized country (G. Miller 2016; Isidore and Luhby 2015). Although women make up nearly half of the workforce today, they are still responsible for a disproportionate share of family caregiving responsibilities. Of the almost seven million jobs lost during the economic recession between 2007 and 2009, over three-fourths of them belonged to men (A Better Balance 2015). Therefore, women's income has become even more essential to many families. When parents are able to spend more time with their children immediately after birth, infant health and mortality rates improve. Fathers who are involved with their children in the first few weeks of their children's lives are more likely to continue to be engaged and active parents. The population is aging at a rapid rate. As baby boomers reach retirement age, there is a growing demand for elder care. For all of these reasons and more, Americans have an ever-increasing need for policies that help them balance work and family life (U.S. Department of Labor 2015a). Such policies have far-reaching effects on families. Child and family health and well-being, family economic security, and gender equality in both the workplace and the home are aided by family leave policies (Fass 2009, 4). However, these policies lose much of their power when they are unpaid. It is therefore imperative that we understand how and why paid family leave policies are able to pass.

The Road to the FMLA

Leading up to the passage of the FMLA in 1993, there were some disagreements within the women's movement on the issue of family leave. On one side, "special-treatment" feminists believed that women face additional obstacles in the workplace as a result of pregnancy that men do not encounter. For this reason, these feminists—including group like the Coalition for Reproductive Equality in the Workplace and 9to5 National Association of Working Women—advocated substantive equality and supported family leave policies targeted specifically at women. On the other side of this debate, "equal-treatment" feminists worried that maternity leave benefits would single out women as more expensive or unreliable employees, as well as reinforce the belief that women are primarily responsible for taking care of the home and family. Therefore, these advocates favored formal equality and leave policies that were equally available to women and men. The National Organization for Women (NOW), which is the largest and most visible women's organization in the United States, would only support such policies. The Women's Legal Defense Fund (WLDF), which led the committee that drafted the first national family leave bill, also favored formal equality.[1] Ultimately, equal-treatment feminists prevailed, and legislative proposals categorized pregnancy and childbirth as a type of disability. Likewise, maternity leave was eschewed in favor of gender-neutral parental leave. Once this decision was made, most women's organizations got behind the idea of equal treatment instead of special treatment. However, the issue of wage replacement became problematic.

NOW strongly supported the inclusion of wage replacement in family leave legislation. The organization felt that unpaid leave would reinforce the male breadwinner model and prevent many women—especially those with low incomes—from taking full advantage of the leave. Most other women's movement actors (WMAs) believed that paid family leave would encounter too much opposition; therefore, they removed it from the first bill drafted in 1984, the Family Employment Security Act. At that time, NOW stood behind the bill even though it did not include wage replacement. But as the bill progressed over the next eight years, the organization became more vocal in its opposition to unpaid leave. Ultimately, NOW rescinded its support for the FMLA because it believed the provisions were not generous enough; it wanted longer leaves, a greater number of covered employees, and—most importantly—wage replacement. Echoing NOW's concerns, the Fund for a Feminist Majority also withdrew its support for the bill.

Although these disagreements within the women's movement were not catastrophic, the lack of internal cohesion undermined the movement's ability to influence legislative behavior to a certain extent. Likewise, the fact that family leave was not a top priority for many WMAs meant that their time was often divided among issues, and policy makers did not feel as much pressure to pass leave legislation. In the two decades leading up the passage of the FMLA, a number of other issues topped the agenda of many women's organizations, including the Equal Rights Amendment, reproductive rights, workplace discrimination unrelated to pregnancy and childbirth, violence against women, marriage and divorce matters, discrimination against women in the military and in education, and discrimination based on sexual orientation. Child care was certainly an issue that took the attention of some family leave advocates, such as the Children's Defense Fund. Once a child care law passed in 1990, such activists were able to devote more of their attention to the FMLA. WLDF was an exception in this regard; family leave was at the top of that organization's agenda from the beginning of the fight for family leave. It is therefore not surprising that WLDF led the coalition that ultimately won family leave for American workers. However, because many other women's organizations did not prioritize the issue in the same way, the movement's overall ability to influence the family leave policy-making process was weakened.

Although there was some dissent within the women's movement during the campaign for the FMLA, WMAs were still crucial to the passage of the law. Indeed, they were the ones who first put the issue on the agenda and often recruited other actors to join the fight for family leave. At the same, it is unlikely that the campaign would have been successful without the additional efforts of unions; critical actors in the legislature; religious groups; and organizations that represented the interests of children, seniors, and the disabled. Ultimately, it took a widespread coalition of activists to overcome the opposition, which came primarily from business interests. Although some were disappointed with the final version of the FMLA, many saw its passage as a victory that would be the first step toward establishing paid family leave in the United States. However, efforts to expand family leave policies at the national level have yielded few results. For this reason, many activists have turned to the subnational level in hopes of enacting paid family leave.

Paid Family Leave in the States and Cities

As a federal system, the task of forming social welfare policies often falls to the subnational governments rather than to the federal government (Vosko 2002). In the case of the United States, "although [the country] has not devolved new formal decision-making powers to the states (for example, the national government still maintains its ability to regulate interstate commerce), a major change since the 1970s has been the downloading of national governmental policy responsibilities to the individual states" (Beckwith 2003, 190). This delegation of power to subnational governments in the United States has been especially prevalent since the era of retrenchment that began with Ronald Reagan's arrival in the White House in 1981. It has also had a significant effect on the development of family leave policies. Subnational governments have greater freedom to design policies that are consistent with the dominant political culture of their state. Local elites and activists may advocate different goals than federal policy makers. As a result of the greater leeway subnational governments have in the policy-making process in the United States, there is considerable variation in family leave policies among states. Some states provide no more coverage than the FMLA, while others provide unpaid leave to a greater number of workers. Ohio, Virginia, and Illinois offer paid parental leave for state employees. Four states have gone even further by passing paid family leave legislation for virtually all workers.

In California, New Jersey, Rhode Island, and New York, women's movement actors worked closely with labor unions and organizations representing families, children, seniors, and people with disabilities to pass paid family leave.[2] They organized rallies, sent letters and e-mails and made calls to their legislators, testified at legislative hearings, wrote letters to the editor, commissioned studies on the potential costs and benefits of paid leave, and worked to educate the community about the need for more extensive work-life policies. Within these state coalitions, each of the individual organizations had its own reasons for supporting paid family leave. For example, 9to5 California stressed the importance of paid leave for working women, especially those with lower incomes. State-level AARP organizations championed the ability for workers to take time to care for an aging parent or spouse. Although coalition members in these states had varying motives, they all came together in support of paid family leave. The cohesion of the activists and their prioritization of the issue help explain why paid family leave passed in these cases.

President Obama's administration has sought to bring greater attention back to the issue of paid family leave in the states. In 2014, the U.S. Department of Labor's Women's Bureau and Employment and Training Administration awarded a total of $500,000 in grants to Massachusetts, Montana, Rhode Island, and Washington, D.C., to study feasibility and execution of paid family leave programs (U.S. Department of Labor 2014a). In September 2015, the Women's Bureau announced the recipients of the 2015 grant program. The following states will each receive a share of $1.55 million "to research and analyze how paid leave programs can be developed and implemented across the country": California, Maryland, New Hampshire, New York, Rhode Island, Tennessee, Vermont, and Washington (U.S. Department of Labor 2015b).[3] The president has also included provisions in his 2016 and 2017 budget proposals that would provide funding to assist states with the initial development costs of a paid family leave program (U.S. Department of Labor 2015d; Lunney 2016).

In the absence of national- and state-level paid family leave, a growing number of municipal governments have adopted their own policies. After Pittsburgh implemented paid parental leave for non-union city workers, Allegheny County announced its own six weeks of paid parental leave for county workers in 2015 (Born 2015). Seattle city employees receive four weeks of paid parental leave (Beekman

2015b), and Austin, Texas, gives its city employees six weeks of paid leave (Coppola 2013). In Massachusetts, Cambridge provides eight weeks for new parents who work for the city, while Boston provides six weeks (Jimenez 2015; A. Ryan 2015). In the Ohio cities of Cincinnati and Dayton, parents can take two weeks of sick or vacation time followed by four weeks of paid leave at 70 percent of their base pay. For the remaining 30 percent, they can borrow against their sick or vacation time (Frolik 2015; Weingartner and Hanselman 2015). In Chicago, women who work for the city receive four to six weeks of paid leave after giving birth; adoptive parents get two weeks, and partners receive one (Dries 2011). In Minnesota, Hennepin County and four cities (Brooklyn Park, Minneapolis, St. Paul, and St. Louis Park) all provide paid parental leave for their employees, ranging from one to four weeks (B. Johnson 2015). Atlanta now offers city employees six weeks of paid leave for a primary caregiver and two weeks for a non-caregiver (Shropshire 2015). St. Petersburg city employees receive six weeks of paid parental leave for men and women (Frago 2014). Multnomah County employees also receive six weeks of paid parental leave (Hernandez 2015).

As of January 1, 2016, city employees in New York City and Portland receive six weeks of paid parental leave ("Mayor de Blasio Announces Paid Parental Leave" 2015; Shine 2015). King County employees in Washington receive twelve weeks of parental leave, but that must include all but one week of their vacation time and all but one week of their sick time (Beekman 2015a). Beginning in May 2016, employees in Kansas City, Missouri, who have worked for the city for at least a year will receive six weeks of paid parental leave. Women who have a C-section or other medical complications following the birth of a child will be eligible for two additional paid weeks (Evans 2015). In April 2016, San Francisco made history by enacting the first city-wide paid parental leave law in the United States. The policy provides six weeks of fully paid leave for new mothers and fathers, including same-sex couples. To be eligible for leave, an employee must have worked for a company for at least 180 days. The law takes effect on January 1, 2017, for companies with more than fifty employees; one year later it will be implemented in companies with twenty or more employees (Fuller 2016).

In Washington, D.C., city workers can take up to eight weeks of paid leave for the birth or adoption of a new child or to care for a seriously ill family member (Covert 2014). In October 2015, the city council introduced a proposal for a paid family leave program. If it passes, it will be the most generous (governmental) paid family leave plan in the country. All full- and part-time workers who live in D.C., as well as those who live in nearby states but work for private companies in D.C., will be eligible for sixteen weeks of paid leave for personal illness or to care for a new child or a seriously ill family member. Benefits will be capped at $3,000 per week. To fund the leave, a new tax will be levied on private D.C. employers, who will contribute between 0.6 and 1 percent of their employees' salaries, determined by a progressive sliding scale. The federal government will not be required to participate, but D.C. residents who are federal employees and self-employed workers can opt into the system with a contribution that will not exceed 1 percent of their salaries (Cauterucci 2015; Gale 2015). On January 14, 2016, the D.C. city council heard testimony from supporters and opponents of the legislation. As the process moves forward, there is significant disagreement over what the cost of implementation will be (A. Davis 2016).

In the current fight for paid leave at the national, state, and municipal levels, the debate over equal treatment versus special treatment has largely disappeared, as most groups involved agree that paid family leave does not only concern women. Indeed, women, men, children, seniors, and businesses are all affected by the availability of paid family leave. However, there is still some disagreement over issues such as length of leave, level of wage replacement, source of funding, and scope of coverage. For example, the Family and Medical Insurance Leave (FAMILY) Act would cover leave for the birth or adoption of a child; the serious illness or injury of a child, parent, spouse, or domestic partner; the employee's own serious illness; and certain military leave and caregiving purposes. On the other hand, the Federal Employees Paid Parental Leave Act would provide paid leave only for new parents. Although this is a necessary benefit for workers, it does not go far enough. It fails to recognize the caregiving responsibility that many people with or without children have to care for a spouse, partner, parent, grandparent, or other family member. As the baby boomers reach retirement age, paid leave for the purposes of elder care has become increasingly important. Moreover, when benefits are set aside solely for parents in this manner, it could breed animosity in the workplace between workers with and without children. As its name implies, the Federal Employees Paid Parental Leave Act would be available only for federal workers; the FAMILY Act would provide nearly universal coverage to employees who pay into and are eligible for Social Security benefits for at least a year. As the campaign for paid family leave moves forward at all levels, disputes over such details could hinder the ability to pass policies. Additionally, paid sick days may continue to overshadow the fight for paid family leave.

The Changing Workplace

Workers' demand for policies that improve work-life balance continues to increase. As government-sponsored policies have lagged behind the realities of most workers, a growing number of companies recognizes the advantages of offering their employees paid family leave. Technology companies in particular are known for their generous leave packages. For example, Google provides up to twenty-two weeks of paid maternity leave and twelve weeks of paid paternity leave (Wojcicki 2014). At Facebook all new parents get four months of paid leave; new moms and dads at Instagram and Reddit get seventeen weeks (Shontell 2013; Liebelson 2013). Spotify provides six months of paid leave for both mothers and fathers, allowing them to break up the time over the first three years of a child's life (Crockett 2016). In March 2015, Vodafone rolled out a global policy on maternity benefits, offering at least sixteen weeks at full pay (Kottasova 2015). Microsoft recently increased paid leave for mothers to twenty weeks; fathers receive twelve weeks of paid leave (Day 2015). Likewise, Adobe has expanded paid maternity leave to sixteen weeks; birth mothers can use it in tandem with ten weeks of paid medical leave. Secondary caregivers receive four weeks of paid leave (Reader 2015). In August 2015, Netflix announced that salaried employees can take as much or as little paid time off as they want during the first year after a child's birth or adoption.[4] Intel recently added eight paid weeks of bonding leave for all new parents in addition to the thirteen weeks that mothers already received (Covert 2015a). In 2016, Twitter became the newest tech company to offer up to twenty weeks of paid parental leave (Lev-Ram 2016).

Generous paid leave policies are becoming more common in large companies outside the technology arena as well. Change.org, which charges organizations and political campaigns to host their petitions, now offers eighteen weeks of paid leave to all new parents (Fairchild 2014). Johnson and Johnson has changed its policy to provide new moms who give birth up to seventeen weeks of paid leave; new fathers and adoptive parents now get nine weeks of paid leave (McGregor 2015). Nestlé offers fourteen weeks of paid parental leave and the right to take an additional six months of unpaid leave (Lindzon 2015). Amazon provides all new parents six weeks of paid leave; birth mothers are offered up to fourteen additional paid weeks. The company also introduced a "leave share program" that allows employees to transfer all or part of the six-week leave to a spouse or partner who works at a company that does not provide paid leave. Under this arrangement, the Amazon employee would go back to work, and his or her partner would be paid by Amazon to stay home and care for the child (Lerman 2015). Bank of America recently increased its paid parental leave from twelve to sixteen weeks for its employees in the United States (Manning 2016). Ernst and Young also announced that it will expand its parental leave to sixteen weeks at full salary for both men and women (Bellstrom 2016b). Etsy now provides up to twenty-six weeks of paid leave for new parents (Deluca 2016). At Anheuser-Busch, birth parents are eligible for up to sixteen weeks of paid leave; the secondary caregiver receives two weeks (Michelson 2016). Starting in 2017, Coca-Cola will provide six weeks of parental leave benefits to employees in the United States who are not covered by collective bargaining. This leave will augment the current six to eight weeks of paid leave that birth mothers can take through short-term disability (Bellstrom 2016a). Wells Fargo has announced that it plans to offer up to sixteen weeks of paid parental leave for employees who have been with the company for at least a year. Notably, it is one of the only companies to include time off for family care as well: workers can take up to five consecutive days off a year to care for a seriously ill family member and up to five days a year to care for an adult (Crosby 2016).

Clearly, companies have realized the value of offering generous family leave policies. Not only do these policies help employees balance their work-life responsibilities, but they also improve overall productivity and profits for businesses. Change.org's COO Jennifer Dulski articulates this logic: "Our goal was to create a real parental leave program that supports all evolving families without creating financial hardship for them. . . . We did a robust financial analysis and having a strong family policy is also good for business" (quoted in Fairchild 2014). Employers recognize the importance of offering paid family leave to attract the best candidates. In July 2015, this was the reason given by secretary of the navy Ray Mabus for tripling paid maternity leave for women in the Navy and Marine Corps to eighteen weeks:

> In the Navy and the Marine Corps, we are continually looking for ways to recruit and retain the best people. We have incredibly talented women who want to serve, and they also want to be mothers and have the time to fulfill that important role the right way. We can do that for them. Meaningful maternity leave when it matters most is one of the best ways that we can support the women who serve our country. This flexibility is an investment in our people and our Services, and a safeguard against losing skilled service members. (U.S. Navy 2015)

In January 2016, defense secretary Ash Carter announced that all uniformed service members would receive twelve continuous weeks of paid maternity leave. Paternity leave would also increase from ten to fourteen days (M. Ryan 2016). While this change in policy will help a significant number of female service members, it does little to alter the portrayal of women as primary caregivers. Recognizing this, in March 2016, Representative Tammy Duckworth (D-IL) introduced legislation to increase paternity leave for service members to twelve weeks (Bushatz 2016).

In the technology industry, employers are especially conscious of the need to attract and retain the greatest technical talent; offering benefits like paid family leave helps to achieve this goal (Lerman 2015). Technology companies are also under pressure to diversify their predominantly male workforces to better reflect society at large (Day 2015). Intel said that its new leave policy is part of its recent efforts to increase diversity in the company by attracting more women and people of color and making the workplace friendlier to them (Covert 2015a).

Although the companies that offer paid leave are providing their employees with a greater ability to balance their work and family lives, most people do not work for such companies. Many businesses—especially small businesses—cannot afford to offer such generous policies on their own (Scaccia 2015). Moreover, the people who have access to paid family leave through these companies are more likely to have higher salaries and more generous benefits packages that make them better able to afford to take unpaid leave if necessary. Emily Peck (2015) describes a "benefits war at the top of the economic pyramid right now." Companies are competing for highly trained and diverse workers, so they are offering generous policies to accommodate parents in addition to high salaries. In companies that cannot afford to offer increased salaries, employers are looking for ways to reward employees without increasing their salaries, such as health care benefits, onetime bonuses, and paid leave from work. These tactics have been generally well received, especially by "the growing workforce of millennials who seem to prize short-term flexibility over long-term financial security" (Mui 2015). Meanwhile, low-income and hourly workers are unlikely to have access to these types of policies.

It is certainly a positive development to see more companies recognize the value of paid family leave policies. At the same time, this expansion of benefits within a small subset of businesses highlights the inadequate paid leave policies for most Americans (Crockett 2016). Moreover, these companies generally only include leave to care for a new child, thereby overlooking the importance of time off to care for elderly or sick family members. However, leave is increasingly available for both women and men in these companies, which helps encourage fathers' participation in caregiving. By offering benefits to men and women, "family leave ceases to be a 'women's issue' and simply becomes normalized as something that most workers are likely to need, and use, at some point in their working years" (Glynn 2015). Of course, this change will occur only if men actually take advantage of available leave.

Office culture has a significant impact on employees' usage of leave. If employees work in a competitive environment, they may feel that they will be penalized for taking leave (Crockett 2016). Many employees—especially men—say that they feel pressure to avoid taking the full leave that is offered in order to demonstrate their dedication to the company (Miller and Streitfeld 2015). Men often report feeling an "unspoken pressure on the job" to limit the amount of paternity leave that they take (Hall 2013). Wage replacement helps alleviate the stigma of taking leave because it provides a value for the care work the employee is doing. As more employees take parental leave, it will also become increasingly socially acceptable. In particular, when men see their coworkers and bosses taking paternity leave, it has a significant effect on their own usage of leave. This is part of the reason that Mark Zuckerberg, the cofounder and chief executive of Facebook, publicly announced that he would take two months of paternity leave after the birth of his daughter in November 2015 (C. Miller 2015a). Indeed, Facebook is known for having "cultivated a culture where it's taboo not to take the full four months or for dads to take less than moms" (Gillett 2015). However, the fact that Zuckerberg took only half of the leave available to him demonstrates that there is still progress to be made.

Millennial men—those who are age eighteen to early thirties—have much more egalitarian attitudes about work, family, and gender roles than previous generations. They typically start their careers and relationships expecting to share caregiving responsibilities. However, they often find that current workplace policies and traditional attitudes about gender roles prevent them from achieving this goal (C. Miller 2015c). As millennial workers make up a greater proportion of the workforce, we are likely to see continuing changes in workplace policies and culture, especially as employers seek to attract such candidates. But increasing the number of companies that provide paid family leave in this piecemeal fashion will not do enough to reach the millions of American workers who lack access to leave benefits. Moreover, headlines about the industry giants that offer paid leave often "[take] heat off the government to help workers at all levels" (Adams 2015). Ultimately, only a federal policy can provide the necessary family leave benefits to all employees. Private companies do not need to fear a loss of competitive edge as a result of a governmental program. Whatever type of paid family leave law the federal government may adopt in the near future will still fall significantly below the benefits that many major companies are already offering. To attract and retain top talent, these companies would need only to continue offering benefits that go above and beyond what the government guarantees.

Continuing Opposition

Family leave policies have proven to be controversial for many reasons. Because they aim to enhance the status of women by allowing them to participate in the labor force more fully, family leave policies challenge traditional gender roles (Dittmar 2008, 9). The fact that wage replacement may induce more men to take leave could lead to further role change. Johns Hopkins labor sociologist Andrew Cherlin claims that "the reluctance of conservatives to incentivize women's work is the only remaining barrier to consensus [on paid leave]. . . . When it gets right down to it, many conservative social policymakers don't want to further discourage mothers from staying home. That's the basic reason we don't have [paid] family leave here when we have it everywhere else" (quoted in Sandler 2015, 35). As Cherlin sees it, policy makers have an ideological aversion to paid family leave because of the gains that would come to women as a result. Deborah J. Anthony points to the "U.S.'s strong liberal foundations and ties to individualism, autonomy, and limited government, along with continued notions of the separation of the public and private spheres," to explain the sustained opposition to paid family leave (2008, 484).

Family leave policies can provoke conflict within the women's movement by dividing it between equal-treatment feminists and those who advocate special treatment, though such schisms are now largely a thing of past. These policies also draw criticism from social conservatives who believe in a limited role for the state in the family and find family leave laws to be an unnecessary intrusion into people's lives. Finally, business interests typically oppose such government mandates, believing they will reduce profits and impede companies' ability to compete. Although current state paid leave programs in the United States are funded solely by employees' contributions, business interests worry about the costs to employers when they have to pay overtime and hire extra help while employees are on leave. However, these concerns have not been borne out by the reality in California, New Jersey, and Rhode Island. Moreover, increasing evidence shows that many businesses support paid family leave. According to internal data leaked from the Council of State Chambers of Commerce, of the one thousand C-level executives surveyed, 72 percent support increased maternity leave, and 82 percent support increased paternity leave. This is surprising, since the organizations that supposedly represent the interests of these executives are the primary opposition to paid family leave legislation. According to Lisa Graves, executive director of the Center for Media and Democracy, "This webinar reveals just how deeply corporate interests and their lobbyists are influencing the priorities of state Chambers of Commerce, even when that agenda contradicts the opinions of their local business members" (PRwatch Editors 2016).

There seems to be a disconnect between the electorate and the opposition in the legislature. Voters have made it clear that paid family leave is important to them and that they want candidates who support the issue. A recent poll of likely 2016 voters found that 79 percent say it is "important for elected officials to update the FMLA to guarantee access to paid family and medical leave" (Ness 2016). Another poll found that 81 percent of likely voters said it was important that lawmakers consider new laws to help working families, such as paid family leave and paid sick days. In addition, 64 percent said that they would be more likely to vote for a candidate who spoke in support of such laws (Lake Research Partners and Tarrance Group 2014). In 2008, women were asked which issue Barack Obama could address if he wanted to do the most to meet the needs of women. More women (35 percent) pointed to family and work-life balance issues than any other answer (Belkin 2009, 9). This issue resonates with voters, and support transcends gender, party, and ideology. Indeed, "it's hard to think of another issue that unites so many voters but remains perennially neglected" (Lerner 2010, B3). This is why we need the activism that WMAs and other grassroots actors can provide. They can help invigorate the voters to make their voices heard and pressure lawmakers, thereby overcoming the various types of opposition.

The Need for Institutional and Cultural Change

Although there have been tremendous strides in the fight for gender equality, sex discrimination is still prevalent in the United States.

Politicians frequently pay lip service to the importance of raising children, yet they have done little to improve parents' ability to balance work and family life. Women are hit hardest by this policy deficiency because much of society still believes they are primarily responsible for raising children and taking care of elderly and disabled relatives; therefore, most women have to choose between having a family and having a career. This is often a false choice because of the enormous amount of pressure on women to have children. Moreover, family leave policies in the United States typically work to reinforce the male breadwinner model, as legislators have consistently tried to shift the responsibility for work-life balance onto the marketplace.

This book focuses primarily on public policy changes as a way to improve women's status. Most research on family leave policies has sought to explain differences across welfare regime types, rather than within the same type. By looking at cases within the United States, I have been able to control for welfare regime type and look more deeply into the explanations for policy differences. Specifically, this work adds to the literature on social movements—and women's movements in particular—and their effects on the policy-making process. The results of this analysis can help explain other governments' experiences with the development of family leave policies. This will be especially useful in the United States as more states work to pass paid family leave. More generally, the findings can be applied to women's movements' experiences with other work-life policies, such as government-sponsored child care. This research also adds to the broader literature on policy making, as it examines the compromises that are often made in the development of policies. Finally, the work expands the existing literature of the growing field of family leave policies. As this analysis demonstrates, the effects of family leave policies are far reaching; therefore, we must continue to study their development throughout the United States.

However, institutional changes can only do so much if they are not accompanied by a change in social practices and attitudes. This can be seen in the (lack of) use of paternity leave in the United States. In an examination of faculty members at a large research university, Jennifer H. Lundquist, Joya Misra, and KerryAnn O'Meara (2012) found that relatively few men take paid leave when it is offered. Most of the men who opt out of parental leave have the support of a stay-at-home spouse or one who is employed part time to provide the necessary caregiving for the family, thus reinforcing their position as the "ideal worker" (J. Williams 2000; Gatta and Roos 2004). But even those without that support often choose not to take leave because they fear being characterized as less dedicated workers. It is often less socially acceptable for men to take leave because it can be seen as detrimental to their breadwinner status. Cultural messages reinforce the stigma of men taking leave for caregiving purposes, which means that fewer men choose to take leave (C. Miller 2014). For this reason, in addition to an expansion of family-friendly policies, "a revamping of gendered family life and the division of labor at home is necessary to afford women the full autonomy in the public sphere that men have enjoyed" (Anthony 2008, 498). Such a change will also benefit men by allowing them the choice to take time for caregiving if they wish.

Looking Ahead

When the FMLA passed in 1993, Republican representative John Boehner, then in his first term in Congress, predicted that it would lead to the "demise" of U.S. business (Sandler 2015, 37). Although that has not happened, the FMLA also has not been the godsend to families that many hoped it would be. Therefore, numerous bills at the federal level have been introduced to expand coverage provided by the FMLA. But the only amendments that have been adopted thus far do not apply to most workers, for they only cover airline flight crewmembers and leave related to military service. The extension of benefits to same-sex spouses came indirectly as the result of the Supreme Court case *United States v. Windsor*. It is unlikely that further expansions at the federal level will be adopted in the current political climate, as "advocates believe any plan that costs anything, no matter how much, or who pays for it, is dead on arrival, especially if it's from the Democratic minority" (39). Therefore, the best course of action seems to be to continue the policy-making process at the state level for the time being.

Family Values @ Work (FV@W) is a "national network of 24 state and local coalitions helping spur the growing movement for family-friendly workplace policies" (Family Values @ Work, n.d.). According to executive director Ellen Bravo, the work done in the states on paid family leave is invaluable.[5] Because the more than two thousand organizations in FV@W's network are rooted in their local communities, they know what will work best in each location. Bravo says that such grassroots activism is vital—that money "can't just go to the organizations in the beltway [in Washington, D.C.]." At the same time, FV@W provides those "groups in the field" a national network and the ability to share resources and strategies. Ultimately, Bravo thinks that the continuing success in the states is essential to the eventual passage of national legislation.

MomsRising is another organization that advocates paid family leave at federal and local levels. Executive director and cofounder Kristin Rowe-Finkbeiner says that MomsRising provides a platform for women to make their voices heard.[6] With over one million members, MomsRising has a significant presence online and "on the ground." According to Rowe-Finkbeiner, the organization works to "break through the beltway bubble to show what's really going on" with issues affecting women and families. Members of MomsRising talk directly with city council members, state legislators, the U.S. Congress, and even the president of the United States. Rowe-Finkbeiner says that the organization opens the door for such interactions. At the same time, they have a substantial grassroots presence. As described in Chapters 4 and 5, MomsRising has played a significant advocacy role in state-level campaigns for paid family leave.

Like Bravo, Rowe-Finkbeiner thinks that success at the state level will ultimately contribute to the success of the national campaign. Indeed, this was a common assertion among the activists I interviewed. Donna Lenhoff, a key figure in the drafting and passage of the FMLA, stated that interaction between national-level and state-level efforts on paid family leave contributes to greater policy success.[7] Linda Meric, executive director of 9to5 National Association of Working Women, said that success at the city and state levels builds momentum at the national level. According to Meric, "State progress has set the stage for a national [paid family leave] law. . . . When we win policies in states, it debunks the claims of critics that it won't work."[8] To explain this policy success, she pointed to the activism on the ground: "It really takes the grassroots efforts to get policies passed. . . . It comes from the members themselves." Vicki Shabo, vice president of the National Partnership for Women and Families, echoed these sentiments: "We're a national organization, so we push for congressional change, but we recognize that so much happens from the ground up."[9] Valerie Young, public policy analyst at Mom-mentum, calls herself "the link between 'normal' mothers who don't necessarily see themselves as political and the government and policy."[10] In addition, she works to educate voters, candidates, politicians, and the public at large about her main priority within the organization, which is the economic security of women. Seeing paid family leave as a way to protect women's economic well-being, she works to educate people on the issue so that they will press their legislators to support it. She stresses her belief that "the only thing that will pass it [paid family leave legislation] is constituents pressuring their legislators." Bravo shares this belief: "Everyday people are the ones who are going to make the change. . . . We [FV@W] are helping to give them a voice."[11]

From April to June 2015, U.S. labor secretary Thomas E. Perez and White House senior advisor Valerie Jarrett went on a Lead on Leave tour around the United States to promote paid leave policies. According to Perez, "I have absolutely no doubt that federal paid leave is a when question, not an if question. The way you build a movement is from the bottom up. Our goal is to amplify and escalate that movement to make sure the 'when' is as soon as possible" (quoted in Dell'Antonia 2015). Indeed, as seen in the various state-level campaigns for paid family leave, those grassroots movements are necessary to overcome opposition and influence legislators to take action. As demonstrated throughout this study, women's movement actors play a necessary role in the passage of family leave policies. But that is not to say that their presence is sufficient to explain the passage or failure of policies. Indeed, no one variable can fully explain policy variation within the United States. A number of factors may influence the passage of paid family leave policies, such as the involvement of unions and other activist organizations, the presence of critical actors in the legislature, and the party in control of both the executive and the legislative branches.

When women's movements can convince other actors to support legislation, there is a greater chance for success. WMAs' ability to persuade these actors increases when the movement is strong and united behind an issue. Moreover, if the issue is high on the movement's agenda, WMAs will exert greater pressure on policy actors. For example, unions have played an important role in influencing the family leave policy-making process. However, it is less likely that they would have prioritized the issue if WMAs had not persuaded them to do so. This can be seen in the actions of women's organizations such as the Coalition of Labor Union Women, which has had a major impact on the passage of paid leave at the state level. If the countermovement is strong—as it has been in the fight for paid family leave—only a similarly strong and united movement will be able to overcome it. Women's movement actors have recognized this problem and have stepped up around the country to pressure lawmakers to address the needs of working families. In the states that have passed paid family leave, women's organizations and women leaders have led coalition efforts and actively lobbied legislators (Dittmar 2008, 29).

It is difficult to build support for government-sponsored family policies in the United States because a number of private solutions exist. For example, because many Americans—especially those in the middle and upper classes—have access to private child care, they do not feel a sense of urgency to lobby lawmakers for government solutions. Moreover, many workers piece together some type of family leave based on the FMLA, state or municipal leave policies, and leave programs provides by employers. However, the people who need job-protected or paid leave the most are usually not employed by businesses that voluntarily offer such benefits. These workers—often women and minorities—are also less likely to meet the eligibility requirements for leave mandated by the federal and state governments. But because some workers can take advantage of these leave programs, it is more difficult to organize a widespread campaign for the expansion of family leave policies in the United States. The grassroots activism of social movement actors is necessary to triumph over this collective action problem. Because a lack of family leave policies disproportionately hurts women, it has often fallen to WMAs to lead the campaign on the issue. In particular, WMAs have a significant role to play in bringing attention to paid family leave, recruiting coalition members, and maintaining pressure on policy makers. Their ability to do this increases when they are united in their support for the legislation and have made it a priority. When that happens, paid family leave has a greater chance of overcoming powerful opposition and becoming law. However, the policy environment will also significantly influence activists' ability to effect change.

There is currently gridlock in Washington, D.C. With a Republican-controlled Congress that has an antagonistic relationship with President Obama, there is virtually no chance of enacting a federal paid family leave law in 2016. For many, the recent legislative victory in New York State has reinforced the belief that activists should keep their focus on the state level. With campaigns making significant progress in states like Connecticut, Massachusetts, and Hawaii, as well as Washington, D.C., there is reason for optimism. At the same time, the remaining state-level campaigns face a significant challenge: the lack of TDI programs. As described in Chapter 4, the states that have implemented paid family leave did so by simply expanding their TDI programs. Although Hawaii technically has TDI, it has largely been privatized and could not implement a new statewide program. Indeed, the recent paid leave bills introduced in Hawaii bypass TDI and call for the development of a new funding mechanism. As we have seen in Washington State, the lack of a funding mechanism can be disastrous. Therefore, perhaps the biggest victory at the state level will be when the first state without existing TDI enacts and implements a functioning paid family leave system that other states can replicate.

Until then, many are speculating about the outcome of the 2016 presidential and congressional elections. Both Hillary Clinton and Bernie Sanders have pledged their support to a federal bill. However, they will have little chance of fulfilling this campaign promise if Republicans keep control of Congress. On the Republican side of the presidential race, none of the remaining candidates at the time of writing (Donald Trump, Ted Cruz, and John Kasich) have given any indication that they would support paid family leave. Ultimately, the results of the election will tell us more about paid family leave policies in the short term than the long term. For even if 2016 ushers in leaders hostile to paid leave, the momentum for the issue will continue to grow. As described throughout this analysis, states, cities, counties, and companies across the country are adopting paid leave at a rapid rate, and public opinion only grows more favorable to family leave. Although we still have a long way to go before all workers in the United States have the access to the paid family leave that they need, we are currently pointed in the right direction.

Notes

Chapter 1

1. For example, Sweden's maternity policies were influenced by the 1934 book *Crisis in the Population Question*, in which Alva and Gunnar Myrdal discuss the declining birthrate in Sweden and propose a number of possible solutions. Such legislative initiatives included financial support for prenatal care and subsidized delivery, as well as maternity leave and bonuses for women after giving birth. For a full discussion of the Myrdals and the development of the Swedish social welfare model, see Carlson 1990.

2. For a full description of women's double burden, see Hochschild 1989.

3. The legislation often only covered specific categories of workers, such as industry workers (Gauthier 1996, 50).

4. For example, the fact that health care benefits are typically available only to full-time employees in the United States hurts women more than men, as women are more likely to work part time (Morgan 2006, 10–12).

5. With regard to care work and labor force participation, there are two opposite models. The "breadwinner model" puts the husband in full-time work outside the home, while his wife stays home to care for the family rather than participating in the paid workforce. The "individual" or "dual earner-carer" model finds both men and women participating in the workforce and in caregiving (Sainsbury 1994, 1996; Lewis 1993, 1997). Unlike in the breadwinner model, the dual earner-carer model often includes care work that is paid and publicly provided.

6. Men often have higher salaries than women; therefore, men would be more likely to take advantage of leave policies that include wage replacement. Similarly, men are more likely to take up leave when the benefits are given exclusively to them, rather than in the form of benefits that can be transferred between partners (Gornick and Meyers 2003, chap. 5; Ray, Gornick, and Schmitt 2009).

7. In 2018, New York will become the fourth state to provide paid family leave.

8. Although Hawaii still has a TDI program, it has largely been privatized (see Chapter 5 in this volume for details).

9. 29 U.S.C. §2601 et seq.

10. An employee can also take up to fifty-two weeks for his or her own disability.

11. Provisions under both are basically the same; however, CFRA does not apply to pregnancy leave. After the FMLA pregnancy leave allowances have been completed, CFRA applies to parental leave for the care of the child (California Department of Fair Employment and Housing, n.d.).

12. An employee can also take up to twenty-six weeks for his or her own disability.

13. The main difference between the state and federal statutes lies in the employee taking leave for his or her own health. Although the FMLA provides leave to care for the employee's own health condition, the NJFLA does not. Therefore, family leave can be taken under NJFLA even if medical leave under the FMLA has been exhausted (New Jersey Department of Law and Public Safety 2008).

14. An employee can also take up to thirty weeks for his or her own disability, but combined benefits for disability and family care cannot exceed thirty weeks.

15. To be considered "explicitly gendered," the language must refer to women as distinct from men (see Katzenstein 1995).

16. My discussion of WMAs and their characteristics in this section relies heavily on the work of the Research Network on Gender Politics and the State (RNGS), which is a network of scholars that conducted a long-term project on late-twentieth-century women's movements and the way governments responded to them. As a result of the efforts of more than forty researchers in thirteen countries, we now have a better understanding of the influence that WMAs and women's policy agencies can and do have on policy-making processes. RNGS completed its work in 2012, but a record of the project can be found at https://pppa.wsu.edu/research-network-on-gender-politics-and-the-state/.

17. This is consistent with the more general literature on social movement theory (Skocpol et al. 1993; Soule et al. 1999; Minkoff 1999) and resource mobilization theory (McCarthy and Zald 1973, 1977; Oberschall 1973; Tilly 1978; Piven and Cloward 1977; Jenkins 1983) that describes a positive correlation between the strength of a social movement and its impact on the policy-making process.

18. The strength of a women's movement can be separated from its policy influence. As S. Laurel Weldon explains, "When women's movement pronouncements and actions command public attention, they are more likely to have an influence on policymaking, because public opinion and attitudes force politicians to pay attention to them. . . . [However,] sometimes policymakers are unable or unwilling to translate these pressures into policy" (2002b, 239). So even though there is often a correlation between women's movement strength and its ability to effect policy change, the two are not synonymous.

19. The language changed again from "parental" to "family" in second half of 1986. This modification reflected the addition of intergenerational leave, which meant that an employee could take time off to care for a sick child, spouse, or an elderly parent. Such a change was necessary to attract support from the American

Association of Retired Persons (AARP). This preference for more inclusive coverage was also gaining traction in the states at that time; in 1987, Connecticut became the first state to introduce and pass an intergenerational family leave bill (see Wisensale 2001, 123–143).

20. Some socially conservative and Christian groups have also opposed leave because they felt it would take women away from their work within the home (Winston and Bane 1993). However, for the most part, antifeminist actors have fought alongside feminists for the passage of family leave policies, arguing that such programs allow parents—especially mothers—more time with their children.

21. Before 1998, the National Partnership for Women and Families was known as the Women's Legal Defense Fund.

Chapter 2

1. "Family member" originally referred only to one's child, parent, or spouse. As a result of *United States v. Windsor* in 2013, same-sex spouses and their children are now included as well.

2. In this context, "liberalism" is understood in the classical sense and opposes excessive government intervention in economic affairs (A. Smith 2008). Classical liberalism most closely resembles political beliefs that are dubbed "conservative" in the United States. On the other hand, the term "liberal" is currently used in the United States to describe a political belief system that favors government action to effect social change (see Hill 1964).

3. Australia, Canada, and the United Kingdom are also included in Gøsta Esping-Andersen's liberal welfare state regime.

4. Surprisingly, Lee Ann Banaszak (2003, 166) found that issues that conflict with neoliberal concerns may not necessarily be more difficult to get passed. Although these issues often inspire great opposition, they are central to major political actors such as businesses and trade unions and therefore will always find a place on the agenda.

5. For a discussion of "private" versus "public," see Thornton 1995 and Boyd 1997.

6. Unless otherwise noted, all statistics for Americans' workforce participation are taken from *Statistical Abstracts of the United States*. For a detailed historical account of women's integration into the workforce in the United States, see Kessler-Harris 1982.

7. 208 U.S. 412 (1908).

8. 198 U.S. 45 (1905).

9. Sex discrimination was not originally included in the language of the Civil Rights Act. Conventional wisdom says that southern legislators added protection from sex discrimination to the bill in order to make its passage less likely. However, Jo Freeman claims that this is an oversimplification, and that the inclusion of sex to the legislative language was "not as thoughtless, or as devious," as previous research has asserted: "Instead it was the product of a small but dedicated group of women, in and out of Congress, who knew how to take advantage of the momentum generated by a larger social movement to promote their own goals, and a larger group of

Congressmen willing to make an affirmative statement in favor of women's rights"
(1991, 183).

10. 417 U.S. 484 (1974).

11. 429 U.S. 125 (1976).

12. 434 U.S. 136 (1977).

13. In 1998, the Women's Legal Defense Fund changed its name to National
Partnership for Women and Families.

14. Pregnancy Discrimination Act, 42 U.S.C. §2000e(k) (1978).

15. Even the issues that have been a top priority for the women's movement are
often low on the policy agenda of the state (Haussman and Sauer 2007, 1).

16. Such beliefs placed special treatment feminists in "an uncomfortable alliance with supporters of a pro-family and conservative position on family leave"
(Mazur 2002, 114).

17. 414 U.S. 632 (1974).

18. 479 U.S. 272 (1987).

19. Joyce Gelb and Marian Lief Palley (1987) label legislation that is perceived
as involving radical change "role change"; incremental change is dubbed "role equity." Gender equality policies aimed at enhancing the status of women are often
put in the "role change" category by opponents. This makes them less likely to be
enacted because Americans tend to shy away from anything considered radical
(Conway, Ahern, and Steuernagel 2005, 10). Moreover, movements that seek to
transform gender and family relations are often accused of threatening the values of
the dominant culture, which makes them prone to provoking strong countermovements (Staggenborg 1998, 123).

20. NOW's website claims that it has more than 500,000 contributing members
and 500 chapters, but Maryann Barakso believes these figures to be overstated. In
1992, NOW reported 275,000 members, and membership has continued to decline.
In 2003, she estimated the number of chapters at 405, with many of them having
fewer than one hundred members (2004, 128).

21. Before 1978, the publication was titled *Do It NOW.*

22. When the PDA was being debated in Congress, NOW rarely addressed the
topic. Indeed, an examination of NOW's newsletter *Do It NOW* from 1970 to 1977
finds that the issue was largely absent. When NOW did discuss the PDA, it was
usually to make it clear that the organization would oppose any bill that included
antiabortion language. Certainly reproductive rights were a much higher priority
than pregnancy-related discrimination in the workforce.

23. For example, the Democratic Party's presidential candidate in 1972, George
McGovern, largely ignored WMAs. In general, the women's movement at that time
had trouble forming close ties with the Democrats and convincing the party to take
up the movement's ideas (Stetson 2001b, 254).

24. Women's organizations can include interest or lobby groups, women's
centers, and cultural institutions such as women's festivals, bookstores, and news-
papers (Weldon 2006, 114). Organizations in the women's movement vary in structure. Some focus on a single issue such as reproductive rights; others have a wider
focus. They may be organized federally or nationally, or by region, community, or

institution. Some organizations provide services, and others fight for services from the government (Briskin 1999, 7).

25. Feminist consciousness can best be thought of "as a lens through which ideas, individuals, and relationships are newly viewed" (Katzenstein 1987, 8).

26. David Meyer (2003, 278) explains that "political institutionalization" refers to the point when "movement actors negotiate some kind of more stable and routinized arrangement with the state and mainstream politics, even as the use of social movement forms and tactics becomes more widely employed and accepted." See also Meyer and Tarrow 1998.

27. In 1972, the ERA passed through Congress and went to the states for ratification. Unable to gain the necessary thirty-eight state ratifications within the seven-year deadline, NOW asked Congress for an extension. The campaign was given until June 30, 1982, to secure the remaining states that it needed; however, the ERA ultimately fell three states short (F. Davis 1991, chap. 18).

28. A few times, family leave was hinted at but not directly addressed. For example, in March 1979 the journal covered the NOW Legal Defense and Education Fund's announcement that it was organizing an assembly about solutions to family problems of the 1980s, such as child care, model marriage and divorce laws, status and security for homemakers, and workplace changes to aid two-breadwinner households.

29. For a detailed history of the bills addressing work-life balance that were introduced in Congress between 1945 and 1990, see Burstein, Bricher, and Einwohner 1995.

30. Before 1998, the National Partnership for Women and Families was known as the Women's Legal Defense Fund.

31. Judith Lichtman, telephone interview by the author, November 24, 2015.

32. The United States actually came close to adopting universal child care in 1971. That year, Congress passed the Comprehensive Child Development Act, which would have created a national network of federally funded child care centers, with bipartisan support. However, President Nixon vetoed it, claiming that it would undermine traditional family structures and likening it to Soviet-style communal approaches to child rearing (Badger 2014).

33. When the bill was introduced in the House in March 1986, it was titled the Parental and Medical Leave Act. By June of that year, it had been renamed the Family and Medical Leave Act in the House (Radigan 1988, 22).

34. Such tactics are common in the policy-making process, because most bills are scaled back from their original form to increase their chances of gaining support from a majority of lawmakers (Radigan 1988, 2).

35. Family leave advocates countered this claim by pointing out that almost all of the rest of the world, including the advanced industrialized nations of the West, had already adopted such policies.

36. The term "New Right" is used to describe the conservative movement that gained increasing power during the 1980s. It combined conservative, religious moral views, such as antifeminism, and laissez-faire economic preferences (Petchesky 1981; Morgan 2001, 2006; Somerville 1992).

37. Kimberly J. Morgan (2006) and Sarah Williamson and Matthew Carnes (2013) point to the influence of religion to explain opposition to both government family policy and shifting gender roles.

38. Anya Bernstein explains the effects of ideology on NOW's policy stances: "NOW leaders are . . . primarily responsible to a mass membership, which in turn is likely to be motivated primarily by ideology and thus is less likely to view a compromise as a win" (2001, 97). This partially explains the fact that NOW revoked its support of the FMLA as the policy-making process advanced.

39. Donna Lenhoff, telephone interview by the author, November 13, 2015.

40. The influence of the Women's Legal Defense Fund can be seen in the fact that Donna Lenhoff was one of the twelve individuals named to the commission to study the effects of the FMLA after its passage in 1993 (Elving 1995, 291).

41. Lenhoff, interview by the author.

42. Although not articulated by members of the coalition, Michael Selmi (2004, 86–89) offers a third possible reason for advocates to accept the legislation in its final form: to receive publicity for their efforts and demonstrate to past and future donors that their organizations were achieving their legislative goals.

Chapter 3

1. 29 U.S.C. §2601 et seq.

2. The twelve weeks of leave do not have to be taken continuously.

3. Public agencies consist of the federal government, state and local governments, and public or private elementary or secondary schools; the District of Columbia and all territories and possessions of the United States are included in the definition of a "state."

4. The employer must notify the employee of the intent to deny restoration on this basis, thereby providing the employee with the opportunity to return to work upon receipt of such notification. If the employee elects not to return to work after receiving such notice, the employer is not required to restore the employee's position.

5. National Defense Authorization Act for Fiscal Year 2008, P.L. 110-181.

6. National Defense Authorization Act for Fiscal Year 2010, P.L. 111-184.

7. Airline Flight Technical Corrections Act, P.L. 111-119.

8. In 1996, a U.S. District Court for Northern Georgia decided that flight attendant Marianne Rich did not qualify for FMLA leave because she had not worked the required 1,250 hours in the previous twelve months (Rich v. Delta Air Lines, Inc., 921 F. Supp. 767 [N.D. Ga. 1996]). She had completed a full-time flight attendant schedule of over 750 hours of "flight time," which measures the hours from departure to arrival, in the year prior to her leave. However, this calculation did not take into account the significant number of hours spent on the job between flights or on "reserve." After the Court's decision, the Association of Flight Attendants-CWA led a campaign to lobby Congress to amend the FMLA so that all flight attendants who work a full-time schedule at their carrier would be covered under the law (Association of Flight Attendants-CWA, n.d.).

9. Although I discuss only four U.S. Supreme Court cases that have directly influenced FMLA policy as it relates to my coverage of the law, the FMLA has

been the subject of approximately one thousand appeals cases. Even though the law has been in place for over two decades, many corporations still have numerous reservations about the FMLA and frequently go to court to fight it. Moreover, the high number of FMLA lawsuits brought on businesses helps in part to explain their rather unwavering opposition to paid family leave at the state level. For a detailed examination of this issue, see Wisensale 1999 and 2001, chap. 7. For information on recent and current FMLA appeals cases, see American Bar Association 2015 and "Archives: FMLA," n.d.

10. Ragsdale v. Wolverine World Wide, Inc., 535 U.S. 81 (2002).

11. 29 CFR 825.208(a).

12. 29 CFR 825.700(a).

13. Nevada Department of Human Resources v. Hibbs, 538 U.S. 721 (2003).

14. Coleman v. Court of Appeals of Maryland, 132 S. Ct. 1327 (2012).

15. United States v. Windsor, 133 S. Ct. 2675 (2013).

16. 1 U.S.C. §7.

17. The report draws on the results of two surveys from 1995: an employee survey conducted by the Institute for Social Research at the University of Michigan and an establishment survey conducted by Westat.

18. The report uses the results of two surveys conducted by Westat Inc. in 2000.

19. Abt Associates conducted both an employee survey and a worksite survey in 2012.

20. The conventional way to measure the wage gap—commonly cited as women earning seventy-seven cents to the male dollar—is to compare annual earnings of men and women who work full-time throughout one complete year. Stephen J. Rose and Heidi I. Hartmann find that this method is misleading because it does not show the difference in men's and women's total lifetime earnings. Therefore, they examine a fifteen-year time frame to account for women's lower work hours and years with no earnings because of family care. This new measure reveals that the wage gap between women and men is closer to 62 percent, rather than 23 percent (2004, iii).

21. Although this change would still require that an employee work approximately twenty-four hours a week, he or she could be eligible for leave six months earlier than the FMLA allows.

22. *United States v. Windsor* (2013) has since mandated the inclusion of domestic partners.

23. Porter groups these abuses into three categories: faking a serious health condition, taking a longer leave than medically necessary so that it will be covered as a "serious health condition," and abusing the intermittent leave provisions of the FMLA (2014, 347). Most of her evidence of these abuses comes from her experience as an employment law attorney prior to her academic career. She also includes data from a 1996 survey conducted by CCH Inc. that finds that only 45 percent of sick days are used for personal illness. According to the study, 27 percent of sick days are taken for family issues; stress and a feeling of entitlement to use the days off primarily account for the other reasons (Sharpe 1996). Overall, there is greater evidence of employers' fear of FMLA abuses and lawsuits against them than of actual abuses. Porter attributes some of this fear to the complicated nature of the FMLA's provisions, which can make it difficult for the employers to understand or implement them (2014, 350–353).

24. S. 1896, 104th Cong. (1996).

25. Family and Medical Leave Expansion Act, S. 3141, 107th Cong. (2002).

26. Family Leave Insurance Act of 2007, S. 1681, 110th Cong. (2007).

27. 135 S. Ct. 2071 (2015).

28. Life-cycle squeeze occurs when the family's consumption goals are likely to exceed the family's resources. The squeeze is typically greatest in the beginning of the family life cycle when setting up a household and having children (see Glick 1947; Oppenheimer 1974).

29. The authors found that the generous parental leave policies and part-time mandates in many of the OECD countries also appear to encourage part-time work and employment in lower-level positions (Blau and Kahn 2013). However, the same pattern is unlikely to develop in the United States if universal paid family leave is adopted, because the benefits proposed by the FAMILY Act—twelve weeks at 66 percent of the employee's salary—are much less generous than those in most OECD states. Moreover, the states in the United States that have already passed paid family leave neither provide overly generous benefits nor have experienced such effects.

30. Some argue that women do not need to stay home to breast-feed because they can use a breast pump at work and take their milk home for the child. Although many women do this, it can be a difficult process, in part because employers often do not provide a private space to use the breast pump or discourage them from taking breaks to do so (Albelda and Mandell 2010).

31. Many Republicans still scoff at the suggestion that other countries that provide paid leave, such as those in Europe, have not suffered significant economic consequences as a result. For example, Representative Charlie Dent (R-PA) said, "I never thought that emulating the European economic model is good for America" (quoted in Marcos 2015).

32. The bill had first been introduced in December 2013 but did not make any progress.

33. Family and Medical Leave Insurance Act, S. 786/H.R. 1439, 114th Cong. (2015).

34. Federal employees receive thirteen days of sick leave per year, with no limit on how much they can accrue. In addition, they receive between thirteen and twenty-six days of annual leave, depending on the length of their federal service. Up to thirty days of annual leave may be carried over to the next leave year.

35. Federal Employees Paid Parental Leave Act of 2015, H.R. 532, 114th Cong. (2015).

36. Federal Employees Paid Parental Leave Act of 2015, S. 2033, 114th Cong. (2015).

37. Working Families Flexibility Act of 2015, H.R. 465, 114th Cong. (2015).

38. Government workers are already allowed to use their overtime toward paid time off (Marcos 2015).

Chapter 4

1. Washington State passed a paid parental leave bill in 2007; however, it was never implemented because of lack of a funding mechanism. In 2015, a completely

revamped bill with expanded coverage and benefits was introduced but has not passed. Therefore, I include Washington as a case study in Chapter 5.

2. For more detailed coverage of state legislative activity on family leave before 1993, see Wisensale 1989a, 1989b, 2001; Bernstein 2001.

3. Established in 1935, the Unemployment Insurance (UI) system is a federal-state program that provides benefits to unemployed workers who meet the requirements of their state's law. Although each state administers a separate UI program, guidelines are established at the federal level and the U.S. Department of Labor has oversight authority (U.S. Department of Labor 2015e).

4. Advocates of this model often point to Canada as an example. Since 1971, Canada has provided paid family leave through the federal government's Employment Insurance (EI) program, which is funded by mandatory employer and employee contributions (Trzcinski 2004).

5. The law that was passed in 2002 did not include care for a seriously ill grandparent, grandchild, sibling, or parent-in-law; SB 770 expanded the law to include them in 2013 (California State Legislature, n.d., "Senate Bill No. 770").

6. On April 11, 2016, Governor Jerry Brown signed into law AB 908, which will expand California's PFL program. Beginning in 2018, weekly benefits will increase from 55 percent of an employee's lost wages to either 60 percent or 70 percent, depending on income. The law will also eliminate the seven-day waiting period for workers taking PFL (Family Values @ Work 2016).

7. Although provisions under both are basically the same, the CFRA does not apply to pregnancy leave. After FMLA pregnancy leave allowances have been completed, CFRA does apply to parental leave for the care of the child (California Department of Fair Employment and Housing, n.d.). In 2015, the California legislature passed a bill that would expand job protection under the CFRA for workers who take leave to care for grandparents, grandchildren, siblings, and in-laws; Democratic governor Jerry Brown vetoed the bill (Siders 2015).

8. Jenya Cassidy, telephone interview by the author, November 22, 2011.

9. Maggie Cook, telephone interview by the author, November 22, 2011.

10. Carol Rosenblatt, telephone interview by the author, November 22, 2011.

11. Mary Bergan, telephone interview by the author, December 1, 2011.

12. Cathy Deppe, telephone interview by the author, December 1, 2011.

13. Cassidy, interview by the author.

14. The primary difference between the state and federal statutes lies in the employee taking leave for his or her own health. Although the FMLA provides leave for an employee because of the employee's own health condition, the NJFLA does not. Therefore, family leave can still be taken under NJFLA, even if medical leave under the FMLA is exhausted. Moreover, to qualify for NJFLA, an employee working for a firm with fifty or more employees must have worked a minimum of 1,000 hours in the previous year, rather than the 1,250 hours required by the FMLA (New Jersey Department of Law and Public Safety 2008).

15. Susan Waldman, telephone interview by the author, December 4, 2011.

16. Adrienne Lesser, telephone interview by the author, November 18, 2011.

17. Marion Johnson, telephone interview by the author, November 18, 2011.

18. Rhode Island also has its own Family and Medical Leave Act, which varies from the FMLA. Rhode Island's law provides thirteen consecutive weeks of leave within a two-year period to full-time employees working on average thirty or more hours per week for twelve consecutive months. The law applies to private employers with fifty or more employees; all state agencies; and any city, town, or municipal agency with thirty or more employees. Leave can be taken for the reasons listed in the FMLA, with the addition of care for parents-in-law (Rhode Island Department of Labor and Training, n.d., "Rhode Island Parental").

19. An employee can also take up to thirty weeks for his or her own disability, but combined benefits for disability and family care cannot exceed thirty weeks.

20. Gayle Goldin, telephone interview by the author, June 1, 2015.

21. Jenn Steinfeld, telephone interview by the author, May 29, 2015.

22. Goldin, interview by the author.

23. As his ancestors had done, Lincoln Chafee began his political career as a Republican. He left the GOP in 2007 and became governor of Rhode Island as in independent in 2010. In May 2013, two months before signing Rhode Island's paid family leave bill, Chafee joined the Democratic Party (Elving 2015).

24. Shanna Pearson-Merkowitz, telephone interview by the author, June 19, 2015.

25. Helen Mederer and Barbara Silver, telephone interview by the author, May 27, 2015.

26. Goldin, interview by the author.

27. Rachel-Lyn Longo, telephone interview by the author, July 9, 2015.

28. Pearson-Merkowitz, interview by the author.

29. Longo, interview by the author.

30. Sherry Leiwant, telephone interview by the author, May 12, 2015.

31. Goldin, interview by the author.

32. Leiwant, interview by the author, May 12, 2015.

33. Steinfeld, interview by the author.

34. Mederer and Silver, interview by the author.

35. Goldin, interview by the author.

36. Steinfeld, interview by the author.

37. Donna Dolan, telephone interview by the author, October 7, 2011.

38. Ibid.

39. Ibid.

40. Such confusion about the differences between paid family leave and paid sick days occurred in Hawaii in 2015, lessening the chances of passing legislation on either issue (see Chapter 5).

41. Sherry Leiwant, telephone interview by the author, November 22, 2011.

42. Marge Ives, telephone interview by the author, December 1, 2011.

43. Hannah Golden, telephone interview by the author, November 22, 2011.

44. Karen DeCrow, telephone interview by the author, November 22, 2011.

45. The paid family leave program adopted in 2016 does not include an increase in TDI; activists in New York continue to fight for the issue.

46. Donna Dolan, telephone interview by the author, May 4, 2015.

47. Ibid.

48. Donna Seymour, e-mail interview by the author, May 26, 2015.
49. Donna Seymour, telephone interview by the author, April 7, 2016.
50. Donna Dolan, telephone interview by the author, April 5, 2016.
51. Seymour, interview by the author, April 7, 2016.
52. Dolan, interview by the author, April 5, 2016.
53. Seymour, interview by the author, April 7, 2016.
54. In her coverage of New York's adoption of paid family leave, Rebecca Traister commented on the effect of men's promotion of the issue: "It seems worth noting that an issue that has been considered third-rail-feminist radicalism for decades, so improbable when it is described as 'maternity leave' that we wave it off as a pipe dream, can gain steam when political men—Barack Obama, Andrew Cuomo, Joe Biden—put their brawn behind it, and begin to describe the ways in which *men* might benefit. It's key to understanding how 'women's issues' can become, simply, issues" (Traister 2016; emphasis in original).

Chapter 5

1. Washington passed a paid parental leave bill in 2007; however, it never took effect because of lack of a funding mechanism. With little hope that the 2007 law will be implemented, most activists have focused their efforts on the passage of more comprehensive family leave legislation. In 2015, a completely revamped bill was introduced but has not passed; I focus on this most recent bill in this chapter.
2. It has since changed its name to the Washington Work and Family Coalition.
3. Marilyn Watkins, telephone interview by the author, September 16, 2011.
4. Lonnie Johns-Brown, e-mail interview by the author, November 24, 2011.
5. Margie Reeves, e-mail interview by the author, November 27, 2011.
6. Watkins, interview by the author, September 16, 2011.
7. Ibid.
8. The funding mechanism must first be approved by the state legislature; payments would begin two years after the plan passes.
9. Marilyn Watkins, telephone interview by the author, May 28, 2015.
10. Ibid.
11. The Washington State FLA provides benefits beyond those guaranteed by the FMLA. Under the FLA, a woman is entitled to time off for any disability related to pregnancy and childbirth, which includes the postpartum recovery period determined by her health-care provider, in addition to the twelve weeks of family leave under the state FLA or federal FMLA. If an employee qualifies for the FMLA and needs time off to care for a registered domestic partner with a serious health condition, the employee can use up to twelve weeks under the FLA and still have twelve weeks of leave available under the FMLA. Likewise, workers may still have access to the FLA after exhausting part of all of FMLA entitlement for a qualifying exigency leave (Washington State Department of Labor and Industries, n.d.).
12. The main difference between the OFLA and the FMLA is that the former applies to employers with twenty-five or more employees in the current or previous year; the latter's threshold is fifty employees. To qualify for most OFLA benefits, employees must have worked at least 180 calendar days and an average of twenty-

five hours a week; parental leave does not require a weekly average. The OFLA also extends leave to care for grandparents, grandchildren, parents-in-law, same-sex domestic partners, and children and parents of same-sex domestic partners (Oregon Secretary of State, n.d.).

13. Regan Gray, telephone interview by the author, September 30, 2011.

14. Ibid.

15. Ibid.

16. Regan Gray, telephone interview by the author, May 20, 2015.

17. Lisa Frack, telephone interview by the author, May 22, 2015.

18. Ibid.

19. Deb Fastino, telephone interview by the author, May 29, 2015.

20. Katie Prisco-Buxbaum, telephone interview by the author, May 29, 2015.

21. Patricia Comfort, telephone interview by the author, July 9, 2015.

22. Fastino, interview by the author.

23. Cathy Betts, telephone interview by the author, May 20, 2015.

24. Lisa Kimura, telephone interview by the author, May 18, 2015.

25. Shay Chan Hodges, telephone interview by the author, April 11, 2016.

26. Betts, interview by the author.

27. Kimura, interview by the author.

28. Shay Chan Hodges, telephone interview by the author, July 16, 2015.

29. Hodges, interview by the author, April 11, 2016.

Chapter 6

1. In 1998, the Women's Legal Defense Fund changed its name to National Partnership for Women and Families.

2. In May 2007, Washington State passed paid parental leave; however, the policy has not been implemented because the legislature has been unable to adopt a funding mechanism for it. After years of stalled progress, most paid leave advocates have abandoned the law in support of new legislation that is significantly wider in scope.

3. Two months after receiving almost $200,000 for the state's Commission on Aging and Disability to study paid family leave, Tennessee announced that it will give back the grant money. Jim Shulman, the commission's executive director, said that the grant focused too much on labor issues instead of caregiving. However, many believe that the motivation for returning the money was more political. Shortly before the commission's announcement, Republican representative Susan Lynn published an op-ed piece calling for the money to be returned because it was part of a larger effort to get states to adopt family leave policies that would be harmful to Tennessee (Covert 2015c).

4. On the surface, this seems like an extremely generous offer. However, without a clear signal from the company about how much leave it feels its employees should take, many new parents will be hesitant to use the full amount of leave available (Covert 2015d).

5. Ellen Bravo, telephone interview by the author, June 12, 2015.

6. Kristin Rowe-Finkbeiner, telephone interview by the author, May 28, 2015.

7. Donna Lenhoff, telephone interview by the author, November 13, 2015.
8. Linda Meric, telephone interview by the author, June 18, 2015.
9. Vicki Shabo, telephone interview by the author, November 25, 2015.
10. Valerie Young, telephone interview by the author, May 22, 2015.
11. Bravo, interview by the author.

References

A Better Balance. 2015. "Investing in Our Families: The Case for Paid Family Leave in New York and the Nation." Available at http://www.abetterbalance.org/web/images/stories/Documents/familyleave/PFL2015.pdf.

———. 2016. "Overview of the New York Paid Family Leave Program." Available at http://www.abetterbalance.org/web/images/stories/Documents/PFLNY.pdf.

Adams, Susan. 2015. "Why Netflix's and Microsoft's New Parental Leave Policies Fall Short of What Parents Need." *Forbes*, August 5. Available at http://www.forbes.com/sites/susanadams/2015/08/05/why-netflixs-and-microsofts-new-parental-leave-policies-fall-short-of-what-parents-need/#6444a5e992d5.

Addati, Laura, Naomi Cassirer, and Katherine Gilchrist. 2014. *Maternity and Paternity at Work: Law and Practice across the World*. Geneva: International Labour Organization.

Albelda, Randy, and Alan Clayton-Matthews. 2015. "Paid Leave Analysis Grant—Massachusetts, Final Memo." Available at http://www.dol.gov/wb/media/MA%20Final%20Policy%20Memo.pdf.

Albelda, Randy, and Betty Reid Mandell. 2010. "Paid Family and Medical Leave." *New Politics* 12 (4): 24–33.

Aldrich, John Herbert. 2011. *Why Parties? A Second Look*. Chicago: University of Chicago Press.

Alesina, Alberto, and Edward L. Glaeser. 2004. *Fighting Poverty in the U.S. and Europe: A World of Difference*. Oxford: Oxford University Press.

Alesina, Alberto, Edward Glaeser, and Bruce Sacerdote. 2001. "Why Doesn't the US Have a European-Style Welfare System?" National Bureau of Economic Research Working Paper 8524. Available at http://www.nber.org/papers/w8524.pdf.

Amenta, Edwin, Neal Caren, Elizabeth Chiarello, and Yang Su. 2010. "The Political Consequences of Social Movements." *Annual Review of Sociology* 36:287–307.

American Association of Retired Persons Public Policy Institute and National Alliance for Caregiving. 2015. "2015 Report: Caregiving in the U.S." Available at http://www.aarp.org/content/dam/aarp/ppi/2015/caregiving-in-the-united-states-2015-report-revised.pdf.

American Bar Association. 2015. "2015 Midwinter Meeting Report of 2014 Cases." Available at http://www.fmlainsights.com/wp-content/uploads/sites/311/2015/03/FMLA-decisions-ABA-2015.pdf.

"Americans' Views on Income Inequality and Workers' Rights." 2015. *New York Times*, June 3. Available at http://www.nytimes.com/interactive/2015/06/03/business/income-inequality-workers-rights-international-trade-poll.html.

Anthony, Deborah J. 2008. "The Hidden Harms of the Family and Medical Leave Act: Gender-Neutral versus Gender-Equal." *Journal of Gender, Social Policy and the Law* 16 (4): 459–501.

Appelbaum, Eileen, and Ruth Milkman. 2011. "Leaves That Pay: Employer and Worker Experiences with Paid Family Leave in California." Available at http://www.cepr.net/documents/publications/paid-family-leave-1-2011.pdf.

"Archives: FMLA." n.d. *Disability, Leave and Health Management Blog.* Available at http://www.disabilityleavelaw.com/articles/fmla/ (accessed May 13, 2015).

Armenia, Amy, and Naomi Gerstel. 2006. "Family Leave, the FMLA and Gender Neutrality: The Intersection of Race and Gender." *Social Science Research* 35:871–891.

Asher, Herbert B., Eric S. Heberlig, Randall B. Ripley, and Karen Snyder. 2001. *American Labor Unions in the Electoral Arena.* Lanham, MD: Rowman and Littlefield.

Asher, Lauren J., and Donna R. Lenhoff. 2001. "Family and Medical Leave: Making Time for Family Is Everyone's Business." *Caring for Infants and Toddlers* 11 (1): 115–121.

Ashley, Laura, and Beth Olson. 1998. "Constructing Reality: Print Media's Framing of the Women's Movement, 1966 to 1986." *Journalism and Mass Communication Quarterly* 75 (2): 263–277.

Associated Press. 2008. "New Jersey Lawmakers Approve Paid Leave for Workers." *New York Times*, April 8. Available at http://www.nytimes.com/2008/04/08/nyregion/08leave.html.

Association of Flight Attendants-CWA. n.d. "FMLA Must Be Clarified to Cover Full Time Flight Attendants." Available at http://files.cwa-union.org/national/issues/osh/afafmla.pdf (accessed February 17, 2016).

Auerbach, Judith D. 1990. "Employer-Supported Child Care as a Woman-Responsive Policy." *Journal of Family Issues* 11 (4): 384–400.

Aumann, Kerstin, Ellen Galinsky, Kelly Sakai, Melissa Brown, and James T. Bond. 2010. "The Elder Care Study: Everyday Realities and Wishes for Change." Families and Work Institute. Available at http://familiesandwork.org/downloads/TheElderCareStudy.pdf.

Auray, Lori. 1994. "A Cost-Shifting Amendment to the Family and Medical Leave Act of 1993: How to Improve upon a Good Thing." *Texas Journal of Women and the Law* 3:403–416.

Avdeyeva, Olga. 2010. "States' Compliance with International Requirements: Gender Equality in EU Enlargement Countries." *Political Research Quarterly* 63 (1): 203–217.

Ayanna, Ariel Meysam. 2007. "Aggressive Parental Leave: A Statutory Proposal toward Gender Equalization in the Workplace." *University of Pennsylvania Journal of Labor and Employment Law* 9:293–324.

Badger, Emily. 2014. "That One Time America Almost Got Universal Child Care." *Washington Post*, June 23. Available at https://www.washingtonpost.com/news/wonk/wp/2014/06/23/that-one-time-america-almost-got-universal-child-care/.

Baird, Chardie L., and John R. Reynolds. 2004. "Employee Awareness of Family Leave Benefits: The Effects of Family, Work, and Gender." *Sociological Quarterly* 45 (2): 325–353.

Baker, Susan. 1999. "Risking Difference: Reconceptualizing the Boundaries between the Public and Private Spheres." In *Women and Public Policy: The Shifting Boundaries between the Public and Private Spheres*, edited by Susan Baker and Anneke van Doorne-Huiskes, 3–31. Brookfield, VT: Ashgate.

Bakst, Dina. 2016. "Leading on Leave in the Empire State." *U.S. News and World Report*, February 9. Available at http://www.usnews.com/opinion/economic-intelligence/articles/2016-02-09/new-yorks-paid-family-leave-proposal-sets-a-strong-example-for-the-nation.

Baldez, Lisa. 2001. *Why Women Protest: Women's Movements in Chile*. New York: Cambridge University Press.

Banaszak, Lee Ann. 1996. *Why Movements Succeed or Fail: Opportunity, Culture, and the Struggle for Woman Suffrage*. Princeton, NJ: Princeton University Press.

———. 2003. "The Women's Movement Policy Successes and the Constraints of State Reconfiguration." In *Women's Movements Facing the Reconfigured State*, edited by Lee Ann Banaszak, Karen Beckwith, and Dieter Rucht, 141–168. New York: Cambridge University Press.

Banaszak, Lee Ann, Karen Beckwith, and Dieter Rucht. 2003. "When Power Relocates: Interactive Changes in Women's Movements and States." In *Women's Movements Facing the Reconfigured State*, edited by Lee Ann Banaszak, Karen Beckwith, and Dieter Rucht, 1–29. New York: Cambridge University Press.

Barakso, Maryann. 2004. *Governing NOW: Grassroots Activism in the National Organization for Women*. Ithaca, NY: Cornell University Press.

Bardasi, Elena, and Janet C. Gornick. 2000. "Women and Part-Time Employment: Workers' 'Choices' and Wage Penalties in Five Industrialized Countries." Luxembourg Income Study Working Paper No. 223. Available at http://www.lisdatacenter.org/wps/liswps/223.pdf.

Bartel, Ann, Charles Baum, Maya Rossin-Slater, Christopher Ruhm, and Jane Waldfogel. 2014. "California's Paid Family Leave Law: Lessons from the

First Decade." Available at http://www.dol.gov/asp/evaluation/reports/PaidLeaveDeliverable.pdf.

Bartlett, Jessica. 2015. "Boston's Paid Parental Leave to Get Statewide Look." *Boston Business Journal*, May 4. Available at http://www.bizjournals.com/boston/blog/health-care/2015/05/bostons-paid-parental-leave-to-get-statewide-look.html.

Bashevkin, Sylvia. 1998. *Women on the Defensive: Living through Conservative Times*. Chicago: University of Chicago Press.

Baum, Charles L., and Christopher J. Ruhm. 2013. "The Effects of Paid Family Leave in California on Labor Market Outcomes." National Bureau of Economic Research Working Paper No. 19741.

Beckwith, Karen. 2003. "The Gendering Ways of States: Women's Representation and State Reconfiguration in France, Great Britain, and the United States." In *Women's Movements Facing the Reconfigured State*, edited by Lee Ann Banaszak, Karen Beckwith, and Dieter Rucht, 169–202. New York: Cambridge University Press.

Beekman, Daniel. 2015a. "King County OKs Paid Parental Leave for Some Employees." *Seattle Times*, December 8. Available at http://www.seattletimes.com/seattle-news/politics/king-county-oks-paid-parental-leave-for-some-employees/.

———. 2015b. "Seattle Council Approves Paid Parental Leave for City Workers." *Seattle Times*, April 13. Available at http://www.seattletimes.com/seattle-news/politics/seattle-council-approves-paid-parental-leave-for-city-workers.

Belkin, Lisa. 2009. "The Senator Track: Why Caroline's 'Experience' Counts." *New York Times Magazine*, January 4, pp. 9–10.

Bell, Lissa, and Sandra Newman. 2003. "Paid Family and Medical Leave: Why We Need It, How We Can Get It." Available at http://www.caregiver.org/jsp/content/pdfs/op_2003_paid_family_medical_leave.pdf.

Bellstrom, Kristen. 2016a. "Coca-Cola Credits Millennials for Its Extended Paid Parental Leave Policy." *Fortune*, April 11. Available at http://fortune.com/2016/04/11/coca-cola-parental-leave-policy/.

———. 2016b. "EY Comes Out Swinging at Other Consulting Firms with New Parental Leave Policy." *Fortune*, April 13. Available at http://fortune.com/2016/04/13/ey-parental-leave-policy/.

Benford, Robert D., and David A. Snow. 2000. "Framing Processes and Social Movements: An Overview and Assessment." *Annual Review of Sociology* 26:611–639.

Berger, Lawrence M., Jennifer Hill, and Jane Waldfogel. 2005. "Maternity Leave, Early Maternal Employment and Child Health and Development in the U.S." *Economic Journal* 115 (501): F29–F47.

Bernstein, Anya. 2001. *The Moderation Dilemma: Legislative Coalitions and the Politics of Family and Medical Leave*. Pittsburgh, PA: University of Pittsburgh Press.

Bianchi, Suzanne M., Liana C. Sayer, Melissa A. Milkie, and John P. Robinson. 2012. "Housework: Who Did, Does or Will Do It, and How Much Does It Matter?" *Social Forces* 91 (1): 55–63.

Blaise, Andre, Donald Blake, and Stephane Dion. 1996. "Do Parties Make a Difference? A Reappraisal." *American Journal of Political Science* 40 (2): 514–520.

Blau, Francine D., Marianne A. Ferber, and Anne E. Winkler. 2002. *The Economics of Women, Men, and Work.* Upper Saddle River, NJ: Prentice Hall.

Blau, Francine D., and Lawrence M. Kahn. 2013. "Female Labor Supply: Why Is the United States Falling Behind?" *American Economic Review* 103 (3): 251–256.

Boles, Janet K. 1991. "Form Follows Function: The Evolution of Feminist Strategies." *Annals of the American Academy of Political and Social Science* 515:38–49.

Born, Molly. 2015. "Allegheny County to Offer Six Weeks of Parental Leave to Employees." *Pittsburgh Post-Gazette*, February 24. Available at http://www.post-gazette.com/local/region/2015/02/24/Allegheny-County-to-offer-six-weeks-of-parental-leve/stories/201502240160.

Bornstein, Lisa. 2000. "Inclusions and Exclusions in Work-Family Policy: The Public Values and Moral Code Embedded in the Family and Medical Leave Act." *Columbia Journal of Gender and Law* 10:77–124.

Boushey, Heather, Jane Farrell, and John Schmitt. 2013. "Job Protection Isn't Enough: Why America Needs Paid Parental Leave." Center for American Progress, December. Available at https://cdn.americanprogress.org/wp-content/uploads/2013/12/ParentalLeave-report-updated-2.pdf.

Boushey, Heather, and Alexandra Mitukiewicz. 2014. "Family and Medical Leave Insurance: A Basic Standard for Today's Workforce." Center for American Progress, April 15. Available at https://www.americanprogress.org/issues/labor/report/2014/04/15/87652/family-and-medical-leave-insurance.

Boyd, Susan B., ed. 1997. *Challenging the Public/Private Divide: Feminism, Law, and Public Policy.* Buffalo, NY: University of Toronto Press.

Brandth, Berit, and Elin Kvande. 2009. "Gendered or Gender-Neutral Care Politics for Fathers?" *Annals of the American Academy of Political and Social Science* 624:177–189.

Bravo, Ellen. 2013. "Rhode Island Becomes the Third State with Paid Family Leave." *Huffington Post*, July 4. Available at http://www.huffingtonpost.com/ellen-bravo/rhode-island-paid-family-leave_b_3543124.html.

Briskin, Linda. 1999. "Mapping Women's Organizing in Sweden and Canada: Some Thematic Considerations." In *Women's Organizing and Public Policy in Canada and Sweden*, edited by Linda Briskin and Mona Eliasson, 3–47. Montreal: McGill-Queen's University Press.

Bronfenbrenner, Urie. 1979. *The Ecology of Human Development: Experiments by Nature and Design.* Cambridge, MA: Harvard University Press.

Brown, Melissa. 2010. "The 'State' of Paid Family Leave: Insights from the 2006 and 2007 Legislative Sessions." In *Innovations in Child and Family Policy: Multidisciplinary Research and Perspectives on Strengthening Children and Their Families*, edited by Emily M. Douglas, 191–210. Lanham, MD: Lexington Books.

Bruinius, Harry. 2016. "Why Cities and States Are Taking the Lead on Paid Family Leave." *Christian Science Monitor*, January 14. Available at http://www.csmonitor.com/USA/Politics/2016/0114/Why-cities-and-states-are-taking-lead-on-paid-family-leave.

Brunell, Don. 2007. "Paid Family Leave Threatens Washington Employers." *Puget Sound Business Journal*, April 8. Available at http://www.bizjournals.com/seattle/stories/2007/04/09/editorial5.html.

Bruning, Gwennaële, and Janneke Plantenga. 1999. "Parental Leave and Equal Opportunities: Experiences in Eight European Countries." *Journal of European Social Policy* 9 (3): 195–209.

Budig, Michelle J., and Paula England. 2001. "The Wage Penalty for Motherhood." *American Sociological Review* 66 (2): 204–225.

Burstein, Paul. 2003. "The Impact of Public Opinion on Public Policy: A Review and an Agenda." *Political Research Quarterly* 56 (1): 29–40.

Burstein, Paul, R. Marie Bricher, and Rachel L. Einwohner. 1995. "Policy Alternatives and Political Change: Work, Family, and Gender on the Congressional Agenda, 1945–1990." *American Sociological Review* 60 (1): 67–83.

Burstein, Paul, and April Linton. 2002. "The Impact of Political Parties, Interest Groups, and Social Movement Organizations on Public Policy: Some Recent Evidence and Theoretical Concerns." *Social Forces* 81 (2): 381–408.

Bushatz, Amy. 2016. "Lawmaker Proposes Bill to Expand Military Paternity Leave to 12 Weeks." *Military.com*, March 22. Available at http://www.military.com/daily-news/2016/03/22/lawmaker-proposes-bill-expand-military-paternity-leave-12-weeks.html.

Business Council of New York State. 2008. "Business Council Launches Electronic Advocacy Campaign on Paid Family Leave." Available at http://www.bcnys.org/whatsnew/2008/052108PFLeadvocacy.htm.

Butts, Cassandra Q. 2004. "Marching on for Equal Pay." Center for American Progress, May 7. Available at https://www.americanprogress.org/issues/women/news/2004/05/07/766/marching-on-for-equal-pay/.

Cabrera, Natasha J., Jacqueline D. Shannon, and Catherine Tamis-LeMonda. 2007. "Fathers' Influence on Their Children's Cognitive and Emotional Development: From Toddlers to Pre-K." *Applied Developmental Science* 11 (4): 208–213.

Caiazza, Amy. 2004. "Does Women's Representation in Elected Office Lead to Women-Friendly Policy? Analysis of State-Level Data." *Women and Politics* 26 (1): 35–70.

California Department of Fair Employment and Housing. n.d. "California Family Rights Act (CFRA)." Available at http://www.dfeh.ca.gov/Publications_CFRADefined.htm (accessed May 7, 2014).

California Employment Development Department. n.d. "State Disability Insurance Frequently Asked Questions." Available at http://www.edd.ca.gov/Disability/Faqs.htm (accessed March 25, 2016).

California State Legislature. n.d. "Complete Bill History." Available at http://www.leginfo.ca.gov/pub/01-02/bill/sen/sb_1651-1700/sb_1661_bill_20020926_history.html (accessed April 6, 2016).

———. n.d. "Senate Bill No. 770." Available at http://leginfo.legislature.ca.gov/faces/billTextClient.xhtml?bill_id=201320140SB770 (accessed April 11, 2016).

Cannonier, Colin. 2014. "Does the Family and Medical Leave Act (FMLA) Increase Fertility Behavior?" *Journal of Labor Research* 35:105–132.

Cantor, David, Jane Waldfogel, Jeff Kerwin, Mareena McKinley Wright, Kerry Levin, John Rauch, Tracey Hagerty, and Martha Stapleton Kudela. 2001. *Balancing the Needs of Families and Employers: Family and Medical Leave Surveys, 2000 Update; A Report.* Washington, DC: U.S. Department of Labor.

Carlson, Allan C. 1990. *The Swedish Experiment in Family Politics: The Myrdals and the Interwar Population Crisis.* New Brunswick, NJ: Transaction.

Carroll, Susan J. 2001. "Representing Women: Women State Legislators as Agents of Policy-Related Change." In *The Impact of Women in Public Office*, edited by Susan J. Carroll, 3–21. Bloomington: Indiana University Press.

———. 2006. "Are Women Legislators Accountable to Women? The Complementary Roles of Feminist Identity and Women's Organizations." In *Gender and Social Capital*, edited by Brenda O'Neill and Elisabeth Gidengil, 357–378. New York: Routledge.

Catlett, Beth Skilken, and Patrick C. McHenry. 2004. "Class-Based Masculinities: Divorce, Fatherhood, and the Hegemonic Ideal." *Fathering: A Journal of Theory, Research, and Practice about Men as Fathers* 2 (2): 165–190.

Cauterucci, Christina. 2015. "All Washington, D.C., Residents May Get 16 Weeks of Paid Family Leave." *Slate*, October 6. Available at http://www.slate.com/blogs/xx_factor/2015/10/06/washington_d_c_residents_may_get_16_weeks_of_paid_family_leave.html.

Cavarero, Adriana. 1992. "Equality and Sexual Difference: Amnesia in Political Thought." In *Beyond Equality and Difference: Citizenship, Feminist Politics, and Female Subjectivity*, edited by Gisela Bock and Susan James, 32–47. New York: Routledge.

Center for State Innovation. 2008. "Paid Family and Medical Leave: Promoting Family Values through Workplace Flexibility." Available at https://www.dropbox.com/s/w3ky1vjnbhpy8s9/Paid_Family_and_Medical_Leave.pdf.

Chatterji, Pinka, and Sara Markowitz. 2012. "Family Leave after Childbirth and the Mental Health of New Mothers." *Journal of Mental Health Policy and Economics* 15 (2): 61–76.

Childs, Sarah, and Mona Lena Krook. 2006. "Should Feminists Give Up on Critical Mass? A Contingent Yes." *Politics and Gender* 2 (4): 522–530.

Chodorow, Nancy, Dierdre English, Arlie Hochschild, Karen Paige, Lillian Rubin, Ann Swindler, and Norma Wikler. 1984. "Feminism 1984: Taking Stock on the Brink of an Uncertain Future." *Ms.*, January, p. 102.

Clausen, Todd. 2015. "Paid Family Leave Poised for Big Debate." *Democrat and Chronicle*, April 20. Available at http://www.democratandchronicle.com/story/money/business/2015/04/16/paid-family-leave-movements/25891009/#.

Clinton, William J. 1999. "Memorandum on New Tools to Help Parents Balance Work and Family." *Weekly Compilation of Presidential Documents* 35 (21): 978–979. Available at https://www.gpo.gov/fdsys/pkg/WCPD-1999-05-31/pdf/WCPD-1999-05-31-Pg978-2.pdf.

Clymer, Adam. 1992a. "Democrats Promise Quick Action on a Clinton Plan." *New York Times*, November 5, p. B6.

Coalition for Social Justice. n.d. "Paid Family Medical Leave." Available at http://coalitionforsocialjustice.org/index.php/paid-family-medical-leave (accessed May 7, 2015).

Cobb, Roger W., and Charles D. Elder. 1972. *Participation in American Politics: The Dynamics of Agenda Building*. Baltimore: Johns Hopkins University Press.

Collier, David. 2011. "Understanding Process Tracing." *PS: Political Science and Politics* 44 (4): 823–830.

Coltrane, Scott. 1996. *Family Man: Fatherhood, Housework, and Gender Equity*. New York: Oxford University Press.

Commission on Family and Medical Leave. 1996. *A Workable Balance: Report to Congress on Family and Medical Leave Policies*. Washington, DC: U.S. Department of Labor.

Conway, M. Margaret, David W. Ahern, and Gertrude A. Steuernagel. 2005. *Women and Public Policy: A Revolution in Progress*. 3rd ed. Washington, DC: CQ Press.

Coppola, Sarah. 2013. "City of Austin Will Offer Paid Parental Leave." *Austin American-Statesman*, June 6. Available at http://www.mystatesman.com/news/news/local/city-of-austin-will-offer-paid-parental-leave/nYD5R.

Costain, Anne N. 1992. *Inviting Women's Rebellion: A Political Process Interpretation of the Women's Movement*. Baltimore: Johns Hopkins University Press.

———. 1998. "Women Lobby Congress." In *Social Movements and American Political Institutions*, edited by Anne N. Costain and Andrew S. McFarland, 171–184. Lanham, MD: Rowman and Littlefield.

Covert, Bryce. 2014. "These Workers Are Now among the Lucky Few Who Can Take Paid Time Off When They Have a Baby." *ThinkProgress*, October 1. Available at http://thinkprogress.org/economy/2014/10/01/3574251/dc-paid-family-leave.

———. 2015a. "How This Major Tech Company Plans to Attract More Female Workers." *ThinkProgress*, January 17. Available at http://thinkprogress.org/economy/2015/01/17/3612837/intel-family-leave/.

———. 2015b. "The Politics of Paid Time Off to Have a Baby." *New York Times*, November 23. Available at http://www.nytimes.com/2015/11/23/opinion/campaign-stops/the-politics-of-paid-time-off-to-have-a-baby.html.

———. 2015c. "State Gives Back Government Money to Study Paid Leave, Says Leave Isn't about Caregiving." *ThinkProgress*, December 2. Available at http://thinkprogress.org/economy/2015/12/02/3725511/tennessee-paid-leave-grant/.

———. 2015d. "Why Spotify's Family Leave Policy Is Actually More Generous than Netflix's." *ThinkProgress*, November 19. Available at http://thinkprogress.org/economy/2015/11/19/3724126/spotify-paid-leave/.

———. 2016. "While Congress Stalls, the Country Has Now Passed 30 Paid Sick Leave Laws." *ThinkProgress*, March 15. Available at http://thinkprogress.org/economy/2016/03/15/3760166/plainfield-paid-sick-leave/.

Crittenden, Ann. 2001. *The Price of Motherhood: Why the Most Important Job in the World Is Still the Least Valued*. New York: Metropolitan Books.

Crockett, Emily. 2016. "America Should Follow Silicon Valley's Lead on Paid Parental Leave." *Vox*, January 12. Available at http://www.vox.com/2015/11/24/9791594/spotify-amazon-paid-leave.

Crosby, Jackie. 2016. "Wells Fargo among Latest Companies to Offer Paid Leave for New Parents." *Star Tribune*, April 13. Available at http://www.startribune.com/wells-fargo-among-latest-companies-to-offer-paid-leave-for-new-parents/375621951/.

Crow, Nick. 2015. "Group Posts Billboards Protesting Paul Ryan's Stance on Family Leave." *GazetteXtra*, November 23. Available at http://www.gazette xtra.com/20151123/group_posts_billboards_protesting_paul_ryans_stance _on_family_leave.

Cummins, Jeff. 2011. "Party Control, Policy Reforms, and the Impact on Health Insurance Coverage in the U.S. States." *Social Science Quarterly* 92 (1): 246–267.

Cuomo, Andrew. 2010. *The New NY Agenda: A Plan for Action*. Available at http:// s3.documentcloud.org/documents/7206/the-new-ny-agenda.pdf.

Dahlerup, Drude. 1986. *The New Women's Movement: Feminism and Political Power in Europe and the U.S.A.* Beverly Hills, CA: Sage.

———. 1988. "From a Small to a Large Minority: Women in Scandinavian Politics." *Scandinavian Political Studies* 11 (4): 275–298.

Daku, Mark, Amy Raub, and Jody Heymann. 2012. "Maternal Leave Policies and Vaccination Coverage: A Global Analysis." *Social Science and Medicine* 74 (2): 120–124.

Damme, Lauren. 2011. "Paid Family Leave: What Could a Federal Paid Leave Insurance Program Look Like?" Washington, DC: New America Foundation.

Dark, Taylor E. 1999. *The Unions and the Democrats: An Enduring Alliance*. Ithaca, NY: ILR Press.

Davis, Aaron. 2016. "Can D.C. Afford 16 Weeks of Paid Leave for Workers? That Depends." *Washington Post*, January 14. Available at https://www.washington post.com/local/dc-politics/can-dc-afford-to-give-all-workers-16-weeks-of -paid-family-leave-depends-on-whom-you-ask/2016/01/14/b7641218-ba36 -11e5-99f3-184bc379b12d_story.html.

Davis, Flora. 1991. *Moving the Mountain: The Women's Movement in America since 1960*. New York: Simon and Schuster.

Day, Matt. 2015. "Microsoft Boosts Paid Leave for New Parents." *Seattle Times*, August 5. Available at http://www.seattletimes.com/business/microsoft -boosts-paid-leave-for-new-parents/.

Day, Shelagh, and Gwen Brodsky. 1998. *Women and the Equality Deficit: The Impact of Restructuring Canada's Social Programs*. Ottawa: Status of Women Canada, Policy Research.

Dell'Antonia, K. J. 2015. "The White House and Paid Leave: Let Flowers Bloom." *New York Times*, March 30. Available at http://parenting.blogs.nytimes .com/2015/03/30/the-white-house-and-paid-leave-let-flowers-bloom/.

Deluca, Matthew. 2016. "Etsy Now Offers More than Six Months of Paid Parental Leave." *NBC News*, March 16. Available at http://www.nbcnews.com/busi ness/business-news/etsy-now-offers-more-six-months-paid-parental-leave -n540176.

Diani, Mario. 1992. "The Concept of Social Movement." *Sociological Review* 40 (1): 1–25.

Dittmar, Kelly. 2008. "A Seat at the Table: The Influence of Women's Political Representation on States' Paid Leave Policy Development." Paper presented at the Eighth Annual State Politics and Policy Conference, Philadelphia, PA, May 30–31.

Dodson, Debra L. 2006. *The Impact of Women in Congress*. New York: Oxford University Press.

Dolan, Donna. 2007. Statement to the New York State Senate, Committee on Labor, June 5. Available at http://timetocareny.org/wp/wp-content/uploads/2013/12/Donna_testimony_revised.doc.

Dorfman, Lori, and Elena O. Lingas. 2003. "Issue 14: Making the Case for Paid Family Leave: How California's Landmark Law Was Framed in the News." Berkeley Media Studies Group, November 1. Available at http://www.bmsg.org/resources/publications/issue-14-making-the-case-for-paid-family-leave.

Drago, Robert. 2011. "What Would They Do? Childcare under Parental Leave and Reduced Hours Options." *Industrial Relations: A Journal of Economy and Society* 50 (4): 610–628.

Dries, Kate. 2011. "City of Chicago Announces Paid Maternity Leave for Workers." WBEZ, September 7. Available at http://www.wbez.org/story/city-chicago-announces-paid-maternity-leave-workers-91641.

Dube, Arindrajit, and Ethan Kaplan. 2002. "Paid Family Leave in California: An Analysis of Costs and Benefits." Available at http://www.paidfamilyleave.org/pdf/dube.pdf.

Eagleton Institute of Politics. 2006. "Summary of Poll Results on Family Leave Insurance." Available at http://njtimetocare.com/sites/default/files/11_Eagleton%20Institute%20of%20Politics%20Poll%20on%20Family%20Leave%20Insurance.pdf.

Economic Opportunity Institute. 2007. "New Poll Shows Strong Support for Family Leave Insurance: State Task Force Encouraged by Results." September 26. Available at http://www.eoionline.org/newsroom/new-poll-shows-strong-support-for-family-leave-insurance-state-task-force-encouraged-by-results/.

Edds, Kimberly. 2002. "California Adopts Family Leave; Law Mandates Paid Time Off." *Washington Post*, September 24, p. A03.

Eisenstein, Hester. 1990. "Femocrats, Official Feminism, and the Uses of Power." In *Playing the State: Australian Feminist Interventions*, edited by Sophie Watson, 87–103. New York: Verso Press.

———. 1996. *Inside Agitators: Australian Femocrats and the State*. Philadelphia: Temple University Press.

Elison, Sonja Klueck. 1997. "Policy Innovation in a Cold Climate: The Family and Medical Leave Act of 1993." *Journal of Family Issues* 18 (1): 30–54.

Elving, Ronald D. 1995. *Conflict and Compromise: How Congress Makes the Law*. New York: Simon and Schuster.

———. 2015. "5 Things You Should Know about Lincoln Chafee." *NPR*, June 3. Available at http://www.npr.org/sections/itsallpolitics/2015/06/03/411327420/5-things-you-should-know-about-lincoln-chafee.

Erickson, Jan. 2003. "Conservatives Pick the Pockets of Most Vulnerable in the U.S." *National NOW Times*, Fall, 11.

Esping-Andersen, Gøsta. 1990. *The Three Worlds of Welfare Capitalism*. Princeton, NJ: Princeton University Press.

Evans, Monica. 2015. "New Provision Will Soon Entitle City Employees to Paid Parental Leave." Fox4, August 25. Available at http://fox4kc.com/2015/08/25/new-provision-will-soon-entitle-city-employees-to-paid-parental-leave/.

Evans, Sara, and Barbara J. Nelson. 1989. *Wage Justice: Comparable Worth and the Paradox of Technocratic Reform.* Chicago: University of Chicago Press.

Executive Office of the President. 2015. "Presidential Memorandum: Modernizing Federal Leave Policies for Childbirth, Adoption and Foster Care to Recruit and Retain Talent and Improve Productivity." *Federal Register* 80 (13): 3135–3137.

Fairchild, Caroline. 2014. "Change.org Boosts Paid Parental Leave Perks for All New Parents." *Fortune,* October 20. Available at http://fortune.com/2014/10/20/paid-parental-leave-tech-companies/.

Faludi, Susan. 1991. *Backlash: The Undeclared War against American Women.* New York: Crown.

Family Values @ Work. n.d. "About Us." Available at http://familyvaluesatwork.org/about-us (accessed April 14, 2016).

———. 2016. "Governor Brown Signs Historic Expansion of California's Paid Family Leave." Available at http://familyvaluesatwork.org/media-center/press-release/ca-paid-leave-expansion.

Farnitano, Andrew. 2015. "Personal Stories Make Clear the Need for Paid Family and Medical Leave in Massachusetts." Raise Up Massachusetts, October. Available at http://raiseupma.org/2015/10/27/press-release-personal-stories-make-clear-the-need-for-paid-family-and-medical-leave-in-massachusetts/.

Fass, Sarah. 2009. "Paid Leave in the States: A Critical Support for Low-Wage Workers and Their Families." National Center for Children in Poverty. Available at http://www.nccp.org/publications/pub_864.html.

"Feminist Leaders Plan Coalition for Law Aiding Pregnant Women." 1976. *New York Times,* December 15, p. 40.

Ferree, Myra Marx, William A. Gamson, Jürgen Gerhards, and Dieter Rucht. 2002. *Shaping Abortion Discourse: Democracy and the Public Sphere in Germany and the United States.* New York: Cambridge University Press.

Ferree, Myra Marx, and Beth B. Hess. 2000. *Controversy and Coalition: The New Feminist Movement across Three Decades of Change.* 3rd ed. New York: Routledge.

Ferree, Myra Marx, and Carol McClurg Mueller. 2004. "Feminism and the Women's Movement: A Global Perspective." In *The Blackwell Companion to Social Movements,* edited by David A. Snow, Sarah A. Soule, and Hanspeter Kriesi, 576–607. Malden, MA: Blackwell.

Fine, Terri Susan. 2006. "The Family and Medical Leave Law: Feminist Social Policy?" *Journal of Policy Practice* 5 (1): 49–66.

Finley, Lucinda M. 1986. "Transcending Equality Theory: A Way Out of the Maternity and the Workplace Debate." *Columbia Law Review* 86 (6): 1118–1182.

Fitzgerald, Wendy A. 1988. "Toward Dignity in the Workplace: *Miller-Wohl* and Beyond." *Montana Law Review* 49 (1): 147–180.

Flora, Peter, and Arnold J. Heidenheimer. 1981. *The Development of Welfare States in Europe and America.* New Brunswick, NJ: Transaction.

Frago, Charlie. 2014. "St. Petersburg Announces Parental Leave Benefit." *Tampa Bay Times,* December 17. Available at http://www.tampabay.com/blogs/bay buzz/st-petersburg-announces-parental-leave-benefit/2210539.

Francia, Peter L. 2006. *The Future of Organized Labor in American Politics*. New York: Columbia University Press.

Frank, Meryl, and Robyn Lipner. 1988. "History of Maternity Leave in Europe and the United States." In *The Parental Leave Crisis: Toward a National Policy*, edited by Edward F. Zigler and Meryl Frank, 3–22. New Haven, CT: Yale University Press.

Fredman, Sandra. 2003. "Beyond the Dichotomy of Formal and Substantive Equality: Towards a New Definition of Equal Rights." In *Temporary Special Measures: Accelerating de Facto Equality of Women under Article 4(1) UN Convention on the Elimination of All Forms of Discrimination against Women*, edited by Ineke Boerefijn, 111–118. New York: Intersensia.

Freedman, Johanna. 1988. "The Changing Composition of the Family and the Workplace." In *The Parental Leave Crisis: Toward a National Policy*, edited by Edward F. Zigler and Meryl Frank, 23–35. New Haven, CT: Yale University Press.

Freeman, Jo. 1991. "How 'Sex' Got into Title VII: Persistent Opportunism as a Maker of Public Policy." *Law and Inequality: A Journal of Theory and Practice* 9 (2): 163–184.

Friedman, Dana E. 1990. "Corporate Responses to Family Needs." *Marriage and Family Review* 15 (1–2): 77–98.

Frolik, Cornelius. 2015. "Dayton First Major Ohio City to Offer Paid Parental Leave." *Dayton Daily News*, August 26. Available at http://www.mydaytondailynews .com/news/news/local/dayton-to-offer-paid-parental-leave/nnRM5/.

Fuller, Thomas. 2016. "San Francisco Approves Fully Paid Parental Leave." *New York Times*, April 5. Available at http://www.nytimes.com/2016/04/06/us/san -francisco-approves-fully-paid-parental-leave.html.

Gale, Rebecca. 2015. "5 Things You Should Know about D.C.'s Proposed Paid Leave." *Roll Call*, October 28. Available at http://www.rollcall.com/news/ policy/five-things-federal-workers-know-dcs-proposed-paid-leave-plan.

Galinsky, Ellen, Kerstin Aumann, and James T. Bond. 2011. "Times Are Changing: Gender and Generation at Work and at Home." Families and Work Institute, August. Available at http://familiesandwork.org/downloads/Times AreChanging.pdf.

Gallagher, Sally K., and Naomi Gerstel. 2001. "Connections and Constraints: The Effects of Children and Caregiving." *Journal of Marriage and Family* 63 (1): 265–275.

Gatta, Mary L., and Patricia A. Roos. 2004. "Balancing without a Net in Academia: Integrating Family and Work Lives." *Equal Opportunities International* 23 (3–5): 124–142.

Gauthier, Anne Hélène. 1996. *The State and the Family: A Comparative Analysis of Family Policies in Industrialized Countries*. New York: Oxford University Press.

Gelb, Joyce. 1989. *Feminism and Politics: A Comparative Perspective*. Berkeley: University of California Press.

Gelb, Joyce, and Marian Lief Palley. 1987. *Women and Public Policies*. Princeton, NJ: Princeton University Press.

George, Alexander L., and Andrew Bennett. 2005. *Case Studies and Theory Development in the Social Sciences.* Cambridge, MA: MIT Press.

George, Alexander L., and Timothy J. McKeown. 1985. "Case Studies and Theories of Organizational Decision Making." In *Advances in Information Processing in Organizations*, vol. 2, edited by Robert F. Coulam and Richard A. Smith, 21–58. Greenwich, CT: JAI Press.

Gerstel, Naomi. 2000. "The Third Shift: Gender and Care Work Outside the Home." *Qualitative Sociology* 23 (4): 467–483.

Gerstel, Naomi, and Sally Gallagher. 1994. "Caring for Kith and Kin: Gender, Employment, and the Privatization of Care." *Social Problems* 41 (4): 519–539.

Gerstel, Naomi, and Katherine McGonagle. 1999. "Job Leaves and the Limits of the Family and Medical Leave Act: The Effects of Gender, Race, and Family." *Work and Occupations* 26 (4): 510–534.

Gilens, Martin. 1999. *Why Americans Hate Welfare: Race, Media, and the Politics of Antipoverty Policy.* Chicago: University of Chicago Press.

Gillett, Rachel. 2015. "Facebook Is at the Forefront of a Radical Workplace Shift—and Every Business in America Should Take Notice." *Business Insider*, August 19. Available at http://www.businessinsider.com/facebook-parental-leave -policy-2015-8.

Glass, Jennifer L., and Sarah Beth Estes. 1997. "The Family Responsive Workplace." *Annual Review of Sociology* 23:289–313.

Glauber, Rebecca. 2007. "Marriage and the Motherhood Wage Penalty among African Americans, Hispanic, and Whites." *Journal of Marriage and Family* 69 (4): 951–961.

Glick, Paul C. 1947. "The Family Cycle." *American Sociological Review* 12 (2): 164–174.

Glynn, Sarah Jane. 2014. "Breadwinning Mothers, Then and Now." Center for American Progress, June 20. Available at https://www.americanprogress.org/ issues/labor/report/2014/06/20/92355/breadwinning-mothers-then-and-now.

———. 2015. "Opinion: Every Worker, Not Just Those at Netflix, Deserves Paid Family Leave." *MarketWatch*, August 12. Available at http://www.market watch.com/story/every-worker-not-just-those-at-netflix-deserves-paid-family -leave-2015-08-12.

Glynn, Sarah Jane, and Jane Farrell. 2012. "Latinos Least Likely to Have Paid Leave or Workplace Flexibility." Center for American Progress, November 20. Available at https://www.americanprogress.org/issues/labor/report/2012/11/20/45394/ latinos-least-likely-to-have-paid-leave-or-workplace-flexibility/.

Glynn, Sarah Jane, and Audrey Powers. 2012. "The Top Ten Facts about the Wage Gap: Women Are Still Earning Less than Men across the Board." Center for American Progress, April 16. Available at https://www.americanprogress.org/ issues/labor/news/2012/04/16/11391/the-top-10-facts-about-the-wage-gap.

Gornick, Janet C., and Marcia K. Meyers. 2003. *Families That Work: Policies for Reconciling Parenthood and Employment.* New York: Russell Sage Foundation.

Grant, Jodi, Taylor Hatcher, and Nirali Patel. 2005. *Expecting Better: A State by State Analysis of Parental Leave Programs.* Washington, DC: National Partnership for Women and Families.

Greenhouse, Linda. 2003. "The Supreme Court: States' Rights; Justices, 6-3, Rule Workers Can Sue States over Leave." *New York Times*, May 28. Available at http://www.nytimes.com/2003/05/28/us/supreme-court-states-rights-justices -6-3-rule-workers-can-sue-states-over-leave.html.

Grossman, Joanna L. 2004. "Job Security without Equality: The Family and Medical Leave Act of 1993." *Washington University Journal of Law and Policy* 15:17–63.

Guendelman, Sylvia, Julia Goodman, Martin Kharrazi, and Maureen Lahiff. 2014. "Work-Family Balance after Childbirth: The Association between Employer-Offered Leave Characteristics and Maternity Leave Duration." *Maternal and Child Health Journal* 18 (1): 200–208.

Guendelman, Sylvia, Michelle Pearl, Steve Graham, Veronica Angulo, and Marin Kharrazi. 2006. "Utilization of Pay in Antenatal Leave among Working Women in Southern California." *Maternal and Child Health Journal* 10 (1): 63–73.

Guerin, Lisa. n.d. "Massachusetts Family and Medical Leave." *Nolo*. Available at http://www.nolo.com/legal-encyclopedia/massachusetts-family-medical -leave.html.

Haas, Linda. 2003. "Parental Leave and Gender Equality: Lessons from the European Union." *Review of Policy Research* 20 (1): 89–114.

Haas, Linda, and C. Philip Hwang. 2008. "The Impact of Taking Parental Leave on Fathers' Participation in Childcare and Relationships with Children: Lessons from Sweden." *Community, Work and Family* 11 (1): 85–104.

Hall, Jason. 2013. "Why Men Don't Take Paternity Leave." *Forbes*, June 14. Available at http://www.forbes.com/sites/learnvest/2013/06/14/why-men-dont-take -paternity-leave/#4de221763270.

Han, Wen-Jui, Christopher Ruhm, and Jane Waldfogel. 2009. "Parental Leave Policies and Parents' Employment and Leave-Taking." *Journal of Policy Analysis and Management* 28 (1): 29–54.

Han, Wen-Jui, and Jane Waldfogel. 2003. "Parental Leave: The Impact of Recent Legislation on Parents' Leave Taking." *Demography* 40 (1): 191–200.

Haussman, Melissa, and Birgit Sauer, eds. 2007. *Gendering the State in the Age of Globalization: Women's Movements and State Feminism in Postindustrial Democracies*. Lanham, MD: Rowman and Littlefield.

Hawaii Department of Health. 2013. "Hawai'i's 2020 Vision: The State of Active Aging." Available at http://www.hawaiiadrc.org/portals/_agencysite/hcbs_1 .pdf.

Hawaii Department of Labor and Industrial Relations, Disability Compensation Division. n.d. "About Temporary Disability Insurance." Available at http:// labor.hawaii.gov/dcd/home/about-tdi/ (accessed May 4, 2015).

Hawaii Department of Labor and Industrial Relations, Wage Standards Division. n.d. "Hawaii Family Leave." Available at http://labor.hawaii.gov/wsd/hawaii -family-leave/ (accessed May 4, 2015).

Hawaii State Legislature. n.d. "HB496 HD1 SD2." Available at http://www .capitol.hawaii.gov/measure_indiv.aspx?billtype=HB&billnumber=496& year= (accessed April 8, 2016).

———. n.d. "SB2961 SD2 HD2." Available at http://www.capitol.hawaii.gov/measure_indiv.aspx?billtype=SB&billnumber=2961&year= (accessed April 8, 2016).

Hayes, Emily A. 2001. "Bridging the Gap between Work and Family: Accomplishing the Goals of the Family and Medical Leave Act of 1993." *William and Mary Law Review* 42:1507–1543.

Hegewisch, Ariane, and Yuko Hara. 2013. "Maternity, Paternity, and Adoption Leave in the United States." *Institute for Women's Policy Research Briefing Paper*, May. Available at http://www.iwpr.org/publications/pubs/maternity-paternity-and-adoption-leave-in-the-united-states-1.

Henderson, Sarah L., and Alana S. Jeydel. 2007. *Participation and Protest: Women and Politics in a Global World*. New York: Oxford University Press.

Hernandez, Tony. 2015. "Multnomah County Adopts Paid Parental Leave Policy." *The Oregonian*, October 8. Available at http://www.oregonlive.com/multnomahcounty/2015/10/multnomah_county_adopts_paid_p.html.

Heymann, Jody. 2005. "Inequalities at Work and Home: Social Class and Gender Divides." In *Unfinished Work: Building Equality and Democracy in an Era of Working Families*, edited by Jody Heymann and Christopher Beem, 89–121. New York: New Press.

Heymann, Jody, and Alison Earle. 2010. *Raising the Global Floor: Dismantling the Myth That We Can't Afford Good Working Conditions for Everyone*. Stanford, CA: Stanford University Press.

Heymann, Jody, and Kristen McNeill. 2013. *Children's Chances: How Countries Can Move from Surviving to Thriving*. Cambridge, MA: Harvard University Press.

Hill, E. Jeffrey, Alan J. Hawkins, Vjollca Märtinson, and Maria Ferris. 2003. "Studying 'Working Fathers': Comparing Fathers' and Mothers' Work-Family Conflict, Fit, and Adaptive Strategies in a Global High-Tech Company." *Fathering* 1 (3): 239–261.

Hill, Lewis E. 1964. "On Laissez-Faire Capitalism and 'Liberalism.'" *American Journal of Economics and Sociology* 23 (4): 393–396.

Hirsch, Barry T., and David A. Macpherson. 2003. "Union Membership and Coverage Database from the Current Population Survey: Note." *Industrial and Labor Relations Review* 56 (2): 349–354.

———. 2015. "Union Membership, Coverage, Density and Employment by State, 2015." *Union Membership and Coverage Database from the CPS*. Available at http://unionstats.com/.

———. 2016. "Union Membership, Coverage, Density, and Employment among All Wage and Salary Workers, 1973–2015." *Union Membership and Coverage Database from the CPS*. Available at http://unionstats.com/.

Hochschild, Arlie. 1989. *The Second Shift: Working Parents and the Revolution at Home*. New York: Viking.

Holmes, Steven A. 1990a. "Bush Vetoes Bill on Family Leave." *New York Times*, June 30, p. 9.

———. 1990b. "House Passes Measure on Family Leave." *New York Times*, May 11, p. B6.

Houser, Linda, and Thomas P. Vartanian. 2012. *Pay Matters: The Positive Economic Impact of Paid Family Leave for Families, Businesses and the Public.* New Brunswick, NJ: Rutgers Center for Women and Work.

Htun, Mala, and Timothy J. Power. 2006. "Gender, Parties, and Support for Equal Rights in the Brazilian Congress." *Latin American Politics and Society* 48 (4): 83–104.

Huang, Rui, and Muzhe Yang. 2015. "Paid Maternity Leave and Breastfeeding Practice before and after California's Implementation of the Nation's First Paid Family Leave Program." *Economics and Human Biology* 16:45–59.

Huber, Evelyne, and John D. Stephens. 2001. *Development and Crisis of the Welfare State: Parties and Policies in Global Markets.* Chicago: University of Chicago Press.

Huckle, Patricia. 1981. "The Womb Factor: Pregnancy Policies and Employment of Women." *Western Political Quarterly* 34 (1): 114–126.

Huerta, Maria del Carmen, Willem Adema, Jennifer Baxter, Wen-Jui Han, Mette Lausten, RaeHyuck Lee, and Jane Waldfogel. 2013. "Fathers' Leave, Fathers' Involvement and Child Development: Are They Related? Evidence from Four OECD Countries." OECD Social, Employment and Migration Working Paper No. 140. Available at http://www.oecd-ilibrary.org/docserver/download/5k4dlw9w6czq.pdf?expires=1455763696&id=id&accname=guest&checksum=6385B7704D626A81965421105A5FBCE7.

Human Rights Watch. 2011. *Failing Its Families: Lack of Paid Leave and Work-Family Supports in the US.* New York: Human Rights Watch. Available at http://www.hrw.org/sites/default/files/reports/us0211webwcover.pdf.

Hyde, Cheryl. 1995. "Feminist Social Movement Organizations Survive the New Right." In *Feminist Organizations: Harvest of the New Women's Movement,* edited by Myra Marx Ferree and Patricia Yancey Martin, 306–322. Philadelphia: Temple University Press.

Institute for Women's Policy Research. 2010. "Majority of Workers Support Workplace Flexibility, Job Quality, and Family Support Policies." Available at http://www.iwpr.org/press-room/press-releases/majority-of-workers-support-workplace-flexibility-job-quality-and-family-support-policies.

Isidore, Chris, and Tami Luhby. 2015. "Turns Out Americans Work Really Hard . . . but Some Want to Work Harder." *CNN Money,* July 9. Available at http://money.cnn.com/2015/07/09/news/economy/americans-work-bush/.

Jacobs, Francine H., and Margery W. Davies. 1994. "Introduction." In *More than Kissing Babies? Current Child and Family Policy in the United States,* edited by Francine H. Jacobs and Margery W. Davies, 1–8. Westport, CT: Auburn.

Jacobs, Jerry A., and Kathleen Gerson. 2004. *The Time Divide: Work, Family, and Gender Inequality.* Cambridge, MA: Harvard University Press.

Jenkins, J. Craig. 1983. "Resource Mobilization Theory and the Study of Social Movements." *Annual Review of Sociology* 9:527–553.

Jimenez, Monica. 2015. "Cambridge Adopts Paid Parental Leave for City Workers." *Wicked Local Cambridge,* October 21. Available at http://cambridge.wickedlocal.com/article/20151021/NEWS/151028998.

Johnson, Ben. 2015. "City of Minneapolis Approves Paid Parental Leave for Employees." *City Pages*, April 28. Available at http://www.citypages.com/news/city-of-minneapolis-approves-paid-parental-leave-for-employees-update-6565852.

Johnson, Tallese. 2008. *Maternity Leave and Employment Patterns of First-Time Mothers: 1961–2003*. Washington, DC: U.S. Census Bureau.

Jordan, Laura. 1999. *Federal Family and Medical Leave Proposals*. Hartford, CT: Connecticut General Assembly Office of Legislative Research.

Jordan, Mike. 2015. "The United States of Get Back to Work: Here's Where the Major Presidential Candidates Stand on Paid Family Leave." *Fatherly*, October 26. Available at https://www.fatherly.com/the-2016-presidential-candidates-policies-on-paid-family-leave-1419122939.html.

Jorgensen, Helene, and Eileen Appelbaum. 2014a. *Documenting the Need for a National Paid Family and Medical Leave Program: Evidence from the 2012 FMLA Survey*. Washington, DC: Center for Economic and Policy Research.

———. 2014b. *Expanding Family and Medical Leave to Small Firms*. Washington, DC: Center for Economic and Policy Research.

———. 2014c. *Expanding Federal Family and Medical Leave Coverage: Who Benefits from Changes in Eligibility Requirements?* Washington, DC: Center for Economic and Policy Research.

Kaitin, Katharine Karr. 1994. "Congressional Responses to Families in the Workplace: The Family and Medical Leave Act of 1987–1988." In *More than Kissing Babies? Current Child and Family Policy in the United States*, edited by Francine H. Jacobs and Margery W. Davies, 91–120. Westport, CT: Auburn.

Kamerman, Sheila, and Peter Moss. 2009. "Introduction." In *The Politics of Parental Leave Policies: Children, Parenting, Gender and the Labour Market*, edited by Sheila Kamerman and Peter Moss, 1–14. Portland, OR: Policy Press.

Kantrowitz, Barbara, and Pat Wingert. 1989. "Parental Leave Cries to Be Born." *Newsweek*, June 5, p. 65.

Katz, Marc D., Isabel Crosby, Michael Mobley, and Britney J. P. Prince. 2016. "New York Is Latest State to Adopt Paid Family Leave Law." *National Law Review*, April 13. Available at http://www.natlawreview.com/article/new-york-latest-state-to-adopt-paid-family-leave-law.

Katzenstein, Mary Fainsod. 1987. "Comparing the Feminist Movements of the United States and Western Europe: An Overview." In *The Women's Movements of the United States and Western Europe: Consciousness, Political Opportunity, and Public Policy*, edited by Mary Fainsod Katzenstein and Carol McClurg Mueller, 3–20. Philadelphia: Temple University Press.

———. 1989. "Organizing against Violence: Strategies of the Indian Women's Movement." *Pacific Affairs* 62 (1): 53–71.

———. 1995. "Discursive Politics and Feminist Activism in the Catholic Church." In *Feminist Organizations: Harvest of the New Women's Movement*, edited by Myra Marx Ferree and Patricia Yancey Martin, 35–52. Philadelphia: Temple University Press.

Katzenstein, Mary Fainsod, and Carol McClurg Mueller, eds. 1987. *The Women's Movements of the United States and Western Europe: Consciousness, Political Opportunity, and Public Policy.* Philadelphia: Temple University Press.

Kaufman, Gayle, Clare Lyonette, and Rosemary Crompton. 2010. "Post-birth Employment Leave among Fathers in Britain and the United States." *Fathering* 8 (3): 321–340.

Kay, Herma Hill. 1985. "Equality and Difference: The Case of Pregnancy." *Berkeley Women's Law Journal* 1:1–37.

Kelly, Erin, and Frank Dobbin. 1999. "Civil Rights Law at Work: Sex Discrimination and the Rise of Maternity Leave Policies." *American Journal of Sociology* 105 (2): 455–492.

Kessler-Harris, Alice. 1982. *Out to Work: A History of Wage-Earning Women in the United States.* New York: Oxford University Press.

Key, V. O., Jr. 1961. *Public Opinion and American Democracy.* New York: Knopf.

Kingdon, John W. 1984. *Agendas, Alternatives and Public Policies.* Boston: Little, Brown.

Kittilson, Miki Caul. 2008. "Representing Women: The Adoption of Family Leave in Comparative Perspective." *Journal of Politics* 70 (2): 323–334.

Klerman, Jacob Alex, Kelly Daley, and Alyssa Pozniak. 2014. *Family and Medical Leave in 2012: Technical Report.* Cambridge, MA: Abt Associates.

Koenig, Robert L. 1993. "Clinton Signs Family Leave, Praises Clay." *St. Louis Post-Dispatch*, February 6, p. 1A.

Koss, Natalie. 2003. "The California Temporary Disability Insurance Program." *Journal of Gender, Social Policy and the Law* 11 (2): 1079–1088.

Kottasova, Ivana. 2015. "Company Offers Moms 16 Weeks Off on Full Pay, Even in the U.S." *CNN Money*, March 6. Available at http://money.cnn.com/2015/03/06/news/companies/vodafone-maternity-leave/.

Krieger, Linda J., and Patricia N. Cooney. 1983. "The Miller-Wohl Controversy: Equal Treatment, Positive Action and the Meaning of Women's Equality." *Golden Gate University Law Review* 13 (3): 513–572.

Labor Project for Working Families. 2003. "Putting Families First: How California Won the Fight for Paid Family Leave." Available at http://www.working-families.org/publications/paidleavewon.pdf.

La Corte, Rachel. 2013. "Dueling Bills Introduced on Paid Family Leave Law." *Washington Examiner*, January 24. Available at http://www.washingtonexaminer.com/dueling-bills-introduced-on-paid-family-leave-law/article/feed/2066554.

Lake Research Partners and Tarrance Group. 2014. "National Partnership for Women and Families/Rockefeller Family Fund Election Eve/Night Omnibus." Available at http://www.nationalpartnership.org/research-library/work-family/lake-research-and-tarrance-group-2014-midterm-election-omnibus-poll-results.pdf.

Lambert, Priscilla A. 2008. "The Comparative Political Economy of Parental Leave and Child Care: Evidence from Twenty OECD Countries." *Social Politics* 15 (3): 315–344.

Langlois, Ed. 2009. "Oregon Legislature to Debate Bill on Family Leave for Employees." *Catholic Sentinel,* April 30. Available at http://www.catholic sentinel.org/main.asp?SectionID=2&SubSectionID=35&ArticleID=10010.

Leira, Arnlaug. 2002. *Working Parents and the Welfare State: Family Change and Policy Reform in Scandinavia.* New York: Cambridge University Press.

Leiwant, Sherry. 2013. "Governor Chafee Signs Paid Family Leave into Law in Rhode Island." *A Better Balance Blog,* July 24. Available at http://www.abetter balance.org/web/blog/entry/rhodeisland.

Leo, John, Val Castronovo, and William Hackman. 1986. "Sexes: Are Women Male Clones?" *Time,* August 18, pp. 63–64.

Lerman, Rachel. 2015. "Amazon Increases Paid Leave for New Parents." *Seattle Times,* November 2. Available at http://www.seattletimes.com/business/amazon/ amazon-increases-paid-leave-for-new-parents/.

Lerner, Sharon. 2010. "Why Unpaid Maternity Leave Isn't Enough." *Washington Post,* June 13, p. B3.

———. 2015. "The Real War on Families: Why the U.S. Needs Paid Leave Now." *In These Times,* August 18. Available at http://inthesetimes.com/article/18151/ the-real-war-on-families.

Lester, Gillian. 2005. "A Defense of Paid Family Leave." *Harvard Journal of Law and Gender* 28 (1): 1–83.

Levenson, Michael. 2015. "AG Healey to Offer Her Employees Paid Parental Leave." *Boston Globe,* May 12. Available at http://www.bostonglobe.com/ metro/2015/05/11/grant-paid-parental-leave-her-employees/Shr5J2W 777agdAmTKptYKK/story.html.

Levine, Linda. 2010. "The Family and Medical Leave Act: Current Legislative Activity." Congressional Research Service, August 3. Available at http://digital commons.ilr.cornell.edu/key_workplace/769/.

Levine, Sam. 2016. "New York Gov. Andrew Cuomo Makes Emotional Plea for Paid Family Leave." *Huffington Post,* January 13. Available at http://www .huffingtonpost.com/entry/andrew-cuomo-paid-family-leave_us_5696b 534e4b0b4eb759cf51a.

Lev-Ram, Michal. 2016. "Twitter to Give All New Parents 20 Weeks of Paid Leave." *Fortune,* April 5. Available at http://fortune.com/2016/04/05/twitter-20-weeks -parental-leave/.

Levs, Josh. 2015. "Paul Ryan, Speaker? Paul Ryan, Hypocrite." *Time,* October 23. Available at http://time.com/4083094/paul-ryan-family-time/.

Lewin, Tamar. 1986. "Debate over Pregnancy Leave." *New York Times,* February 3, p. D1.

Lewis, Jane, ed. 1993. *Women and Social Policies in Europe: Work, Family and the State.* Brookfield, VT: Edward Elgar.

———, ed. 1997. *Lone Mothers in European Welfare Regimes: Shifting Policy Logics.* Philadelphia: Kingsley.

Liebelson, Dana. 2013. "Can Facebook and Reddit Fix America's Maternity Leave Problem?" *Mother Jones,* May 28. Available at http://www.motherjones.com/ politics/2013/05/silicon-valley-maternity-leave-paternity-leave.

Lindzon, Jared. 2015. "How Nestlé Plans to Prove That Paid Parental Leave Makes Business Sense." *Fortune*, September 29. Available at http://fortune .com/2015/09/29/how-nestle-plans-to-prove-that-paid-parental-leave-makes -business-sense/.

Lipset, Seymour Martin. 1990. *Continental Divide: The Values and Institutions of the United States and Canada*. New York: Routledge.

Livio, Susan K. 2008a. "Divided NJ Senate Approves Family Leave Bill." *NJ.com*, April 8. Available at http://www.nj.com/business/index.ssf/2008/04/divided _nj_senate_approves_fam.html.

———. 2008b. "Gov. Corzine Signs Paid Family Leave Act." *NJ.com*, May 2. Available at http://www.nj.com/news/index.ssf/2008/05/corzine_signs _family_leave_act.html.

Lovenduski, Joni. 1986. *Women and European Politics: Contemporary Feminism and Public Policy*. Amherst: University of Massachusetts Press.

———. 2005. "Introduction: State Feminism and the Political Representation of Women." In *State Feminism and Political Representation*, edited by Joni Lovenduski, 1–19. New York: Cambridge University Press.

Lundquist, Jennifer H., Joya Misra, and KerryAnn O'Meara. 2012. "Parental Leave Usage by Fathers and Mothers at an American University." *Fathering* 10 (3): 337–363.

Lunney, Kellie. 2015. "Feds Would Get Sex Weeks of Paid Parental Leave under Bill." *Government Executive*, September 15. Available at http://www.gov exec.com/pay-benefits/2015/09/feds-would-get-six-weeks-paid-parental-leave -under-bill/121025/.

———. 2016. "Obama Again Urges Paid Parental Leave for Federal Employees." *Government Executive*, February 9. Available at http://www.govexec.com/pay -benefits/2016/02/obama-again-urges-paid-parental-leave-federal-employees /125812/.

MacKinnon, Catharine A. 1989. *Toward a Feminist Theory of the State*. Cambridge, MA: Harvard University Press.

———. 1991. "Reflections on Sex Equality under Law." *Yale Law Journal* 100 (5): 1281–1328.

Malin, Martin H. 1994. "Fathers and Parental Leave." *Texas Law Review* 72 (5): 1047–1095.

———. 1998. "Fathers and Parental Leave Revisited." *Northern University Law Review* 19 (1): 25–56.

Manning, Margie. 2016. "Why the Biggest Bank in Tampa Is Changing Its Parental Leave Policy." *Tampa Bay Business Journal*, March 31. Available at http://www .bizjournals.com/tampabay/blog/morning-edition/2016/03/why-the-biggest -bank-in-tampa-is-changing-its.html.

Mansbridge, Jane J. 1986. *Why We Lost the ERA*. Chicago: University of Chicago Press.

———. 1995. "What Is the Feminist Movement?" In *Feminist Organizations: Harvest of the New Women's Movement*, edited by Myra Marx Ferree and Patricia Yancey Martin, 27–34. Philadelphia: Temple University Press.

———. 1999. "Should Blacks Represent Blacks and Women Represent Women? A Contingent 'Yes.'" *Journal of Politics* 61 (3): 628–657.

Mapes, Jeff. 2009. "Proponents of Paid Family Leave Seek Support in Oregon Legislature." *The Oregonian*, April 8. Available at http://www.oregonlive.com/business/index.ssf/2009/04/proponents_of_paid_family_leav.html.

Marchbank, Jennifer. 2000. *Women, Power and Policy: Comparative Studies of Childcare*. New York: Routledge.

Marcos, Cristina. 2015. "GOP Pans Push for Paid Leave." *The Hill*, January 22. Available at http://thehill.com/regulation/230359-gop-pans-push-for-paid-leave.

Massachusetts State Legislature. n.d. "Bill H.1718." Available at https://malegislature.gov/Bills/189/House/H1718 (accessed April 8, 2016).

———. n.d. "Bill H.809." Available at https://malegislature.gov/Bills/189/House/H809 (accessed April 8, 2016).

Mayer, Gerald. 2013. "The Family and Medical Leave Act (FMLA): Policy Issues." Congressional Research Service, September 4. Available at http://digitalcommons.ilr.cornell.edu/cgi/viewcontent.cgi?article=2316&context=key_workplace.

"Mayor de Blasio Announces Paid Parental Leave for NYC Employees—Putting NYC at the Forefront of Cities and States around the Country." 2015. *NYC*, December 22. Available at http://www1.nyc.gov/office-of-the-mayor/news/968-15/mayor-de-blasio-paid-parental-leave-nyc-employees---putting-nyc-the-forefront-of.

Mazur, Amy G. 2001. "Introduction." In *State Feminism, Women's Movements, and Job Training: Making Democracies Work in the Global Economy*, edited by Amy Mazur, 3–27. New York: Routledge.

———. 2002. *Theorizing Feminist Policy*. New York: Oxford University Press.

McAdam, Doug, John D. McCarthy, and Mayer N. Zald. 1996. "Introduction: Opportunities, Mobilizing Structures, and Framing Processes—toward a Synthetic, Comparative Perspective on Social Movements." In *Comparative Perspectives on Social Movements: Political Opportunities, Mobilizing Structures, and Cultural Framings*, edited by Doug McAdam, John D. McCarthy, and Mayer N. Zald, 1–20. New York: Cambridge University Press.

McBride, Dorothy E. 2007. "Welfare Reform: America's Hot Issue." In *Gendering the State in the Age of Globalization: Women's Movements and State Feminism in Postindustrial Democracies*, edited by Melissa Haussman and Birgit Sauer, 281–300. Lanham, MD: Rowman and Littlefield.

McBride, Dorothy E., and Amy G. Mazur. 2010. *The Politics of State Feminism: Innovation in Comparative Research*. Philadelphia: Temple University Press.

McCarthy, John D., and Mayer N. Zald. 1973. *The Trend of Social Movements in America: Professionalization and Resource Mobilization*. Morristown, NJ: General Learning Press.

———. 1977. "Resource Mobilization and Social Movements: A Partial Theory." *American Journal of Sociology* 82 (6): 1212–1241.

McConnell, Grant. 1966. *Private Power and American Democracy*. New York: Knopf.

McDonald, Daniel A., and David M. Almeida. 2004. "The Interweave of Fathers' Daily Work Experiences and Fathering Behaviors." *Fathering: A Journal of Theory, Research, and Practice about Men as Fathers* 2 (3): 235–251.

McGovern, Patricia, Bryan Dowd, Dwenda Gjerdingen, Ira Moscovice, Laura Kockevar, and Sarah Murphy. 2000. "The Determinants of Time Off Work after Childbirth." *Journal of Health Politics, Policy and Law* 25 (3): 527–564.

McGregor, Jena. 2015. "A Smart Way to Help Mothers Return to Work after Maternity Leave." *Washington Post*, May 7. Available at https://www.washingtonpost.com/news/on-leadership/wp/2015/05/07/a-smart-way-to-ease-mothers-return-to-work-after-maternity-leave/.

McIntosh, Don. 2013. "Unanimous City Council: Portland Workers Will Have Sick Leave." *nwLaborPress.org*, April 3. Available at http://nwlaborpress.org/2013/04/city-council-portland-sick-leave/.

McKay, Lindsey, and Andrea Doucet. 2010. "'Without Taking Away Her Leave': A Canadian Case Study of Couples' Decisions on Fathers' Use of Paid Parental Leave." *Fathering* 8 (3): 300–320.

Medoff, Marshall H., Christopher Dennis, and Kerri Stephens. 2011. "The Impact of Party Control on the Diffusion of Parental Involvement Laws in the U.S. States." *State Politics and Policy Quarterly* 11 (3): 325–347.

Mei, Michelle. 2016. "Raise Up Massachusetts! Community Forums with State Legislators." American Friends Service Committee, March 24. Available at http://afscwm.org/blog/event/raise-up-massachusetts-community-forums-with-state-legislators/.

Melnick, Erin R. 2000. "Reaffirming No-Fault Divorce: Supplementing Formal Equality with Substantive Change." *Indiana Law Journal* 75 (2): 711–729.

Meyer, David S. 2003. "Restating the Woman Question: Women's Movements and State Restructuring." In *Women's Movements Facing the Reconfigured State*, edited by Lee Ann Banaszak, Karen Beckwith, and Dieter Rucht, 275–294. New York: Cambridge University Press.

Meyer, David S., and Suzanne Staggenborg. 1996. "Movements, Countermovements, and the Structure of Political Opportunity." *American Journal of Sociology* 101 (6): 1628–1660.

Meyer, David S., and Sidney Tarrow, eds. 1998. *The Social Movement Society: Contentious Politics for a New Century*. Lanham, MD: Rowman and Littlefield.

Mezey, Susan Gluck. 2011. *Elusive Equality: Women's Rights, Public Policy, and the Law*. 2nd ed. Boulder, CO: Lynne Rienner.

Michelson, Spencer. 2016. "Anheuser-Busch Introduces New Paid Parental Leave Policy." *KMOV.com*, April 15. Available at http://www.kmov.com/story/31737078/anheuser-busch-introduces-new-paid-paternal-leave-policy.

Milkman, Ruth, and Eileen Appelbaum. 2004. "Paid Family Leave in California: New Research Findings." In *The State of California Labor 2004*, edited by Ruth Milkman, 45–67. Berkeley: University of California Press. Available at http://www.irle.ucla.edu/publications/documents/StateofCALabor_2004.pdf.

———. 2013. *Unfinished Business: Paid Family Leave in California and the Future of U.S. Work-Family Policy*. Ithaca, NY: ILR Press.

Miller, Claire Cain. 2014. "Paternity Leave: The Rewards and the Remaining Stigma." *New York Times*, November 7. Available at http://www.nytimes.com/2014/11/09/upshot/paternity-leave-the-rewards-and-the-remaining-stigma.html.

———. 2015a. "How Mark Zuckerberg's Example Helps Fight Stigma of Family Leave." *New York Times*, December 2. Available at http://www.nytimes .com/2015/12/03/upshot/how-mark-zuckerbergs-example-helps-fight-stigma -of-family-leave.html.

———. 2015b. "Marco Rubio's Plan for Paid Leave Does Not Require Paid Leave." *New York Times*, September 28. Available at http://www.nytimes .com/2015/09/29/upshot/rubios-plan-for-paid-leave-depends-on-the-kind ness-of-business.html.

———. 2015c. "Millennial Men Aren't the Dads They Thought They'd Be." *New York Times*, July 30. Available at http://www.nytimes.com/2015/07/31/upshot/ millennial-men-find-work-and-family-hard-to-balance.html.

Miller, Claire Cain, and David Streitfeld. 2015. "Big Leaps for Parental Leave, if Workers Actually Take It." *New York Times*, September 15. Available at http://www.nytimes.com/2015/09/02/upshot/big-leaps-for-parental-leave-if -workers-actually-follow-through.html.

Miller, G. E. 2016. "The U.S. Is the Most Overworked Developed Nation in the World— When Do We Draw the Line?" *20 Something Finance*, January 4. Available at http://20somethingfinance.com/american-hours-worked-productivity -vacation/.

Minkoff, Debra. 1999. "Bending with the Wind: Strategic Change and Adaptation by Women's and Racial Minority Organizations." *American Journal of Sociology* 104 (6): 1666–1703.

Minnick, Thomas R. 2007. Statement to the New York State Senate, Committee on Labor, June 5. Available at http://www.bcnys.org/inside/labor/2007/family leavetestimony060507.pdf.

Minow, Martha. 1990. "Adjudicating Differences: Conflicts among Feminist Lawyers." In *Conflicts in Feminism*, edited by Marianne Hirsch and Evelyn Fox Keller, 149–163. New York: Routledge.

Mishel, Lawrence R., Jared Bernstein, and John Schmitt. 2001. *The State of Working America, 2000–2001*. Ithaca, NY: ILR Press.

MomsRising. n.d. "The Power of ONEsie!" Available at http://www.momsrising .org/page/moms/PowerofONEsie (accessed February 17, 2016).

———. 2007a. "MomsRising Executive Director Testifies in Support of Washing- ton State Paid Leave Bill." Available at http://www.momsrising.org/page/ moms/020607PressRelease.

———. 2007b. "MomsRising Helps Make Washington Second State to Adopt Paid Leave." Available at http://www.momsrising.org/page/moms/050807 PressRelease_2.

———. 2007c. "Taking Action, Making Changes." Available at http://www.moms rising.org/page/moms/MakingChanges.

———. 2008. "Go New Jersey! Family Leave Insurance." Available at http://www .momsrising.org/page/moms/NewJersey.

Morgan, Kimberly J. 2001. "A Child of the Sixties: The Great Society, the New Right, and the Politics of Federal Child Care." *Journal of Policy History* 13 (2): 215–250.

———. 2006. *Working Mothers and the Welfare State: Religion and the Politics of Work-Family Policies in Western Europe and the United States.* Stanford, CA: Stanford University Press.

———. 2009. "Caring Time Policies in Western Europe: Trends and Implications." *Comparative European Politics* 7 (1): 37–55.

Morgan, Kimberly J., and Kathrin Zippel. 2003. "Paid to Care: The Origins and Effects of Care Leave Policies in Western Europe" *Social Politics* 10 (1): 49–85.

Molyneux, Maxine. 1998. "Analyzing Women's Movements." In *Feminist Visions of Development: Gender Analysis and Policy*, edited by Cecile Jackson and Ruth Pearson, 65–88. London: Routledge.

Mui, Ylan Q. 2015. "Companies Have Found Something to Give Their Workers Instead of Raises." *Washington Post*, July 28. Available at https://www.washing tonpost.com/news/wonk/wp/2015/07/28/companies-have-found-something -to-give-their-workers-instead-of-raises/.

Myles, John. 1998. "How to Design a 'Liberal' Welfare State: A Comparison of Canada and the United States." *Social Policy and Administration* 32 (4): 341–364.

Naples, Michelle, and Meryl Frank. 2001. "The Fiscal Viability of New Jersey Family Leave Insurance." Institute for Women's Policy Research. Available at http://www.iwpr.org/publications/pubs/the-fiscal-viability-of-new-jersey -family-leave-insurance.

National Council of Jewish Women–New York Section. n.d. "Advocacy." Available at http://www.ncjwny.org/advocacy.

National Organization for Women. 1973. "Mandatory Pregnancy Leaves." *Do It NOW*, December, pp. 6–7.

———. 1977. "Legislation to Prohibit Sex Discrimination on the Basis of Pregnancy." *Do It NOW*, September–October, p. 6.

———. 1985. "Parental and Disability Leave Act." *National NOW Times*, August–September, p. 5.

———. 1986. "FMLA Poised for House Passage." *National NOW Times*, July–September, p. 8.

———. 1989. "Legislative Updates." *National NOW Times*, July–September, pp. 10–11.

———. 1990. "FMLA Undergoes Last Minute Changes." *National NOW Times*, Fall, p. 13.

———. 1991. "NOW Calls for Strong Family Medical Leave." *National NOW Times*, December, p. 12.

———. 2002. "Good News for Women: California Governor Gray Davis Signs Bill Allowing Paid Family Leave." Previously available at http://www.now.org/ issues/wfw/0930021eave.html.

———. 2003. "NOW Opposed the Rescinding of 'Baby UI,' Calls for Comprehensive Paid Family Leave Programs." Previously available at http://www.now.org/ issues/family/013003ui-comments.html.

———. 2006. "NOW-NJ: Calling All Feminist Business Owners." Previously available at http://www.nownj.org/njIssues/Paid%20Family%20Leave/NOW_NJ _small_business2.pdf.

———. 2007a. "New Jersey Family Leave Alert." Previously available at http://morris countynow.org/familyleavealert.htm.

———. 2007b. "Testimony: Family Leave Insurance, Senate Bill 2249." Previously available at http://www.nownj.org/Press,%20Speeches/2007/070524%20 Testimony%20Family%20Leave%20Insurance%20Senate%20bill%202249 .htm.

National Partnership for Women and Families. 2013. "Fact Sheet: Work and Family Agenda for the 113th Congress." Available at http://www.nationalpartnership .org/research-library/work-family/work-and-family-agenda-113th-congress .pdf.

———. 2014. "Expecting Better: A State-by-State Analysis of Laws That Help New Parents." 3rd ed. Available at http://www.nationalpartnership.org/research -library/work-family/expecting-better-2014.pdf.

———. 2015a. "Fact Sheet: An Empty Promise: The Working Families Flexibility Act Would Give Workers Less Flexibility and Less Pay." Available at http:// www.nationalpartnership.org/research-library/work-family/other/an-empty -promise-the-working-families-flexibility-act.pdf.

———. 2015b. "Fact Sheet: The Family and Medical Insurance Leave Act (The FAMILY Act)." Available at http://www.nationalpartnership.org/research -library/work-family/paid-leave/family-act-fact-sheet.pdf.

———. 2015c. "The Family and Medical Leave Act at 22: 200 Million Reasons to Celebrate and Move Forward." Available at http://www.nationalpartnership.org/ research-library/work-family/fmla/the-family-and-medical-leave-at-22.pdf.

———. 2016. "Current Paid Sick Days Laws." Available at http://www.nationalpart nership.org/research-library/work-family/psd/current-paid-sick-days-laws .pdf.

Naumann, Ingela K. 2005. "Child Care and Feminism in West Germany and Sweden in the 1960s and 1970s." *Journal of European Social Policy* 15 (1): 47–63.

Nepomnyaschy, Lenna, and Jane Waldfogel. 2007. "Paternity Leave and Fathers' Involvement with Their Young Children." *Community, Work and Family* 10 (4): 427–453.

Ness, Debra L. 2016. "Voters Say It's Time for Paid Family and Medical Leave." National Partnership for Women and Families, February 5. Available at http://www.nationalpartnership.org/blog/general/voters-say-its-time-for-paid -family-and-medical-leave.html.

New Jersey Department of Labor and Workforce Development. n.d. "Family Leave Insurance." Available at http://lwd.dol.state.nj.us/labor/fli/fliindex.html (accessed April 2, 2016).

New Jersey Department of Law and Public Safety. 2008. "New Jersey Family Leave Act Regulations." Available at http://www.nj.gov/oag/dcr/downloads/ FamilyLeaveAct-Regulations%20.pdf.

New Jersey Legislature. n.d. "Assembly Committee Substitute for Assembly, No. 873." Available at http://www.njleg.state.nj.us/2008/Bills/A1000/873_U1.PDF (accessed April 6, 2016).

———. n.d. "Assembly, No. 873." Available at http://www.njleg.state.nj.us/2008/ Bills/A1000/873_I1.PDF (accessed April 6, 2016).

———. n.d. "Senate, No. 786." Available at http://www.njleg.state.nj.us/2008/Bills/S1000/786_I1.PDF (accessed April 6, 2016).

———. n.d. "Senate, No. 2249." Available at http://www.njleg.state.nj.us/2006/Bills/S2500/2249_I1.PDF (accessed April 6, 2016).

New Jersey Time to Care. n.d. "Coalition Members." Available at http://www.nj timetocare.com/about/coalition-members (accessed February 17, 2016).

New York State Assembly. n.d. "Bill No. A03870." Available at http://assembly.state.ny.us/leg/?default_fld=&bn=A03870&term=2015&Summary=Y&Actions=Y&Votes=Y&Memo=Y (accessed April 6, 2016).

———. n.d. "Bill No. A08742." Available at http://assembly.state.ny.us/leg/?default_fld=&bn=A08742&term=2009&Summary=Y&Actions=Y&Votes=Y&Memo=Y&Text=Y (accessed April 6, 2016).

New York State Workers' Compensation Board. n.d. "Disability Benefits." Available at http://www.wcb.ny.gov/content/main/offthejob/IntroToLaw_DB.jsp (accessed April 11, 2016).

Nussbaum, Karen. 1992. "This Is a Sound Start." *USA Today*, August 10, p. 6A.

Obama, Barack H. 2015. "Remarks by the President in State of the Union Address." Available at https://www.whitehouse.gov/the-press-office/2015/01/20/remarks-president-state-union-address-january-20-2015.

Oberschall, Anthony. 1973. *Social Conflicts and Social Movements*. Englewood Cliffs, NJ: Prentice Hall.

O'Brien, Margaret. 2009. "Fathers, Parental Leave Policies, and Infant Quality of Life: International Perspectives and Policy Impact." *Annals of the American Academy of Political and Social Science* 624:190–213.

O'Brien, Margaret, Berit Brandth, and Elin Kvande. 2007. "Fathers, Work and Family Life." *Community, Work and Family* 10 (4): 375–386.

O'Connor, Julia S., Ann Shola Orloff, and Sheila Shaver. 1999. *States, Markets, Families: Gender, Liberalism, and Social Policy in Australia, Canada, Great Britain, and the United States*. New York: Cambridge University Press.

Office of Senator Kirsten Gillibrand. n.d. "American Opportunity Agenda." Available at http://www.gillibrand.senate.gov/imo/media/doc/American%20Opportunity%20Agenda.pdf (accessed May 21, 2015).

Okin, Susan Moller. 1989. *Justice, Gender, and the Family*. New York: Basic Books.

O'Leary, Ann. 2007. "How Family Leave Laws Left Out Low-Income Workers." *Berkeley Journal of Employment and Labor Law* 28:1–62.

Oliver, Melvin L., and Thomas M. Shapiro. 2006. *Black Wealth, White Wealth: A New Perspective on Racial Inequality*. 10th anniversary ed. New York: Routledge.

Olson, Mancur. 1965. *The Logic of Collective Action: Public Goods and the Theory of Groups*. Cambridge, MA: Harvard University Press.

O'Malley, Martin. 2015. "America Succeeds When Women and Families Succeed." *The Gazette*, September 14. Available at http://www.thegazette.com/subject/opinion/america-succeeds-when-women-and-families-succeed-20150914.

Oppenheimer, Valerie Kincade. 1974. "The Life-Cycle Squeeze: The Interaction of Men's Occupational and Family Life Cycles." *Demography* 11 (2): 227–245.

Oregon Secretary of State. n.d. "Oregon Family Leave Act." Available at http://
arcweb.sos.state.or.us/pages/rules/oars_800/oar_839/839_009.html (accessed
April 13, 2016).

Oregon State Legislature. n.d. "SB 966 A." Available at https://olis.leg.state.or.us/
liz/2009R1/Measures/Overview/SB966 (accessed April 6, 2016).

———. 2009. Senate Committee on Commerce and Workforce Development, public hearing on SB 966, April 8. Available at http://oregon.granicus.com/Media
Player.php?view_id=18&clip_id=5536 (accessed April 6, 2016).

Orloff, Ann Shola. 1993. "Gender and the Social Rights of Citizenship: The Comparative Analysis of Gender Relations and Welfare States." *American Sociological Review* 58 (3): 303–328.

Otani, Akane. 2015. "The 10 U.S. Companies with the Best Paternity Leave Benefits." *Bloomberg Business*, April 30. Available at http://www.bloomberg
.com/news/articles/2015-04-30/the-10-u-s-companies-with-the-best-pater
nity-leave-benefits.

Outshoorn, Joyce. 2004. "Introduction: Prostitution, Women's Movements and
Democratic Politics." In *The Politics of Prostitution: Women's Movements,
Democratic States and the Globalisation of Sex Commerce*, edited by Joyce
Outshoorn, 1–20. New York: Cambridge University Press.

Padavic, Irene, and Barbara F. Reskin. 2002. *Women and Men at Work*. 2nd ed.
Thousand Oaks, CA: Pine Forge Press.

Page, Benjamin I., and Robert Y. Shapiro. 1983. "Effect of Public Opinion on
Policy." *American Political Science Review* 77 (1): 175–190.

Palazzari, Kari. 2007. "The Daddy Double-Bind: How the Family and Medical
Leave Act Perpetuates Sex Inequality across All Class Levels." *Columbia
Journal of Gender and Law* 16:429–470.

Pappas, Marcia A. 2007. Statement to the New York State Senate, Committee
on Labor, June 5. Available at http://timetocareny.org/wp/wp-content/
uploads/2013/12/now_testimony.doc.

Pateman, Carole. 1989. *The Disorder of Women: Democracy, Feminism and Political
Theory*. Cambridge, NY: Polity Press.

———. 1992. "Equality, Difference, Subordination: The Politics of Motherhood
and Women's Citizenship." In *Beyond Equality and Difference: Citizenship,
Feminist Politics, and Female Subjectivity*, edited by Gisela Bock and Susan
James, 14–27. New York: Routledge.

Peck, Emily. 2015. "Accenture Just Upped the Ante on Benefits for New Moms and
Dads." *Huffington Post*, August 26. Available at http://www.huffingtonpost
.com/entry/accenture-parental-benefits_us_55dc8595e4b08cd3359d504c.

Pedriana, Nicholas. 2009. "Discrimination by Definition: The Historical and Legal
Paths to the Pregnancy Discrimination Act of 1978." *Yale Journal of Law and
Feminism* 21:1–14.

Petchesky, Rosalind Pollack. 1981. "Antiabortion, Antifeminism, and the Rise of
the New Right." *Feminist Studies* 7 (2): 206–246.

Pew Research Center. 2015. "Raising Kids and Running a Household: How
Working Parents Share the Load." Available at http://www.pewsocialtrends
.org/files/2015/11/2015-11-04_working-parents_FINAL.pdf.

Piccirillo, Mary. 1988. "The Legal Background of a Parental Leave Policy and Its Implications." In *The Parental Leave Crisis: Toward a National Policy*, edited by Edward F. Zigler and Meryl Frank, 293–314. New Haven, CT: Yale University Press.

Pierson, Paul. 1995. "The Scope and Nature of Business Power: Employers and the American Welfare State, 1900–1935." Paper presented at the Annual Conference of the American Political Science Association, Chicago, IL, August 30–September3.

Piven, Frances Fox, and Richard A. Cloward. 1977. *Poor People's Movements: Why They Succeed, How They Fail*. New York: Pantheon Books.

Porter, Nicole B. 2010. "Why Care about Caregiving? Using Communitarian Theory to Justify Protection of 'Real' Workers." *Kansas Law Review* 58:355–414.

———. 2014. "Finding a Fix for the FMLA: A New Perspective, A New Solution." *Hofstra Labor and Employment Law Journal* 31:327–366.

Prohaska, Ariane, and John F. Zipp. 2011. "Gender Inequality and the Family and Medical Leave Act." *Journal of Family Issues* 32 (11): 1425–1448.

PRWatch Editors. 2016. "Exposed: Most CEOs Support Paid Sick Leave, Increased Minimum Wage, and More but Chamber Lobbyists Told How to 'Combat' These Measures." *PRWatch*, April 4. Available at http://www.prwatch.org/news/2016/04/13075/top-gop-pollster-chamber-commerce-lobbyists-poll-shows-your-members-support.

Pyle, Jean L., and Marianne S. Pelletier. 2003. "Family and Medical Leave Act: Unresolved Issues." *New Solutions* 13 (4): 353–384.

Radigan, Anne L. 1988. *Concept and Compromise: The Evolution of Family Leave Legislation in the U.S. Congress*. Washington, DC: Women's Research and Education Institute.

Raise Up Massachusetts. n.d. "Paid Family and Medical Leave Campaign." Available at http://raiseupma.org/paid-family-and-medical-leave-campaign/ (accessed April 9, 2016).

Randall, Vicki. 1991. "Feminism and Political Analysis." *Political Studies* 39 (3): 513–532.

Ray, Rebecca, Janet C. Gornick, and John Schmitt. 2009. "Parental Leave Policies in 21 Countries: Assessing Generosity and Gender Equality." Center for Economic and Policy Research. Available at http://www.cepr.net/documents/publications/parental_2008_09.pdf.

Reader, Ruth. 2015. "Adobe Joins Netflix, Microsoft in Expanding Maternity Leave." *Venture Beat*, August 10. Available at http://venturebeat.com/2015/08/10/adobe-joins-netflix-microsoft-in-expanding-maternity-leave/.

Rebouché, Rachel. 2009. "The Substance of Substantive Equality: Gender Equality and Turkey's Headscarf Debate." *American University International Law Review* 24 (5): 711–737.

Rhode Island Department of Labor and Training. n.d. "Rhode Island Parental and Family Medical Leave Act." Available at http://www.dlt.ri.gov/ls/pdfs/MedicalLeave_rr02.pdf (accessed May 23, 2014).

———. n.d. "Temporary Disability Insurance/Temporary Caregiver Insurance Frequently Asked Questions." Available at http://www.dlt.ri.gov/tdi/tdifaqs.htm (accessed February 2, 2016).

Rhode Island General Assembly. n.d. "2013—H 5889." Available at http://webserver .rilin.state.ri.us/billtext13/housetext13/h5889.pdf (accessed April 11, 2016).

——. n.d. "2013—H 5889 Substitute A as Amended." Available at http://webserver .rilin.state.ri.us/billtext13/housetext13/h5889aaa.pdf (accessed April 11, 2016).

——. n.d. "2013—S 0231." Available at http://webserver.rilin.state.ri.us/billtext13/ senatetext13/s0231.pdf (accessed April 11, 2016).

——. n.d. "2013—S 0231 Substitute A as Amended." Available at http://webserver .rilin.state.ri.us/billtext13/senatetext13/s0231aaa.pdf (accessed April 11, 2016).

——. n.d. "2013—S 0231 Substitute B." Available at http://webserver.rilin.state .ri.us/billtext13/senatetext13/s0231b.pdf (accessed April 11, 2016).

Rochon, Thomas R., and Daniel A. Mazmanian. 1993. "Social Movements and the Policy Process." In *Citizens, Protest, and Democracy*, edited by Russell J. Dalton, 75–87. Newbury Park, CA: Sage.

Rose, Stephen J., and Heidi I. Hartmann. 2004. "Still a Man's Labor Market: The Long Term Earnings Gap." Institute for Women's Policy Research. Available at http://www.iwpr.org/publications/pubs/still-a-mans-labor-market-the-long -term-earnings-gap.

Rosenfeld, Michel. 1986. "Substantive Equality and Equal Opportunity: A Jurisprudential Appraisal." *California Law Review* 74 (5): 1687–1712.

Rosenfeld, Rachel A., and Kathryn B. Ward. 1996. "Evolution of the Contemporary U.S. Women's Movement." In *Research in Social Movements, Conflict and Change*, vol. 19, edited by Michael N. Dobkowski and Isidor Wallimann, 51–73. Greenwich, CT: JAI Press.

Rossin-Slater, Maya, Christopher J. Ruhm, and Jane Waldfogel. 2013. "The Effects of California's Paid Family Leave Program on Mothers' Leave-Taking and Subsequent Labor Market Outcomes." *Journal of Policy Analysis and Management* 32 (2): 224–245.

Rovner, Julie. 1987. "'Compromise' Wins Few Republican Friends: Revised Family-Leave Measure OK'd by Divided House Panel." *CQ Weekly*, November 21, p. 2884.

Ruhm, Christopher. 1998. "Parental Leave and Child Health." National Bureau of Economic Research Working Paper 6554. Available at http://www.nber.org/ papers/w6554.pdf.

Ryan, Andrew. 2015. "City Council Approves Paid Parental Leave Measure." *Boston Globe*, April 29. Available at https://www.bostonglobe.com/metro/2015/ 04/29/city-council-approves-paid-parental-leave-for-municipal-employees/ 6JZ4eVovEtrX7CKDWgWKhP/story.html.

Ryan, Barbara. 1992. *Feminist and the Women's Movement: Dynamics of Change in Social Movement Ideology and Activism*. New York: Routledge.

Ryan, Missy. 2016. "Pentagon Extends Maternity and Paternity Leave for Military Families." *Washington Post*, January 28. Available at https://www.washington post.com/news/checkpoint/wp/2016/01/28/pentagon-extends-maternity-and -paternity-leave-for-military-families/.

Sabatini, Joshua. 2015. "Parental Leave Rights Increased." *San Francisco Examiner*, November 4. Available at http://www.sfexaminer.com/parental-leave-rights -increased/.

Sainsbury, Diane. 1994. *Gendering Welfare States*. Thousand Oaks, CA: Sage.

———. 1996. *Gender, Equality, and Welfare States.* New York: Cambridge University Press.

Saluter, Arlene F., and Terry A. Lugaila. 1998. "Marital Status and Living Arrangements: March 1996." *Current Population Reports*, March. Available at https://www.census.gov/prod/3/98pubs/p20-496.pdf.

Sandler, Lauren. 2015. "Taking Care of Our Own: Paid Leave Goes from Progressive Pipe Dream to Political Reality." *New Republic* 246 (5): 32–41.

Sawer, Marian. 1990. *Sisters in Suits: Women and Public Policy in Australia.* Sydney: Allen and Unwin.

———. 1996. "Femocrats and Ecorats: Women's Policy Machinery in Australia, Canada and New Zealand." United Nations Research Institute for Social Development Occasional Paper 6. Available at http://www.unrisd.org/ 80256B3C005BCCF9/httpNetITFramePDF?ReadForm&parentunid=D1A254 C22F3E5CC580256B67005B6B56&parentdoctype=paper&netitpath=80256B 3C005BCCF9/%28httpAuxPages%29/D1A254C22F3E5CC580256B67005B6B 56/$file/opb6.pdf.

Sawyers, Traci M., and David S. Meyer. 1999. "Missed Opportunities: Social Movement Abeyance and Public Policy." *Social Problems* 46 (2): 187–206.

Sayer, Liana C. 2005. "Gender, Time and Inequality: Trends in Women's and Men's Paid Work, Unpaid Work and Free Time." *Social Forces* 84 (1): 285–303.

Scaccia, Annamarya. 2015. "What Does Parental Leave Look Like in NYC's Silicon Alley?" *City Limits*, December 2. Available at http://citylimits.org/2015/12/02/ what-does-parental-leave-look-like-in-nycs-silicon-alley/.

Schattschneider, Elmer Eric. 1960. *The Semisovereign People: A Realist's View of Democracy in America.* New York: Holt, Rinehart, and Winston.

Schlafly, Phyllis. 1986. "Parental Leave—a Windfall for Yuppies." *Phyllis Schlafly Report* 20 (4): Section 1.

Schneider, Anne, and Helen Ingram. 1993. "Social Construction of Target Populations: Implications for Politics and Policy." *American Political Science Review* 87:334–347.

Schroeder, Patricia. 1988. "Parental Leave: The Need for a Federal Policy." In *The Parental Leave Crisis: Toward a National Policy*, edited by Edward F. Zigler and Meryl Frank, 326–332. New Haven, CT: Yale University Press.

Schwarz, Eleanor Bimla, Roberta M. Ray, Alison M. Stuebe, Matthew A. Allison, Roberta B. Ness, Matthew S. Freiberg, and Jane A. Cauley. 2009. "Duration of Lactation and Risk Factors for Maternal Cardiovascular Disease." *Obstetrics and Gynecology* 113 (5): 974–982.

Selmi, Michael. 2004. "Is Something Better than Nothing? Critical Reflections on Ten Years of the FMLA." *Washington University Journal of Law and Policy* 15:65–91.

Service Canada. 2016. "Employment Insurance Compassionate Care Benefits." Available at http://www.esdc.gc.ca/en/reports/ei/compassionate_care .page#Definition.

Sevos, Carolyn. 2007. Statement to the New York State Senate, Committee on Labor, June 5. Available at http://timetocareny.org/wp/wp-content/uploads/2013/12/ Carolyn-Sevos.doc.

Shapiro, Robert Y., and John T. Young. 1989. "Public Opinion and the Welfare State: The United States in Comparative Perspective." *Political Science Quarterly* 104 (1): 59–89.

Sharpe, Rochelle. 1996. "Work Week: A Special News Report about Life on the Job—and the Trends Taking Shape There." *Wall Street Journal*, February 27, p. A1.

Shine, Nicole Knight. 2015. "Portland City Employees to Get Paid Parental Leave." *Rewire*, December 8. Available at https://rewire.news/article/2015/12/08/portland-city-employees-get-paid-parental-leave/.

Shiner, Meredith. 2015. "Bernie Sanders Wants to Take Back 'Family Values' from the GOP." *Yahoo! Politics*, June 11. Available at https://www.yahoo.com/politics/bernie-sanders-wants-to-take-back-family-values-121276760221.html.

Shontell, Alyson. 2013. "Biological Moms Get Preferential Treatment over Parents Who Adopt at Companies Like Yahoo and Google." *Business Insider*, August 16. Available at http://www.businessinsider.com/maternity-paternity-leave-policies-at-google-facebook-yahoo-twitter-microsoft-2013-8.

Shropshire, Terry. 2015. "Mayor Reed and White House Agree on Paid Family Leave." *Atlanta Daily World*, July 9. Available at http://atlantadailyworld.com/2015/07/09/mayor-reed-white-house-agree-on-family-paid-leave/.

Shuit, Douglas. 2002. "Are You Ready for Paid Family Leave." *Workforce*, December 23. Available at http://www.workforce.com/articles/are-you-ready-for-paid-family-leave.

Siders, David. 2015. "Jerry Brown Vetoes Expanded Family Leave." *Sacramento Bee*, October 11. Available at http://www.sacbee.com/news/politics-government/capitol-alert/article38755236.html.

Silver, Barbara. 2013. "In Support of RI Senate Bill 231: Temporary Disability Insurance." Schmidt Labor Resource Center, June 27. Available at http://uri-slrc.blogspot.com/2013/06/barbara-ph.html.

Skocpol, Theda, Marjorie Abend-Wein, Christopher Howard, and Susan Goodrich Lehmann. 1993. "Women's Associations and the Enactment of Mothers' Pensions in the United States." *American Political Science Review* 87 (3): 686–701.

Smith, Adam. 2008. *An Inquiry into the Nature and Causes of the Wealth of Nations: A Selected Edition.* Edited by Kathryn Sutherland. New York: Oxford University Press.

Smith, Belinda. 2002. "Time Norms in the Workplace: Their Exclusionary Effect and Potential for Change." *Columbia Journal of Gender and Law* 11 (2): 271–360.

Snow, David A., and Robert D. Benford. 1992. "Master Frames and Cycles of Protest." In *Frontiers in Social Movement Theory*, edited by Aldon D. Morris and Carol McClurg Mueller, 133–155. New Haven, CT: Yale University Press.

Somerville, Jennifer. 1992. "The New Right and Family Politics." *Economy and Society* 21 (2): 93–128.

Soule, Sarah A., Doug McAdam, John McCarthy, and Yang Su. 1999. "Protest Events: Cause or Consequence of the U.S. Women's Movement and Federal Congressional Activities, 1956–1979." *Mobilization* 4 (2): 239–256.

Soule, Sarah A., and Susan Olzak. 2004. "When Do Movements Matter? The Politics of Contingency and the Equal Rights Amendment." *American Sociological Review* 69 (4): 473–497.

Spalter-Roth, Roberta, and Ronnee Schreiber. 1995. "Outsider Issues and Insider Tactics: Strategic Tensions in the Women's Policy Network during the 1980s." In *Feminist Organizations: Harvest of the New Women's Movement*, edited by Myra Marx Ferree and Patricia Yancey Martin, 105–127. Philadelphia: Temple University Press.

Staff, Jeremy, and Jeylan T. Mortimer. 2012. "Explaining the Motherhood Wage Penalty during the Early Occupational Career." *Demography* 49 (1): 1–21.

Staggenborg, Suzanne. 1991. *The Pro-Choice Movement: Organization and Activism in the Abortion Conflict*. New York: Oxford University Press.

———. 1998. *Gender, Family, and Social Movements*. Thousand Oaks, CA: Pine Forge Press.

Stearns, Jenna. 2015. "The Effects of Paid Maternity Leave: Evidence from Temporary Disability Insurance." *Journal of Health Economics* 43:85–102.

Stetson, Dorothy McBride. 1995. "The Oldest Women's Policy Agency: The Women's Bureau in the United States." In *Comparative State Feminism*, edited by Dorothy McBride Stetson and Amy G. Mazur, 254–271. Thousand Oaks, CA: Sage.

———. 2001a. "Federal and State Women's Policy Agencies Help to Represent Women in the United States." In *State Feminism, Women's Movements, and Job Training: Making Democracies Work in the Global Economy*, edited by Amy G. Mazur, 271–292. New York: Routledge.

———. 2001b. "US Abortion Debates, 1959–1998: The Women's Movement Hold On." In *Abortion Politics, Women's Movements, and the Democratic State: A Comparative Study of State Feminism*, edited by Dorothy McBride Stetson, 247–266. New York: Oxford University Press.

———. 2004. *Women's Rights in the USA*. 3rd ed. New York: Routledge.

Stetson, Dorothy McBride, and Amy G. Mazur. 1995. "Introduction." In *Comparative State Feminism*, edited by Dorothy McBride Stetson and Amy G. Mazur, 1–21. Thousand Oaks, CA: Sage.

Steves, David. 2007. "Senate Says No to Paid Family Leave." *Register-Guard*, June 28. Available at http://www.thefreelibrary.com/Senate+says+no+to+paid+family+leave.-a0166463737.

Stewart, David O. 1987. "Equal Treatment for Pregnant Workers." *ABA Journal* 73 (3): 40–47.

Stuebe, Alison M., Walter C. Willett, Fei Xue, and Karin B. Michels. 2009. "Lactation and Incidence of Premenopausal Breast Cancer: A Longitudinal Study." *Archives of Internal Medicine* 169 (15): 1364–1371.

Sussman, Anna Louie, and Laura Meckler. 2016. "Clinton Offers New Details about Paid Family Leave Plan." *Wall Street Journal*, January 7. Available at http://www.wsj.com/articles/clinton-offers-new-details-about-paid-family-leave-plan-1452212973.

Swarns, Rachel L. 2015. "Advocates Press Cuomo to Take Action on Paid Family Leave Legislation." *New York Times*, March 15. Available at http://www

.nytimes.com/2015/03/16/nyregion/advocates-press-cuomo-to-support-paid
-family-leave-legislation.html.

Sweeney, John J. 2002. "Statement by AFL-CIO President John J. Sweeney on
California Paid Family Leave Law." AFL-CIO, September 23. Available
at http://ftp.workingamerica.org/Press-Room/Press-Releases/Statement-by
-AFL-CIO-President-John-J.-Sweeney-on122.

Swers, Michele L. 2002. *The Difference Women Make: The Policy Impact of Women
in Congress.* Chicago: University of Chicago Press.

Symes, Beth. 1987. "Equality Theories and Maternity Benefits." In *Equality and
Judicial Neutrality,* edited by Sheilah L. Martin and Kathleen E. Mahoney,
207–217. Toronto: Carswell.

Tanaka, Sakiko. 2005. "Parental Leave and Child Health across OECD Countries."
Economic Journal 115 (501): F7–F28.

Tanaka, Sakiko, and Jane Waldfogel. 2007. "Effects of Parental Leave and Work
Hours on Fathers' Involvement with Their Babies." *Community, Work and
Family* 10 (4): 409–426.

Tarrow, Sidney G. 1994. *Power in Movement: Social Movements, Collective Action
and Politics.* New York: Cambridge University Press.

Taub, Nadine. 1985. "From Parental Leaves to Nurturing Leaves." *New York
University Review of Law and Social Change* 13:381–405.

Taylor, Joan Kennedy. 1991. "Protective Labor Legislation." In *Freedom, Feminism,
and the State: An Overview of Individualist Feminism.* 2nd ed., edited by
Wendy McElroy, 187–192. New York: Holmes and Meier.

Taylor, Verta, and Nancy Whittier. 1997. "The New Feminist Movement." In
Feminist Frontiers IV, edited by Laurel Richardson, Verta Taylor, and Nancy
Whittier, 544–561. New York: McGraw-Hill.

Teghtsoonian, Katherine. 1993. "Neo-Conservative Ideology and Opposition to
Federal Regulation of Child Care Services in the United States and Canada."
Canadian Journal of Political Science 26 (1): 97–121.

Teske, Robin L., and Mary Ann Tétreault. 2000. *Conscious Acts and the Politics of
Social Change: Feminist Approaches to Social Movements, Community, and
Power.* Columbia: University of South Carolina Press.

Thomas, Sue. 1994. *How Women Legislate.* New York: Oxford University Press.

Thornton, Margaret. 1995. "The Cartography of Public and Private." In *Public and
Private: Feminist Legal Debates,* edited by Margaret Thornton, 2–16. New York:
Oxford University Press.

Tilly, Charles. 1978. *From Mobilization to Revolution.* Reading, MA: Addison-
Wesley.

———. 1984. "Social Movements and National Politics." In *Statemaking and Social
Movements: Essays in History and Theory,* edited by Charles Bright and Susan
Harding, 297–317. Ann Arbor: University of Michigan Press.

———. 1995. *European Revolutions, 1492–1992.* Cambridge, MA: Blackwell.

Tilly, Chris. 1996. *Half a Job: Bad and Good Part-Time Jobs in a Changing Labor
Market.* Philadelphia: Temple University Press.

Time to Care. n.d. "Coalition Partners." Available at http://timetocareny.org/
coalition-partners/ (accessed February 17, 2016).

Time to Care for Oregon Families. n.d. "SB 966—Oregon Family Leave Insurance." Available at https://oregonpaidfamilyleave.files.wordpress.com/2009/03/paid -family-leave-2009-fact-sheet-time-to-care3.pdf (accessed April 6, 2016).

Traister, Rebecca. 2016. "New York Just Created a Revolutionary Family-Leave Policy." *The Cut*, April 1. Available at http://nymag.com/thecut/2016/03/new -york-revolutionary-family-leave-paid-time-off.html.

Trzcinski, Eileen. 2004. "The Employment Insurance Model: Maternity, Parental, and Sickness Benefits in Canada." In *Equity in the Workplace: Gendering Workplace Policy Analysis*, edited by Heidi Gottfried and Laura Reese, 243–280. Lanham, MD: Lexington Books.

Tsebelis, George. 1995. "Decision Making in Political Systems: Veto Players in Presidentialism, Parliamentarism, Multicamerlism and Multipartyism." *British Journal of Political Science* 25 (3): 289–325.

United Press International. 1984. "Maternity-Leave Law Found Illegal by Judge." *New York Times*, March 22, p. C5.

U.S. Department of Health and Human Services, Administration on Aging. 2014. "A Profile of Older Americans: 2014." Available at http://aoa.gov/Aging _Statistics/Profile/2014/docs/2014-Profile.pdf.

U.S. Department of Labor. n.d. "Labor Force by Sex, 2014 and Projected 2022." Available at http://www.dol.gov/wb/stats/laborforce_sex_projected _2014_2022_txt.htm (accessed May 7, 2015).

———. n.d. "Women in the Labor Force." Available at http://www.dol.gov/wb/stats/ stats_data.htm (accessed May 21, 2015).

———. 1993. "The Family and Medical Leave Act of 1993, as Amended." Available at http://www.dol.gov/whd/fmla/fmlaAmended.htm.

———. 2000. "Birth and Adoption Unemployment Compensation." *Federal Register*, June 13. Available at https://www.federalregister.gov/articles/ 2000/06/13/00-14801/birth-and-adoption-unemployment-compensation.

———. 2003. "Unemployment Compensation—Trust Fund Integrity Rule; Birth and Adoption Unemployment Compensation; Removal of Regulations." *Federal Register*, October 9. Available at http://www.gpo.gov/fdsys/pkg/FR-2003-10-09/ pdf/03-25507.pdf.

———. 2010. "Administrator's Interpretation No. 2010-3." Available at http://www .dol.gov/WHD/opinion/adminIntrprtn/FMLA/2010/FMLAAI2010_3.pdf.

———. 2014a. "$500K for Studies on Expanding Paid Family and Medical Leave Provided by US Labor Department Grants." Available at http://www.dol.gov/ opa/media/press/wb/WB20141206.htm.

———. 2014b. "National Compensation Survey: Employee Benefits in the United States, March 2014." Available at http://www.bls.gov/ncs/ebs/benefits/2014/ ebb10055.pdf.

———. 2015a. "The Cost of Doing Nothing: The Price We All Pay without Paid Leave Policies to Support America's 21st Century Working Families." Available at http://www.dol.gov/featured/paidleave/cost-of-doing-nothing-report.pdf.

———. 2015b. "Department Awards $1.55M to Study Paid Family, Medical Leave Implementation." Available at http://www.dol.gov/opa/media/press/wb/ WB20151927.htm.

————. 2015c. "Fact Sheet: Final Rule to Amend the Definition of Spouse in the Family and Medical Leave Act Regulations." Available at http://www.dol.gov/whd/fmla/spouse/factsheet.htm.

————. 2015d. "FY 2016 Department of Labor Budget in Brief." Available at http://www.dol.gov/dol/budget/2016/PDF/FY2016BIB.pdf.

————. 2015e. "State Unemployment Insurance Benefits." Available at http://workforcesecurity.doleta.gov/unemploy/uifactsheet.asp.

U.S. General Accounting Office. 1988. *Parental Leave: Estimated Cost of Revised Parental and Medical Leave Act Proposal.* Washington, DC: U.S. Government Printing Office.

U.S. House Committee on Education and Labor. 1977. *Legislation to Prohibit Sex Discrimination on the Basis of Pregnancy: Hearing Before the Subcommittee on Employment Opportunities of the Committee on Education and Labor.* 95th Cong. (hearing on H.R. 5055 and H.R. 6075).

U.S. House Committee on Ways and Means. 2000. *Unemployment Compensation and the Family and Medical Leave Act: Hearing Before the Subcommittee on Human Resources.* 106th Cong.

U.S. Navy. 2015. "SECNAV Announces New Maternity Leave Policy." Available at http://www.navy.mil/submit/display.asp?story_id=87987.

U.S. Social Security Administration, Office of Retirement and Disability Policy. 2014. "Temporary Disability Insurance Program Description and Legislative History." Available at http://www.ssa.gov/policy/docs/statcomps/supplement/2014/tempdisability.html.

Vahratian, Anjel, and Timothy R. B. Johnson. 2009. "Maternity Leave Benefits in the United States: Today's Economic Climate Underlines Deficiencies." *Birth* 36 (3): 177–179.

Valenti, Catherine. 2003. "Is Paid Family Leave Coming to Your State?" *ABC News*, October 2. Available at http://abcnews.go.com/Business/story?id=89931&page=1#.TrR9F3ImuQw.

Van Doorne-Huiskes, Anneke. 1999. "Work-Family Arrangements: The Role of the State versus the Role of the Private Sector." In *Women and Public Policy: The Shifting Boundaries between the Public and Private Spheres,* edited by Susan Baker and Anneke van Doorne-Huiskes, 93–110. Brookfield, VT: Ashgate.

Vogel, Lise. 1990. "Debating Difference: Feminism, Pregnancy, and the Workplace." *Feminist Studies* 16 (1): 9–32.

————. 1995. "Considering Difference: The Case of the U.S. Family and Medical Leave Act of 1993." *Social Politics* 2:111–120.

Vosko, Leah F. 2002. "Mandatory 'Marriage' or Obligatory Waged Work: Social Assistance and Single Mothers in Wisconsin and Ontario." In *Women's Work Is Never Done: Comparative Studies in Caregiving, Employment, and Social Policy Reform,* edited by Sylvia Bashevkin, 165–199. New York: Routledge.

Voss, Gretchen. 2015. "Mother F*cker." *Women's Health* 12 (8): 162–167.

Waldfogel, Jane. 1997. "The Effect of Children on Women's Wages." *American Sociological Review* 62 (2): 209–217.

————. 1998. "Understanding the 'Family Gap' in Pay for Women with Children." *Journal of Economic Perspectives* 12 (1): 137–156.

———. 1999. "The Impact of the Family and Medical Leave Act." *Journal of Policy Analysis and Management* 18 (2): 281–302.

———. 2001. "International Policies toward Parental Leave and Child Care." *Caring for Infants and Toddlers* 11 (1): 99–111.

Wallace, Rachel. 2014. "By the Numbers: A Look at the Gender Pay Gap." American Association of University Women, September 18. Available at http://www.aauw.org/2014/09/18/gender-pay-gap/.

Walsh, Ed. 2007. "Paid Family Leave Bill Dies." *The Oregonian*, June 28. Available at http://blog.oregonlive.com/politics/2007/06/paid_family_leave_bill_dies.html.

Washington State Department of Labor and Industries. n.d. "Washington State Family Leave Act." Available at http://www.lni.wa.gov/WorkplaceRights/LeaveBenefits/FamilyCare/LawsPolicies/FamilyLeave/default.asp (accessed June 9, 2014).

Washington State Legislature. n.d. "Family Leave Insurance." Available at http://apps.leg.wa.gov/rcw/default.aspx?cite=49.86 (accessed May 17, 2014).

———. n.d. "HB 1273." Available at http://apps.leg.wa.gov/billinfo/summary.aspx?bill=1273 (accessed April 11, 2016).

———. n.d. "HB 1457." Available at http://apps.leg.wa.gov/billinfo/summary.aspx?bill=1457&year=2013 (accessed April 11, 2016).

———. n.d. "HB 2044." Available at http://apps.leg.wa.gov/billinfo/summary.aspx?bill=2044&year=2013 (accessed April 11, 2016).

———. n.d. "SB 5159." Available at http://apps.leg.wa.gov/billinfo/summary.aspx?bill=5159&year=2013 (accessed April 11, 2016).

———. n.d. "SB 5659." Available at http://apps.leg.wa.gov/billinfo/summary.aspx?year=2007&bill=5659 (accessed April 11, 2016).

———. n.d. "SB 6570." Available at http://apps.leg.wa.gov/billinfo/summary.aspx?bill=6570&year=2011 (accessed April 11, 2016).

Washington Work and Family Coalition. n.d. "About." Available at http://waworkandfamily.org/about (accessed February 17, 2016).

———. 2012. "New Name, Same Values—and More Progress for Washington Families!" February 28. Available at https://familyleave.wordpress.com/page/4/.

Weingartner, Tana, and Jay Hanselman. 2015. "Cincinnati Approves Paid Parental Leave Program." WVXU Cincinnati, September 30. Available at http://wvxu.org/post/cincinnati-approves-paid-parental-leave-program#stream/0.

Weir, Margaret. 2002. "Income Polarization and California's Social Contract." In *The State of California Labor 2002*, edited by Ruth Milkman, 97–131. Berkeley: University of California Institute for Labor and Employment.

Weldon, S. Laurel. 2002a. "Beyond Bodies: Institutional Sources of Representation for Women in Democratic Policymaking." *Journal of Politics* 64 (4): 1153–1174.

———. 2002b. *Protest, Policy, and the Problem of Violence against Women: A Cross-national Comparison.* Pittsburgh, PA: University of Pittsburgh Press.

———. 2006. "Women's Movements, Identity Politics, and Policy Impacts: A Study of Policies on Violence against Women in the 50 United States." *Political Research Quarterly* 59 (1): 111–122.

———. 2011. *When Protest Makes Policy: How Social Movements Represent Disadvantaged Groups*. Ann Arbor: University of Michigan Press.

White, Linda A. 2006. "Institutions, Constitutions, Actor Strategies, and Ideas: Explaining Variation in Paid Parental Leave Policies in Canada and the United States." *International Journal of Constitutional Law* 4 (2): 319–346.

Whittier, Nancy. 1995. *Feminist Generations: The Persistence of the Radical Women's Movement*. Philadelphia: Temple University Press.

Williams, Joan. 2000. *Unbending Gender: Why Family and Work Conflict and What to Do about It*. New York: Oxford University Press.

Williams, Wendy. 1984–1985. "Equality's Riddle: Pregnancy and the Equal Treatment/Special Treatment Debate." *New York University Review of Law and Social Change* 13:325–380.

Williamson, Sarah, and Matthew Carnes. 2013. "Partisanship, Christianity, and Women in the Legislature: Determinants of Parental Leave Policy in the U.S. States." *Social Science Quarterly* 94 (4): 1084–1101.

Willis, Joseph. 1997. "The Family and Medical Leave Act of 1993: A Progress Report." *Brandeis Journal of Family Law* 36:95–108.

Wines, Michael. 1992. "Bush Vetoes Bill Making Employers Give Family Leave." *New York Times*, September 23, p. A1.

Winston, Kenneth, and Mary Jo Bane, eds. 1993. *Gender and Public Policy: Cases and Comments*. Boulder, CO: Westview Press.

Wisensale, Steven K. 1989a. "Family Leave Legislation: State and Federal Initiatives." *Family Relations* 38 (2): 182–189.

———. 1989b. "Family Policy in the State Legislature: The Connecticut Agenda." *Policy Studies Review* 8 (3): 622–637.

———. 1999. "The Family and Medical Leave Act in Court: A Review of Key Appeals Court Cases Five Years After." *Working USA: The Journal of Labor and Society* 3 (4): 96–119.

———. 2001. *Family Leave Policy: The Political Economy of Work and Family in America*. Armonk, NY: Sharpe.

———. 2003. "Two Steps Forward, One Step Back: The Family and Medical Leave Act as Retrenchment Policy." *Review of Policy Research* 20 (1): 135–152.

———. 2006. "California's Paid Leave Law: A Model for Other States?" In *Families and Social Policy: National and International Perspectives*, edited by Linda Haas and Steven K. Wisensale, 177–195. Binghamton, NY: Haworth Press.

———. 2009. "Aging Policy as Family Policy: Expanding Family Leave and Improving Flexible Work Policies." In *Boomer Bust? Economic and Political Issues of the Graying Society*, vol. 1, *Perspectives on the Boomers*, edited by Robert B. Hudson, 253–269. Westport, CT: Praeger Perspectives.

Wojcicki, Susan. 2014. "Paid Maternity Leave Is Good for Business." *Wall Street Journal*, December 16. Available at http://www.wsj.com/articles/susan-wojcicki-paid-maternity-leave-is-good-for-business-1418773756.

Wolbrecht, Christina, and Rodney Hero, eds. 2005. *The Politics of Democratic Inclusion*. Philadelphia: Temple University Press.

Women's Bureau, U.S. Department of Labor. 1993. *State Maternity/Family Leave Law*. Washington, DC: U.S. Department of Labor.

Wooldridge, Scott. 2015. "Paid Family Leave Becoming Hot Political Topic." *BenefitsPro*, November 9. Available at http://www.benefitspro.com/2015/11/09/paid-family-leave-becoming-hot-political-topic.

World Policy Analysis Center. n.d. "Is Paid Leave Available to Mothers and Fathers of Infants?" Available at http://worldpolicyforum.org/policies/is-paid-leave-available-to-mothers-and-fathers-of-infants (accessed May 12, 2015).

Wright, John R. 1996. *Interest Groups and Congress: Lobbying, Contributions, and Influence.* Boston: Allyn and Bacon.

Ybarra, Marci. 2013. "Implications of Paid Family Leave for Welfare Participants." *Social Work Research* 37 (4): 375–387.

Zald, Mayer N., and Bert Useem. 1987. "Movement and Countermovement Interaction: Mobilization, Tactics, and State Involvement." In *Social Movements in an Organizational Society*, edited by Mayer N. Zald and John D. McCarthy, 247–272. New Brunswick, NJ: Transaction.

Index

fornia, 113, 162; San Jose chapter of,
113
Nojay, Bill, 130
Nontraditional Employment for Women,
126
Northwest Women's Law Center, 138
Nursing Mothers Counsel of Oregon,
145
Nussbaum, Karen, 67

Obama, Barack, 69–70, 73, 98–99, 133,
162, 171, 177, 189n54
Obergefell v. Hodges, 89
Ohio, 106, 161, 163
Older Women's League, 110, 116, 126
O'Leary, Ann, 99
O'Malley, Martin, 100
Oregon, paid family leave in, 27, 135–137,
144–147
Oregon Center for Public Policy, 144
Oregon Family Leave Act (OFLA), 137,
144, 189–190n12
Organisation for Economic Co-operation
and Development (OECD), 92

Paid family leave, 1–3, 5, 7, 87, 98–99,
133–135, 157, 161–162, 186n29, 189n54;
and Barack Obama, 69, 98–99, 133,
162; benefits of, for business, 95–96;
and Bill Clinton, 104–105; in companies, 165–170; and gender equality in
the home, 90–91, 172–173; and gender
equality in the workplace, 91–93,
172–173; health benefits of, for mothers and children, 93–94; and increased
economic security, 87–90; and labor
unions, 21–22; for military service
members, 167; at the municipal level,
162–164; opposition to, 111–112, 114,
117–118, 122, 127, 129–131, 140–141,
145–146, 151, 154, 170–171, 184–185n9,
186n31; at the state level, 3, 13–15, 27,
102–103, 105–157, 161–162, 174–175;
in 2016 elections, 99–101, 177–178;
and United States as exception, 2, 26,
29–30; and women's movement, 18–20,
46, 48, 51, 58, 66–67, 105, 159, 176. *See
also specific companies, municipalities,
and states*

Paid sick days, 95, 99, 106, 171; in Hawaii,
153–154, 188n40; as issue priority, 128–
129, 143, 146–147, 149, 157, 165; in Massachusetts, 149–151; in New York, 129;
in Oregon, 146–147; as parental leave,
98; in San Francisco, 128; in Washington State, 143; and WMAs, 128
Paiva Weed, Teresa, 121–123
Palau, 2
Paluso, Andrea, 147
Pappas, Marcia, 126
Papua New Guinea, 2
Parental and Disability Leave Act of
1985, 49–51, 56
Parental and Medical Leave Act of 1986,
52–54, 183n33
Parental leave, 32, 43, 52, 64, 97; and
CFRA, 180n11, 187n7; in companies,
101, 165–167, 169; definition of, 4; in
equal treatment versus special treatment debate, 19, 50–51, 159; and fathers, 6, 169, 172; Federal Employees
Paid Parental Leave Act of 2015, 98,
164–165; and health, 7; in Massachusetts, 148, 151; at municipal level,
162–163; in New York, 133; OFLA,
189–190n12; and party in power, 23;
and Phyllis Schlafly, 55; policies on,
around the world, 1–2, 92, 186n29; in
Rhode Island, 120; at state level, 161;
and UI system, 104; in Washington,
D.C., 164; in Washington State, 3, 27,
106, 186–187n1, 189n1, 190n2. *See also*
Family leave; Maternity leave; Paid
family leave; Paternity leave
Partnership for Working Families, 116
Paternity leave, 1–2, 4–6, 32, 62, 91, 165,
167, 169, 171–172. *See also* Family leave;
Paid family leave; Parental leave
Paul, Alice, 34
Pearson-Merkowitz, Shanna, 121–122
Pennsylvania, 104
Perez, Thomas E., 132, 175
Peterson, Gretchen, 145
Pettine, Laurie, 116
PHOCUSED (Protecting Hawaii's Ohana,
Children, Under-Served, Elderly and
Disabled), 155
Pittsburgh, Pennsylvania, 162

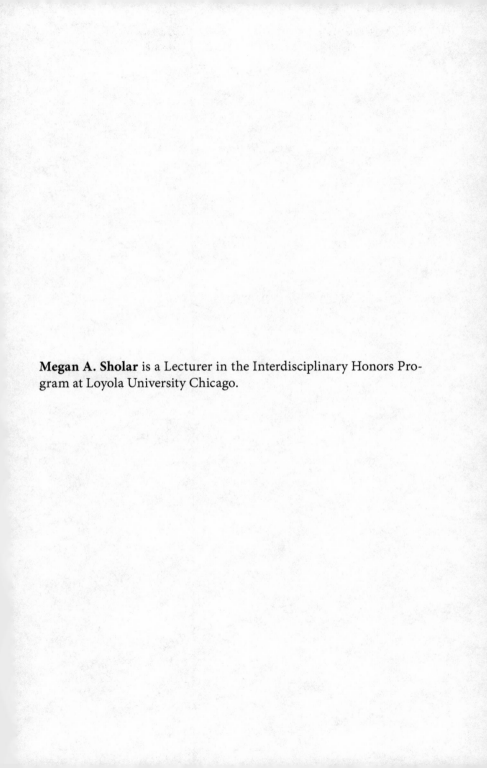

Megan A. Sholar is a Lecturer in the Interdisciplinary Honors Program at Loyola University Chicago.